Parallel Database Techniques

Mahdi Abdelguerfi
Kam-Fai Wong

IEEE
COMPUTER
SOCIETY

Los Alamitos, California

Washington • Brussels • Tokyo

Library of Congress Cataloging-in-Publication Data

Parallel database techniques / [edited by] Mahdi Abdelguerfi, Kam-Fai Wong.
     p.   cm.
    Includes bibliographical references.
    ISBN 0-8186-8398-8
    1. Parallel processing (Electronic computers)   2. Database
management.   I. Abdelguerfi, Mahdi.   II. Wong, Kam-Fai.
QA76.58.P3762   1998
005.75 ' 6 ' 0285435—dc21

                       97-51310
                       CIP

IEEE Computer Society Press Order Number BP08398
Library of Congress Number 98-51310
ISBN 0-8186-8398-8

Additional copies may be ordered from:

IEEE Computer Society Press	IEEE Service Center	IEEE Computer Society	IEEE Computer Society
Customer Service Center	445 Hoes Lane	13, Avenue de l'Aquilon	Ooshima Building
10662 Los Vaqueros Circle	P.O. Box 1331	B-1200 Brussels	2-19-1 Minami-Aoyama
P.O. Box 3014	Piscataway, NJ 08855-1331	BELGIUM	Minato-ku, Tokyo 107
Los Alamitos, CA 90720-1314	Tel: +1-732-981-1393	Tel: +32-2-770-2198	JAPAN
Tel: +1-714-821-8380	Fax: +1-732-981-9667	Fax: +32-2-770-8505	Tel: +81-3-3408-3118
Fax: +1-714-821-4641	mis.custserv@computer.org	euro.ofc@computer.org	Fax: +81-3-3408-3553
Email: cs.books@computer.org			tokyo.ofc@computer.org

Publisher: Matt Loeb
Developmental Editor: Cheryl Baltes
Advertising/Promotions: Tom Fink
Production Editor: Lisa O'Conner
Copy Editor: Kathryn Lewis

IEEE
COMPUTER
SOCIETY

IEEE

Contents

1 Introduction   **1**
  1.1 Background 1
  1.2 Parallel Database Systems 2
      1.2.1 Computation Model 2
      1.2.2 Engineering Model 4
  1.3 About this Manuscript 8
  Bibliography 9

I Request Manager   **13**

2 Designing an Optimizer for Parallel Relational Systems   **15**
  2.1 Introduction 15
  2.2 Overall Design Issues 16
      2.2.1 Design a Simple Parallel Execution Model 16
      2.2.2 The Two-Phase Approach 17
      2.2.3 Parallelizing is Adding Information! 17
      2.2.4 Two-Phase versus Parallel Approaches 18
  2.3 Parallelization 19
      2.3.1 Kinds of Parallelism 19
      2.3.2 Specifying Parallel Execution 21
  2.4 Search Space 22
      2.4.1 Slicing Hash Join Trees 23
      2.4.2 Search Space Size 24
      2.4.3 Heuristics 25
      2.4.4 The Two-Phase Heuristics 26
  2.5 Cost Model 28
      2.5.1 Exceptions to the Principle of Optimality 28
      2.5.2 Resources 30
      2.5.3 Skew and Size Model 31
      2.5.4 The Cost Function 32
  2.6 Search Strategies 34
      2.6.1 Deterministic Search Strategies 35
      2.6.2 Randomized Strategies 35
  2.7 Conclusion 37
  Bibliography 38

3 New Approaches to Parallel Join Utilizing Page Connectivity Information **43**

   3.1 Introduction 43

   3.2 The Environment and a Motivating Example 46

   3.3 The Methodology 48

      3.3.1 Definition of Parameters 49

      3.3.2 The Balancing Algorithm 50

      3.3.3 Schedules for Reading Join Components and Data Pages 54

   3.4 Performance Analysis 57

      3.4.1 The Evaluation Method 57

      3.4.2 Evaluation Results 59

   3.5 Concluding Remarks and Future Work 71

   Bibliography 73

4 A Performance Evaluation Tool for Parallel Database Systems **77**

   4.1 Introduction 77

   4.2 Performance Evaluation Methods 78

      4.2.1 Analytical Modeling 78

      4.2.2 Benchmarks 79

      4.2.3 Observations 80

   4.3 The Software Testpilot 81

      4.3.1 The Experiment Specification 81

      4.3.2 The Performance Assessment Cycle 83

      4.3.3 The System Interface 84

   4.4 The Software Testpilot and Oracle/Ncube 84

      4.4.1 Database System Performance Assessment 85

      4.4.2 The Oracle/Ncube Interface 87

   4.5 Preliminary Results 89

   4.6 Conclusion 91

   Bibliography 92

5 Load Placement in Distributed High-Performance Database Systems **93**

   5.1 Introduction 93

   5.2 Investigated System 94

      5.2.1 System Architecture 94

      5.2.2 Load Scenarios 97

      5.2.3 Trace Analysis 97

      5.2.4 Load Setup 99

   5.3 Load Placement Strategies Investigated 100

   5.4 Scheduling Strategies for Transactions 102

   5.5 Simulation Results 103

      5.5.1 Influence of Scheduling 103

      5.5.2 Evaluation of the Load Placement Strategies 104

      5.5.3 Lessons Learned 109

      5.5.4 Decision Parameters Used 111

   5.6 Conclusion and Open Issues 113

Bibliography 114

II Parallel Machine Architecture 117

6 Modeling Recovery in Client-Server Database Systems 119
6.1 Introduction 119
6.2 Uniprocessor Recovery and Formal Approach to Modeling Recovery 120
    6.2.1 Basic Formal Concepts 121
    6.2.2 Logging Mechanisms 123
    6.2.3 Runtime Policies for Ensuring Correctness 124
    6.2.4 Data Structures Maintained for Efficient Recovery 125
    6.2.5 Restart Recovery—The ARIES Approach 126
6.3 LSN Sequencing Techniques for Multinode Systems 128
6.4 Recovery in Client-Server Database Systems 129
    6.4.1 Client-Server EXODUS (ESM-CS) 130
    6.4.2 Client-Server ARIES (ARIES/CSA) 133
    6.4.3 Shared Nothing Clients with Disks (CD) 135
    6.4.4 Summary of Recovery Approaches in Client-Server Architectures . 136
6.5 Conclusion 136
Bibliography 137

7 Parallel Strategies for a Petabyte Multimedia Database Computer 139
7.1 Introduction 140
7.2 Multimedia Data Warehouse, Databases, and Applications 141
    7.2.1 Three Waves of Multimedia Database Development 141
    7.2.2 National Medical Practice Knowledge Bank Application 142
7.3 Massively Parallel Architecture, Infrastructure, and Technology 144
    7.3.1 Parallelism 145
7.4 Teradata-MM Architecture, Framework, and New Concepts 146
    7.4.1 Teradata-MM Architecture 146
    7.4.2 Key New Concepts 146
    7.4.3 SQL3 151
    7.4.4 Federated Coordinator 151
    7.4.5 Teradata Multimedia Object Server 152
7.5 Parallel UDF Execution Analysis 155
    7.5.1 UDF Optimizations 155
    7.5.2 PRAGMA Facility 158
    7.5.3 UDF Value Persistence Facility 159
    7.5.4 Spatial Indices for Content-Based Querying 160
7.6 Conclusion 162
Bibliography 162

8 The MEDUSA Project   **165**
   8.1   Introduction 165
   8.2   Indexing and Data Partitioning 166
       8.2.1   Standard Systems 166
       8.2.2   Grid Files 167
   8.3   Dynamic Load Balancing 167
       8.3.1   Data Access Frequency 168
       8.3.2   Data Distribution 168
       8.3.3   Query Partitioning 168
   8.4   The MEDUSA Project 169
       8.4.1   The MEDUSA Architecture 169
       8.4.2   Software 169
       8.4.3   Grid File Implementation 172
       8.4.4   Load Balancing Strategy 174
   8.5   MEDUSA Performance Results 174
       8.5.1   Test Configuration 174
       8.5.2   Transaction Throughput 175
       8.5.3   Speedup 177
       8.5.4   Load Balancing Test Results 180
   8.6   Conclusions 180
   Bibliography 181

III   Partitioned Data Store   **183**

9 System Software of the Super Database Computer SDC-II   **185**
   9.1   Introduction 185
   9.2   Architectural Overview of the SDC-II 186
   9.3   Design and Organization of the SDC-II System Software 188
       9.3.1   Parallel Execution Model 188
       9.3.2   I/O Model and Buffer Management Strategy for Bulk Data Transfer 189
       9.3.3   Process Model and Efficient Flow Control Mechanism 191
       9.3.4   Structure of the System Software Components 192
   9.4   Evaluation of the SDC-II System 193
       9.4.1   Details of a Sample Query Processing 193
       9.4.2   Comparison with Commercial Systems 197
   9.5   Conclusion 200
   Bibliography 200

10 Data Placement in Parallel Database Systems   **203**
   10.1   Introduction 203
   10.2   Overview of Data Placement Strategies 204
       10.2.1   Declustering and Redistribution 204
       10.2.2   Placement 205
   10.3   Effects of Data Placement 208
       10.3.1   STEADY and TPC-C 208

10.3.2 Dependence on Number of Processing Elements 209
10.3.3 Dependence on Database Size 212
10.4 Conclusions 216
Bibliography 218

Contributors **221**

Chapter 1

Introduction

Mahdi Abdelguerfi and Kam-Fai Wong

1.1 Background

There has been a continuing increase in the amount of data handled by database management systems (DBMSs) in recent years. Indeed, it is no longer unusual for a DBMS to manage databases ranging in size from hundreds of gigabytes to terabytes. This massive increase in database sizes is coupled with a growing need for DBMSs to exhibit more sophisticated functionality such as the support of object-oriented, deductive, and multimedia-based applications. In many cases, these new requirements have rendered existing DBMSs unable to provide the necessary system performance, especially given that many mainframe DBMSs already have difficulty meeting the I/O and CPU performance requirements of traditional information systems that service large numbers of concurrent users and/or handle massive amounts of data [13].

To achieve the required performance levels, database systems have been increasingly required to make use of parallelism. As noted in [1], the traditional approach to parallelism for conventional DBMSs which use industry-standard database models such as the relational, can take one of two forms. The first is through the use of massively parallel general-purpose hardware platforms. As an example of this, commercial platforms such as nCube and SP1 are now supporting Oracle's parallel server [5]. Also, the Distributed Array Processor marketed by Cambridge Parallel Processing is now being used to produce a commercial massively parallel database system [4]. The second approach makes use of arrays of off-the-shelf components to form custom massively parallel systems. For the most part, these hardware systems are based on MIMD parallel architectures. The NCR 3700 [1] and the Super Database Computer II (SDC-II) [27] are two such systems. The NCR 3700 uses a high-performance multistage interconnection network known as Bynet and RAIDS (Redundant Arrays of Inexpensive Disks [11]). This system can now run a parallel version of Sybase relational DBMS [5, 26]. The SDC-II consists of eight data processing modules, where each module is composed of seven processors and five disk drives. The data processing modules communicate through an omega interconnection network.

The use of clusters of workstations as virtual parallel systems is a more recent approach that is already impacting the DBMS industry. These networks of workstations provide enormous amounts of aggregate computational power, often rivaling that of tightly coupled multiprocessor systems. They provide a viable high-performance computing environment and have several benefits over large, dedicated parallel machines, including cost, elimination of central point of failure, and scalability. Their use as a virtual parallel machine does not preclude the use of individual machines in more traditional ways. As an example of this, parallel versions of relational DBMSs, such as Oracle, are now even available on clusters of PC-compatible systems [2], thereby providing high performance at a relatively low cost.

The number of general purpose or dedicated parallel database computers is increasing each year. It is not unrealistic to envisage that all high-performance database management systems in the year 2010 will support parallel processing. The high potential of parallel databases in the future urges both the database vendors and practitioners to understand the concept of parallel database systems in depth.

1.2   Parallel Database Systems

The parallelism in databases is inherited from their underlying data model. In particular, the relational data model (RDM) provides many opportunities for parallelization. For this reason, existing research projects, academic and industrial alike, on parallel databases are nearly exclusively centered on relational systems. In addition to the parallel potential of the relational data model, the worldwide utilization of relational database management systems has further justified the investment in parallel relational databases research. It is, therefore, the objective of this book to review the latest techniques in parallel relational databases.

The topic of parallel databases is large and no single manuscript could be expected to cover this field in a comprehensive manner. In particular, this manuscript does not address parallel object-oriented database systems. However, it is noteworthy that several projects described in this manuscript make use of hybrid relational DBMSs. The emergence of hybrid relational DBMSs such as multimedia object/relational [10] database systems has been made necessary by new database applications as well as the need for commercial corporations to preserve their initial investment in the RDM. These hybrid systems require an extension to the underlying structure of the RDM to support unstructured data types such as text, audio, video, and object-oriented data. Towards this end, many commercial relational DBMSs are now offering support for large data types (also known as binary large objects, or BLOBs) that may require several gigabytes of storage space per row.

1.2.1   Computation Model

In relational databases, the mutual independence between two tables as well as between two tuples within a table, makes simultaneous processing of multiple tables and/or tuples possible. A database request often involves the processing of multiple tables. The ways in which a request accesses these tables and combines the intermediate results are defined by the computation model. Based on this model, one can understand the potential parallelism embedded in a database request.

Computation of a database request is modeled by an extended dataflow graph (EDG) [29]. The idea is to extend a conventional dataflow graph (that is, data operation nodes interconnected by data communication arcs) with partition parallelism; as such, one data operation node may be made up of multiple subnodes. As a result, complex and time consuming database operations, such as join, can be executed concurrently in a divide-and-conquer manner. For example, a join operation between (A join B) can be executed by performing N subjoins (Ai join Bi, where i = 1 to N) in parallel and later combining the results to produce the final answer of the join operation. The EDG model is the basis of FAD [12] and LERA [8], the query languages of the BUBBA and EDS parallel database servers. To better understand the concept of EDG, let us consider the SQL request below:

```
SELECT   *
FROM     employee, department
WHERE    (employee.dept_no = department.dept_no) AND
         (employee.position = "manager")
```

Assuming that the employee relation is partitioned in three fragments (that is, E1, E2, and E3) and the department relation in two (that is, D1 and D2), this request can be represented in the EDG shown in Figure 1.1(b). The control of the execution of the EDG is completely data driven. Referring to the example, when a START signal is received by the SW (single wait), it will initiate the query execution process. It will send a trigger signal to the two SCAN operators which then commence the scanning of the employee table seeking for the tuples whose position matches with the string "manager." Those tuples which satisfy the condition are distributed, by hashing on the dept_no attribute, to the JOIN operators. Conceptually, as soon as one of the employee tuples appears at any one of the JOIN operators, the join operation with the department tuples can proceed without delay. The results of the join operation are assumed to be stored on the same nodes which store the department table. Finally, once the last tuple on each JOIN operator is processed, a signal from each of them will be sent to the GW (global wait) operator. Upon receiving these three end signals, GW will terminate the execution process. It is shown from the above that the EDG is a self-scheduling structure such that once the START signal is sent, the execution of the EDG will run to completion by itself without any external control such as a program counter.

Furthermore, if the underlying execution platform is comprised of multiple processing units, a set of similar database requests can be executed in parallel as follows:

Interquery parallelism. More than one database request can be executed at one time. This will lead to increased throughput—that is, the number of requests processed per second, an important metric in on-line transaction application.

Interoperation parallelism. Within one request more than one operation can be performed simultaneously. In this example both the SCAN and JOIN operations can be executed in parallel. Notice that this form of parallelism is also referred to as pipeline parallelism since the result tuples from the SCAN operator can be processed by the JOIN operator as soon as they are available.

```
SELECT      *
FROM        employee, department
WHERE       (employee.dept_no = department.dept_no) AND (employee.position = "manager")
```

(a)   SQL Request

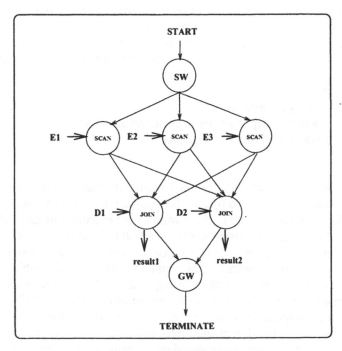

(b)   An equivalent Extended Dataflow Graph.

Figure 1.1: An Extended Dataflow Graph example.

Intraoperation parallelism. This is the parallelism offered by data partitioning. An operation can be split into smaller suboperations if the data that it processes are partitioned. This form of parallelism is the key to response time reduction.

An EDG only shows the potential parallelism of a database request. The actual parallelism depends on the implementation. Realization of the parallelism is a complicated engineering task whose primary objective is to achieve high performance in a cost-effective manner.

1.2.2 Engineering Model

To achieve a high-performance parallel database system, one must provide an efficient environment for EDG execution. This will require a thorough understanding of the parallel database systems engineering model [29]. The engineering model defines how an EDG is physically executed on a parallel database environment. The main target of this book focuses on the engineering model and presents a number of state-of-the-art techniques which can either directly or indirectly lead to high-performance parallel database implementation.

In some practical situations, due to various physical constraints, certain forms of parallelism in an EDG are simply "restricted." In the above example, if there are only four processing units in the underlying parallel platform, two of the five data fragments, E1, E2, E3, D1, and D2 (see Figure 1.1(b)), must then be placed together on the same processing unit. This, inevitably, limits parallelism; but for cost-effectiveness reasons, the parallel database designer may, however, choose to do this. In other situations, parallelism may be "reduced." In the above example, if the communication cost (for example, in setting up a message packet) is high, the SCAN operator may bundle several tuples together before sending them out to the downstream JOIN operator. Effectively, this reduces the pipeline parallelism. In yet other situations, parallelism may be "eliminated" deliberately by the system. In the above example, if the sizes of the employee and the department relations are small, the communication cost between the SCAN and JOIN operators may undermine the processing time of the two operations. In that case, one may group the operators together to avoid the communication overhead. The above are just a few examples depicting how the execution environment can hinder the exploitation of the potential parallelism embedded in an EDG.

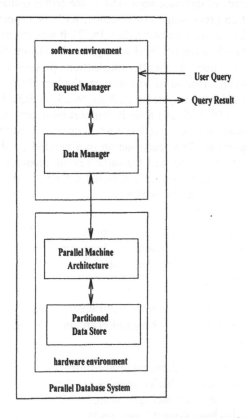

Figure 1.2: Overall internal architecture of a parallel database system.

Software Execution Environment. The top-level architecture of a typical parallel database system (such as the EDS parallel database server [8]) consisting of the software and hardware execution environments is shown in Figure 1.2. The software part is comprised of the request manager and the data manager.

Request Manager. The role of the request manager is (a) to transform a user's request into a set of semantic equivalent EDGs; (b) to select the "best" EDG from the set; and (c) finally, to translate the EDG into an executable object file. For a single request, there is usually more than one way of execution. Query optimization is the process of determining the best execution path. This is a complicated process even for sequential databases. Conventional parallel database systems (such as XRPS) adopt a two-phase optimization approach. In the first phase, the "best" sequential execution plan is determined and in the second, this plan is parallelized. Recent query optimization techniques are presented in [23].

Data Manager. This can be regarded as the parallel database operating system whose major responsibility is to execute the object file produced by the request manager. As pointed out by Stonebraker [24], conventional operating systems (OS) are inefficient for database applications. Some of the traditional features of OS that, generally, do not meet the needs of database applications are buffer management, load placement, and transaction processing. For instance, KEV is a special OS designed for the BUBBA parallel database machine [28]. In [2], it was observed that well-known load balancing methods at the OS level were generally unsuitable and that database-specific schemes were needed. Parallel transactions processing exploits interquery parallelism extensively. Due to its importance, the kernel of a number of existing commercial parallel database systems such as NonStop SQL [5, 9], Oracle Parallel Server [5, 3], and DB2 [5, 20] already support interquery parallelism. Furthermore, parallel transaction processing has opened up many new technical issues, such as recovery management. Data partitioning in a parallel database system renders data more vulnerable to failure. For the same reason, recovery in parallel database platforms is more difficult than in conventional database systems. Researchers are actively investigating techniques to provide reliable yet fast recovery environments (see, for example, [30, 22]).

In addition to the classical database requirements, special features must be provided by the OS for high-performance parallel database implementations. These include interprocessor communications, distributed/shared memory management, multithreading, and group communications.

Hardware Execution Environment. To realize parallelism, suitable hardware must be employed. This includes both a machine with a parallel architecture and a data store supported with the data partition model.

Parallel Machine Architecture. For database applications, machine architectures are classified according to the way in which resources are shared. The classification scheme, first introduced by Stonebraker, includes: shared nothing, shared memory, and shared disk. In a parallel database system based on the shared nothing concept, each system's node has its own main memory and secondary storage devices. Communication between the different nodes is achieved through message-passing across an interconnection network. This lack of resource sharing reduces nodes contention and permits a high degree of scalability. A parallel version of IBM's DB2 [7] running on the RS/6000-based POWERparallel multiprocessor system [14] is one such machine. This version of DB2 has the added advantage of providing advanced features such as support for binary large objects (for compressed video, images, and audio), and character large objects (for text documents) [5]. Despite their popularity [25], shared nothing parallel database systems suffer, in general, from a load balancing problem. In shared disk systems, each node has its private main memory but secondary storage, usually a disk array, is a shared resource. Because the disk data is shared by all nodes, these systems tend to have limited load imbalance but require a global lock manager to preserve the data consistency. Shared memory systems make use of a global main memory shared by all of the system's nodes. The use of a global memory eliminates the load balancing problem. The XPRS running Postgres [17, 15] is an example of such systems. However, these systems do not scale up well, as an increase in the number of nodes leads to more contention over the shared memory. Commercial database systems such as the NCR 3700 tend to have a hybrid architecture that combines some of the above features.

It is noteworthy that in recent years, due to the advancement in operating system and high-speed networking technologies, the differences between distributed and parallel computing are gradually disappearing. Many parallel processing techniques can be applied to distributed computer systems. For example, a shared nothing parallel database system could be developed on a cluster of high performance workstations interconnected by an asynchronous transfer mode (ATM) network by using a parallel OS kernel which supports physical virtual machine (PVM), multithreading, remote procedural call, as well as efficient message passing, and so forth.

Partitioned Data Store. Multiple disks are often used to minimize the data I/O overhead in a parallel database system. In a shared nothing architecture, each processing node is mounted with a local disk and in the shared disk environment the multiple disks are shared among the processing nodes. In the former case, the process of partitioning a database across the processing nodes is a performance-critical design issue. Data partitioning and allocation determine how much work needs to be performed by each node (for example, each subjoin operator), as well as how much communication overhead is incurred during the transfer of intermediate results from one node to another. Common partitioning techniques include range, round-robin, and hash partitioning [13]. These partitioning techniques generally perform the declustering based on a single attribute and, as a result, cannot support multiattribute declustering [6]. Additionally, they do not provide an effective solution for the imbalance caused by insertions and deletions [6]. The grid file declustering (GFD) technique [18] elevates these shortcomings. Other data partitioning techniques are presented and compared in [31]. Similarly, in a shared disk environment, improper partitioning will lead to high data contention rates. This causes reduced concurrency and as a result the system performance can be drastically affected.

1.3   About this Manuscript

Database technology is now rapidly expanding into new application areas such as multimedia, digital libraries, and data warehousing. These new applications areas bring with them many challenging new requirements—such as increased functionality and the efficient handling of very large heterogeneous databases—that need to be addressed by next-generation database management systems (DBMSs).

This manuscript describes how the use of parallel processing technology has made it possible to meet these new challenges. It includes nine invited papers that emphasize techniques for achieving high performance in parallel database systems. This will be beneficial to designers in the areas of database and parallel processing who intend to design their own parallel database products as well as to database practitioners who are contemplating migrating their sequential database systems to parallel platforms.

Because of its increased importance, the body of research in the area of parallel databases has become a large one. As a result, several manuscripts, such as [1, 16, 19], dealing with this topic have appeared recent years. In particular, [1] focuses on the architectures of various parallel database systems such as DBC/1012, NCR 3700, IDIOMS, MDBS, IFS2, and the Datacycle project. Consequently, [1] is a good complement to this book.

The body of this manuscript is structured according to the overall architecture of a parallel database system (see Figure 1.2). The nine chapters in this book present a number of state-of-the-art techniques which can be adopted in the design of parallel database software and hardware execution environments. Chapters 2, 3, and 4 are related to the request manager; Chapters 5 and 6 to the data manager; Chapters 7, 8, and 9 to the parallel machine architecture; and finally, Chapter 10 addresses concerns about different techniques for the partitioned data store.

Chapter 2 (request manager related). A survey of parallel query optimization techniques for requests involving multiway joins is presented in this chapter. In particular, the two-phase heuristics algorithm designed for the XPRS shared memory parallel database system is emphasized. In the first phase, the optimizer identifies the "best" sequential execution plan; and in the second phase, the optimized parallelized version of the plan is derived.

Chapter 3 (request manager related). In database query optimization, in addition to selecting the "best" execution plan, the optimizer is also required to select the best algorithm for the operations involved in the plan. The former step is often referred to as global optimization and the latter, local optimization. This chapter introduces a new technique for the time-consuming join operation. This can be adopted in the local optimization stage. Page connectivity information [21] is used extensively in this new technique.

Chapter 4 (request manager related.) In the process of designing new parallel query optimization techniques (such as designing a new cost model), it is important that the design choices (for example, communication cost) are valid. This chapter describes the Test Pilot system—a performance evaluation tool for parallel databases. Such a tool can be used to serve the above-mentioned purpose. Furthermore, it can be used for performance tuning—a critical step to be taken by the database engineers after a database system has been commissioned.

Chapter 5 (data manager related). This chapter gives insight into the behavior of buffering and locking mechanisms for parallel database applications. It includes a case study where traditional load balancing techniques are shown to be unsuitable for such applications. This study stresses the need for database-specific load balancing techniques. The results of this study will be beneficial for the development of intelligent load balancing schemes.

Chapter 6 (data manager related). This chapter introduces a framework for recovery in parallel database systems using the ACTA formalism [22]. This approach enables concise description of the recovery mechanism in a parallel database environment. This is essential for database designers in working out new parallel recovery techniques.

Chapter 7 (parallel machine architecture related). This chapter describes the architecture of the NCR's new Petabyte multimedia parallel system [10]. This is a commercial product. The architectural features of the machine to support multimedia applications as well as the object/relational data model are outlined in this chapter.

Chapter 8 (parallel machine architecture related). The Medusa parallel database system is described in this chapter. It is a transputer-based shared nothing system. It was designed with a new technique for self-managing its own data partitions, with minimal impact to transaction processing [6].

Chapter 9 (parallel machine architecture related). This chapter describes the Super Database Computer, SDC-II. It was designed with a special hardware support for the bucket spreading hash join algorithm. This novel hardware-supported join technique is the key to the high performance rate for complex queries offered by SDC-II.

Chapter 10 (partitioned data store related). This chapter presents a case study for a shared nothing parallel database server. It analyzes and compares the effectiveness of five data placement techniques under different environmental settings, such as number of nodes, the database size, and the relative frequency of queries. The analytical results are helpful to database designers for choosing suitable data placement techniques for his/her environment.

Bibliography

[1] M. Abdelguerfi and S. Lavington, *Emerging Trends in Database and Knowledge-Base Machines: the Application of Parallel Architectures to Smart Information Systems*, IEEE CS Press, Los Alamitos, CA, 1995.

[2] L. Borrmann, B. Shiemann, and E. Born, "Load Placement in Distributed High-Performance Database Systems," *Parallel Database Techniques*, M. Abdelguerfi and K.F. Wong, eds., chapter 5, IEEE CS Press, Los Alamitos, CA, 1998, pp. 93–115.

[3] S. Bobrowski, "Bobrowski, S.," *DBMS*, Dec. 1993.

[4] N. Bond and S. Reddaway, "A Massively Parallel Indexing Engine Using dap," *Emerging Trends in Database and Knowledge-Base Machines: the Application of Parallel Architectures to Smart Information Systems*, M. Abdelguerfi and S. Lavington, eds., chapter 9, IEEE CS Press, 1995, pp. 159–179.

[5] C.J. Bontempo and C.M. Saracco, *Database Management Principles and Products*, Prentice Hall, 1995.

[6] G.M. Bryan and W.E. Moore, "The Medusa Project," *Parallel Database Techniques*, M. Abdelguerfi and K.F. Wong, eds., chapter 8, IEEE CS Press, Los Alamitos, CA, 1998, pp. 165–182.

[7] C. Baru et al., "An Overview of DB2 Parallel Edition," *Proc. ACM SIGMOD Conf.*, pp. 460–462, 1985.

[8] P. Borla-Salamet, C. Chachty, and B.B. Bergsten, "Capturing Parallel Data Processing Strategies within a Compiled Language," *Parallel Processing and Data Management*, P. Valduriez, ed., Chapman-Hall, 1992, pp. 295–316.

[9] C. Mala et al., *Enhancing Availability, Management, and Performance for Nonstop tm/mp*, tech. report, Tandem Systems Review, Tandem, July 1994.

[10] F. Carino and W. Sterling, "Parallel Strategies and New Concepts for a Petabyte Multimedia Database Computer," *Parallel Database Techniques*, M. Abdelguerfi and K.F. Wong, eds., chapter 7, IEEE CS Press, Los Alamitos, CA, 1998, pp. 139–164.

[11] D. Patterson et al., "The Case for Redundant Arrays of Inexpensive Disks (RAID)," *Proc. ACM SIGMOD Conf.*, Vol. 6, 1988, pp. 109–116.

[12] S. Danforth and P. Valduriez, "A Fad for Data Intensive Applications," *IEEE Trans. Knowledge and Data Eng.*, Vol. 4, No. 1, 1992, pp. 34–51.

[13] D. DeWitt and J. Gray, "Parallel Database Systems: The Future of High Performance Database Systems," *Comm. ACM*, Vol. 35, No. 6, 1992, pp. 85–91.

[14] G. Fecteau, "Database 2 AIX/6000 Parallel Technology," tech. report, IBM Software Solution Laboratory, Ontario, Canada, Mar. 1994.

[15] G. Graefe et al., "Tuning a Parallel Database Algorithm on a Shared-Memory Multiprocessor," *Software—Practice and Experience*, Vol. 22, No. 7, 1992, pp. 495–571.

[16] H. Lui et al., *Query Processing in Parallel Relational Database Systems*, IEEE CS Press, Los Alamitos, CA, 1994.

[17] W. Hong, "Exploiting Inter-Operation Parallelism in XPRS," *Proc. ACM SIGMOD Conf.*, 1992, pp. 19–28.

[18] K.A. Hua and C. Lee, "An Adaptive Data Placement Schemes for Parallel Database Computer Systems," *Proc. 16th VLDB Conf.*, 1990, pp. 493–506.

[19] A.R. Hurson, *IEEE Tutorial: Parallel Architectures for Database Systems*, IEEE CS Press, Los Alamitos, CA, 1989.

[20] *IBM DATABASE 2 Version 3, Administrative Guide Volumes I, II and III*, IBM Corp., SC26-4888, Dec. 1993.

[21] C. Lee, "New Approaches to Join Optimization in Parallel Database Systems Utilizing Page Connectivity Information," *Parallel Database Techniques*, M. Abdelguerfi and K.F. Wong, eds., chapter 3, IEEE CS Press, Los Alamitos, CA, 1998, pp. 43–75.

[22] L.D. Molesky and K. Ramamritham, "Modeling Recovery in Client-Server Database Systems," *Parallel Database Techniques*, M. Abdelguerfi and K.F. Wong, eds., chapter 6, IEEE CS Press, Los Alamitos, CA, 1998, pp. 119–138.

[23] M. Zait, M. Ziane, and P. Valduriez, "Optimization for Parallel Execution," *Parallel Database Techniques*, M. Abdelguerfi and K.F. Wong, eds., chapter 2, IEEE CS Press, Los Alamitos, CA, 1998, pp. 15–41.

[24] M. Stonebraker, "Operating System Support for Database Management," *Comm. ACM*, Vol. 24, No. 7, 1981, pp. 412–418.

[25] M. Stonebraker, "The Case for Shared Nothing," *Database Engineering*, Vol. 9, No. 1, 1986, pp. 4–9.

[26] *Sybase Navigation Server: Delivering the Promise of Parallel High-Performance*, Technical Paper Series, Sybase, 1994.

[27] T. Tamura and M. Kitsuregawa, "System Software of the Super Database Computer SDC-II," *Parallel Database Techniques*, M. Abdelguerfi and K.F. Wong, eds., chapter 9, IEEE CS Press, Los Alamitos, CA, 1998, pp. 185–201.

[28] K. Wilkinson and H. Boral, "Kev—A Kernel for Bubba," *Proc. 5th Int'l Workshop on Database Machines*, Japan, Oct. 1987, pp. 109–116.

[29] K.F. Wong, "Parallel Database Systems Engineering," *Tutorial Notes in 1995 EuroPar Conf.*, Stockholm, Sweden, Aug. 29–31, 1995.

[30] K.F. Wong, "Performance Evaluation of Three Logging Schemes for a Shared-Nothing Database Server," *Proc. 1995 Int'l Conf. on Distributed Computing Systems (ICDCS'95)*, Vancouver, Canada, May 30–June 2, 1995, pp. 221–228.

[31] S. Zhou and M.H. Williams, "Data Placement in Parallel Database Systems," *Parallel Database Techniques*, M. Abdelguerfi and K.F. Wong, eds., chapter 10, IEEE CS Press, Los Alamitos, CA, 1998, pp. 203–219.

Part I

Request Manager

Chapter 2

Designing an Optimizer for Parallel Relational Systems

Patrick Valduriez, Mohamed Zaït, and Mikal Ziane

Abstract. *In this chapter we address the problem of query optimization in parallel relational systems and highlight the differences with the sequential case. We first define the new task of the optimizer, namely parallelization, and then discuss the pros and cons of several heuristics which address the problem of a large search space. Special attention is given to the two-phase heuristics used in XPRS. Finally, we expose the problems related to the design of a cost model in a parallel environment and the impact on the search strategies.*

2.1 Introduction

This chapter is based on the experience we gained in designing and implementing the optimizers of the Bubba [4] and then the DBS3 [3, 40, 25] parallel relational systems. It concerns people who are already familiar with sequential (one-processor) cost-based optimization [22, 31] and would like either to build a parallel optimizer (that is, an optimizer for parallel execution, not an optimizer running on several processors) or would like to understand the main design issues. Note that it is not a survey of parallel query processing techniques: we assume that the reader is already familiar with the basic techniques to parallelize relational operators. Also, our examples and some of the analysis will essentially deal with multijoin queries. This is a natural (and quite usual) decision: first, multijoin optimization is by far the most important task of relational optimizers, second, its issues and solutions can easily be adapted to other relational operators.

Before we summarize these issues, let us recall the basic terms of query optimization. The objective of a database optimizer is to produce a good execution plan for a given query. The quality of a plan is defined by a *cost function* which estimates response time or the amount of resources used (sometimes called total work) or a combination of both. The optimizer searches a set of candidate plans which can be generated thanks to transformation rules (for example, moving a selection before a join). The set of candidate plans is called the *search space*.

A good optimizer balances the potentially tremendous optimization effort and the quality of the resulting execution plan. It would be much too complex to design an optimizer including all the low-level execution techniques available on a given system. In particular, designing and validating the cost model would simply be intractable. This was already true with sequential optimization but parallelism severely aggravates this problem. It is therefore vital to carefully choose heuristics to reduce the search space as well as simplify the design of the optimizer.

In this chapter we will review some of the most important simplifying heuristics which were evaluated in various research prototypes. We will especially focus on the two-phase approach [18] which splits parallel optimization into a classical sequential phase and a parallelization phase. Section 2.2 will present this approach which requires that we first define parallelization as constraining the execution of a dataflow tree of operators. Section 2.3 will define more precisely typical decisions to be taken in the parallelization phase. Section 2.4 will discuss the interest of typical heuristics in shared memory and distributed memory architectures. Finally, the issues related to the cost model will be addressed in Section 2.5 and issues related to the search strategies in Section 2.6. Section 2.7 concludes the chapter.

2.2 Overall Design Issues

2.2.1 Design a Simple Parallel Execution Model

The first thing to do to build a parallel optimizer is to define an *abstract parallel execution model* which will be the abstract machine on which the execution plans will run. This abstract execution model is not to be confused with the "real" (or low-level) execution model of the parallel machine: it is similar to an algebraic machine (that is, a set of algorithms for relational operators) with more complex rules to combine these algorithms and execute them in parallel.

A mistake which is crucial to avoid here would be to define a too complex model. It is not only useless but in fact dramatically inefficient to include in the optimizer's execution model all the low-level options that the target machine supports. First, it is difficult to design such a model. Second, it is extremely difficult, if only practically possible, to design and validate a cost model for a complex execution model. Third, it can dramatically increase the search space to let the optimizer decide among two options, while it might not greatly improve the quality of the plan produced.

Suppose, for example, that for each relational operation you want to let the optimizer decide, say, among two ways to manage pipeline queues. If, on the average, both options are valid for, say, three nodes of a query, then your search space is eight times larger than if you had a priori decided to discard one of the options! And there are simply too many of those parameters to consider. Well, of course if the execution model is too simple it will be impossible to design a good cost function because it will simply lack information to make good predictions. It is a good idea though to start with an oversimplified model and then add features one by one until an acceptable cost function can be produced.

2.2.2   The Two-Phase Approach

Once you get the execution model, you can deal with the overall architecture of the optimizer, that is, define which modules will do what and how they will interact. At this point, it is useful to notice that, as pointed out in [18], a parallel plan can be viewed as a parallelization of some sequential plan. Hence, optimization for parallel optimization could be decomposed into two phases: classical sequential optimization and parallelization. As we will see, these phases can heuristically be considered as independent and it would then greatly simplify your task since it might be possible to reuse an existing sequential optimizer or at least well-known sequential optimization techniques. You could then concentrate your efforts on the parallelization phase.

More precisely, the *two-phase hypothesis* introduced by [18] states that the parallelization of the best sequential plan is the best parallel plan. If this hypothesis is true in your system, then you can safely reuse a sequential optimizer and easily plug it into a parallelization module. If the hypothesis does not hold on your system, then you can still conceptually distinguish two modules but you will need a more complex design or have to accept suboptimal parallel plans. This overall decision is maybe the most important issue of parallel optimizer design since it can either save you a lot of effort or lead to a low-quality optimizer.

There is now a potential confusion which must be dispelled. Defining an abstract parallel execution model for the optimizer does not mean that there is no *low-level* parallelization module in the execution system, that is, after the two phases of parallel optimization. This is sort of a third phase which does exist in the DBS3 [3, 5] system for example, and there is a priori no limit to the number of abstraction layers. The real question is whether or not these layers are independent, that is, whether or not the search space can be pruned with limited impact on the quality of the resulting execution plan.

2.2.3   Parallelizing is Adding Information!

To say that a parallel plan is a parallelization of some sequential plan is in fact quite ambiguous, and it is necessary to precisely define what *parallelization* means. If a parallelization is any transformation of a sequential plan which produces an equivalent parallel plan (that is, a plan producing the same results) then of course any parallel plan is equivalent to some sequential plan. But such a definition is too general: two completely different sequential algorithms computing the same function could lead to the same parallel plan. This is not the kind of transformation that we had in mind: it is usually assumed that parallelizing a sequential plan keeps something of it.

This ambiguity explains super-linear speedups which often surprise the newcomers to parallelism. Suppose, for example, that a nested-loop join is parallelized by cloning, using a hash-function on the join attribute to distribute tuples of both relations. It should not be surprising that a super-linear speedup is achieved, since the parallel algorithm had better been compared to a sequential hash join. This example might seem a bit trivial, but suppose now that a sequential hash-based join is parallelized. Super-linear speedups can also be achieved in some cases if the degree of fragmentation (that is, the number of hash buckets) of the parallel algorithm (a typical decision of the parallelization phase), is different from the degree of the sequential version.

So, if the parallelization phase can lead to super-linear speedups what is the limit? What decisions should be made in the parallelization phase and what decisions should be left to the sequential optimization phase? Remember that it was for the sake of simplicity that we decided to distinguish, conceptually at least and maybe in the implementation, two phases. It would then not be consistent to let the parallelization phase do most of the job. Worse, it would then have to undo what was done in the first phase. So, to avoid that, we will define parallelization as the mere addition of information. There is however a problem then, since obviously there is something of sequential plans that parallel execution models do not respect: scheduling for example. This leads to *abstract execution plans* which represent the part of sequential plans which are not to be changed by the parallelization phase.

Like sequential plans, abstract execution plans can be defined as dataflow trees whose leaves represent database relations and whose nonleaf nodes are algorithms for relational operators (such as hash join). A typical sequential system would be able to execute such a tree without any additional information. This does not mean that all sequential systems would execute a given tree the same way. For example, System R would rely on synchronous pipelining [29] to avoid intermediate results while some other systems might materialize them, that is, wait until they are completely produced (that is, store them) before consuming them.

Since part of the execution (especially the scheduling of tuple consumption) is often implicitly constrained by the execution system (rather than explicitly in the plan), a sequential optimizer might produce sequential execution plans which are simply abstract plans. It is nevertheless more correct to say that abstract plans (rather than sequential plans) are parallelized, and if a sequential plan does explicitly bear additional information we assume that it could be easily removed or ignored.

To summarize, the parallelization phase takes as input sequential plans produced by the sequential optimization phase, and only considers their dataflow tree of operators, removing or ignoring any additional information. The parallelization phase will only add information to it, that is, further constrain execution. This information depends on the abstract parallel execution model which has been designed for the optimizer. Before we focus on the parallelization phase it is necessary to give a more precise picture of how the two phases can be incorporated into an optimizer's design.

2.2.4   Two-Phase versus Parallel Approaches

Up to now we have decomposed parallel optimization into two *phases* (the accepted term). This term is a bit misleading though, since it seems to presuppose that in the implementation the first phase will be finished before the second phase starts. To clearly indicate that we make no such assumption, we prefer to use the term *module*.[1] It is convenient to consider that each of these modules is further decomposed into two modules: the first one produces alternatives (execution plans at various abstraction levels), and the second one discards some of them. Optimization for parallel execution is then seen as a dataflow chain of four modules.

---

[1] These modules are in fact operators which take as input a set of plans (or a query) and produce plans. We use "module" to avoid confusion with relational operators.

It is now easy to represent the *two-phase approach* which consists of using a sequential optimizer to produce one single plan which is then parallelized (right side of Figure 2.1). The main alternative approach, which we will call the *parallel optimization* approach, does not discard any abstract plan before parallelization (left side of Figure 2.1).

In Figure 2.1 the two-phase approach might look more complex, but it is indeed easier to implement and much less resource-consuming. If a sequential optimizer can be reused then only the parallelization and choice modules have to be implemented. Even if such an optimizer is not available it is still easier to pass a single abstract plan on to the parallelization module than to deal with a set of abstract plans.

In the parallel approach, the parallelization module is typically called for each abstract plan which is obviously quite time-consuming. Intermediate approaches are of course possible which would filter the set of abstract plans more or less severely using heuristics. More generally, all the classical optimization techniques can be applied. For instance, the global space of parallel plans, that is, the set of all the parallelizations of all the abstract plans can be searched using randomized techniques [20, 36, 24].

One might wonder how it can make sense to discard sequential plans when the target system is not sequential. It should not be a problem, though, to define a sequential cost function for a multiprocessor system by simply instantiating the general cost function with appropriate parameters (the number of processors will of course be set to one).

The first system for which the two-phase approach was implemented is the XPRS research prototype. On this shared memory system, each processor runs a Postgres [35] relational execution engine. It was then of course the original optimizer of Postgres which was used in the first phase. [18] reports only an 8 percent loss of optimality due to the two-phase approach, but XPRS, as we will show in Section 2.4.4, was an especially favorable case. Before we shed some light on the domain of validity of the two-phase hypothesis we need to make more precise the typical decisions that the parallelization phase will take.

2.3 Parallelization

2.3.1 Kinds of Parallelism

When we interpreted parallelization as the addition of information to abstract execution plans rather than as a complete transformation, we assumed that *algorithms are black boxes*, which means that the algorithms of an abstract plan will still be present, intact, in the parallel plan. This might be a bit surprising but [14] did describe an elegant model in which sequential plans are parallelized by the introduction of so-called *exchange operators*. This approach allows the implementation of sequential algorithms which can then very easily be parallelized.

Parallelism occurs at a given instant when several units of work are in progress. If the algorithms are black boxes, does it mean then that the units of work are the instances of algorithms in the abstract plan? Not really, because if the optimizer cannot break down the code of an algorithm into pieces,[2] it can still fragment its input data.

---

[2]It is often convenient to distinguish two operators in hash-based join algorithms: build and probe. The optimizer, however, does not need to be aware of them but merely whether or not one argument must be materialized.

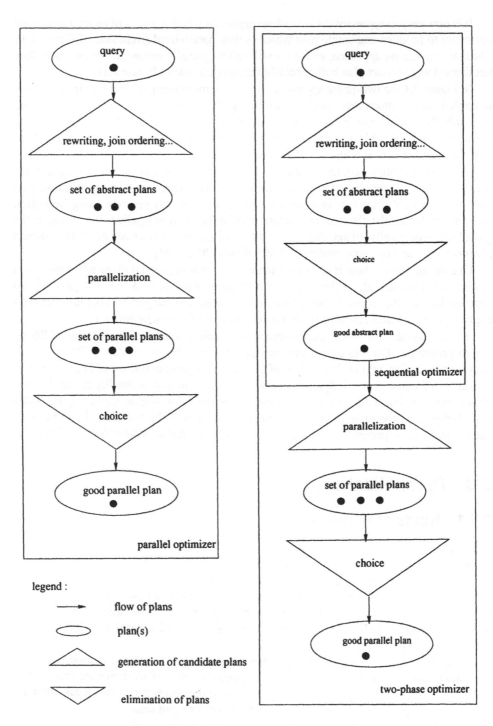

Figure 2.1: Parallel versus two-phase approaches.

This leads to *intraoperation parallelism* which is achieved by replicating the algorithm's code, each clone being allocated to one processor along with a fraction of the input data. The set of processors which will execute the operation is called the *home* of the operation [41]. In shared memory systems it is usually not wise to let the optimizer choose the operations' homes because the execution system will do it dynamically for better load balancing. In distributed memory, on the other hand, the cost of communication is much higher and it might be a good idea to let the optimizer specify these homes.

Interoperation parallelism occurs when units of work in progress at the same time belong to several operations. *Asynchronous pipelining* occurs when two parallel operations are linked by a dataflow arc, while *independent parallelism* occurs when they are not. Interoperation parallelism should not be confused with overlapping the execution of several operations such as in synchronous pipelining. Synchronous pipelining [29] can be useful to avoid storing large intermediate results but does not reduce response time the way parallelism can.

Since relational plans usually involve many more tuples than operations, data fragmentation is by far the most interesting source of parallelism. The interest of interoperation parallelism is much more difficult to assess. In particular, load balancing is more difficult to achieve with interoperator parallelism.

2.3.2 Specifying Parallel Execution

We now make more precise the kind of information which is to be added by the parallelization module (which we will now call *parallelizer*). It would be difficult, if only possible, to give an exhaustive review of all the decisions which a parallelizer could take. We will then simply give a very general and informal specification of the set of possibilities which the parallelization information constrains, and then mention a few examples of what is done in practice.

The first thing to identify is the atomic actions which can be used to execute a given abstract plan. Since we decided to consider the code of algorithms as black boxes, the parallelizer cannot break it down. On the other hand, as was already said, the input relations can be fragmented or replicated, and each fragment passed on to one or several clones of the algorithms' code, provided that the algorithms accept anonymous inputs [14]. Note that such transformations are not necessarily related to parallelism and hash-based join algorithms, for example, can be obtained from an initial nested-loop algorithm by fragmenting both input relations with a hash function on join attributes.

For a given abstract plan there are many ways to decompose it into atomic actions, and for each set of actions the parallelizer still has to choose a scheduling, that is, to specify a partial order on this set. This makes so many possibilities that it would, of course, be ridiculous for the parallelizer to generate each one of them and compute its cost. On the contrary, the typical optimizer will rely on a limited set of well-known general strategies, some of which will be discussed below.

The ideal parallelizer would rely on a general model on which a declarative language would allow the specification of these strategies. Quite ideally too, the constraints imposed by the semantics of relational operations, the dataflow constraints of the abstract plan to parallelize, the semantics of relational algorithms, the execution model, and the resources available would also be specified declaratively. While we are not aware of the existence of such a wonder, the parallelizer's designer should, however, clearly identify these constraints and what level of extensibility is worth the effort.

Some people think, for example, that a relational difference cannot start the consumption of its second argument before its first argument has been completely consumed. In fact this constraint is not intrinsic to the difference operation but to some of its algorithms. Another example of constraint which is sometimes badly specified is the impossibility to execute a join in pipeline with the production of both its arguments. While many systems forbid the specification of two pipeline inputs in any operation, some other systems do allow such executions [2, 38]. It would be too bad to compromise the portability of a parallelizer by overestimating the generality of such constraints.

The most obvious constraint imposed by a dataflow execution tree is that an operation cannot consume tuples which have not yet been produced and made available to it. Let us recall that a relation is said to be *materialized* when all its tuples must be produced before the consumption of any of them can start. The simplest way to constrain the scheduling (ordering) of tuple consumptions is to specify which relations will be materialized and which ones will be consumed in pipeline with their production.

Some execution models impose that plans be sliced into sequential phases. In such models, each operation of the execution plan is completely executed during one specific phase, thereby imposing that the execution of an operation cannot overlap with two phases. Consequently, the parallelizer must then specify a *slicing strategy* [41], which will determine nonoverlapping subtrees of the execution plan, whose operations are executed simultaneously. Depending on the *shape* of the execution tree, specifying materialized and pipelined intermediate results may or may not be enough to determine a slicing strategy. The issues related to the shape of execution trees are presented in the next section.

Memory allocation will not generally be explicitly mentioned by the parallelizer but the cost model must be able to predict how much of it will be necessary. This does not mean that these predictions need to be made statically, since the decisions which depend on this information could be postponed at runtime, using, for example, choose-plan operators [15, 9]. Note that this has nothing to do with the two-phase approach which we mentioned above. The two-phase approach heuristically discards sequential plans and a priori (unless the two-phase assumption is proven) compromises optimality. On the contrary, the solution introduced by [15] only discards plans which are known to be dominated and preserves optimality.

The degree of parallelism[3] of each operation, as well as the number of fragments of the data, are often specified by parallelizers. On the other hand, in shared memory it is usually not a good idea to assign specific processors to operations (when it is possible). More generally, in shared memory, the execution system rather than the parallelizer, should take load-balancing-related decisions [6].

2.4 Search Space

In this section we investigate the size of the different search spaces of parallel plans, then, we present the most usual heuristics used to restrict the large search space of parallel op-

---

[3] That is, the number of processors, or sometimes threads.

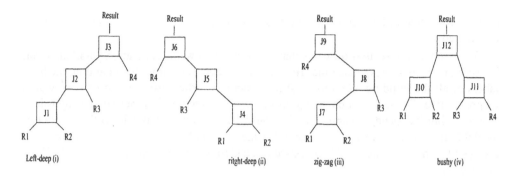

Figure 2.2: Execution plans of various shapes.

timization. These heuristics concern the shape of the execution trees and the two-phase approach.

2.4.1 Slicing Hash Join Trees

For linear trees, that is, trees in which at least one argument of each join operation is a base relation (as opposed to an intermediate relation), specifying which operations are materialized is enough to determine a slicing strategy. However, this is not the case of bushy (that is, nonlinear) trees and either the execution sysi 1 or the optimizer has to further constrain their scheduling. In this section we analyze the problem of choosing a slicing strategy for a tree of hash joins, and its relationship with the shape (linear, bushy, ...) of the tree. Consider the following example,

Example 2.4.1

    Select R_2.* from R_1, R_2, R_3, R_4
    where $R_1.A=R_2.A$ and $R_2.B=R_3.B$ and $R_3.C=R_4.C$

Figure 2.2 shows the different tree shapes for this example.

[30] adopted a convenient notation for capturing trees of hash join algorithms in which the right operand is consumed in pipeline (it is called the probing operand) while the left operand is blocked (it is called the building operand). The authors then compared the advantages of two extreme cases among the different slicing strategies of linear trees, namely the strategies associated with left-deep and right-deep trees. In a left-deep tree, each probing operand is a base relation, so that pipeline is not possible between joins. With these trees, only intraoperation parallelism is possible. In a right-deep tree, each materialized operand is a base relation and all the joins can be evaluated in pipeline if enough memory is available.

The size of available main memory is indeed a crucial factor which must be taken into account. Recent relational systems are expected to have enough memory to load one or more relations although probably not enough to load all the relations of a very complex query. [18] experimentally demonstrated that, at least in the context of their shared memory system (XPRS), the size of main memory, as long as it is above the hash join threshold [32], has little impact on the choice of the best plan. This is due to the fact that their search space is restricted to left-deep trees and this is no longer valid when other tree shapes are considered.

To be more precise, in some cases that we discuss below, interoperation parallelism can be useful to decrease response time. However, to execute several joins in parallel, the hash tables of all the building relations must fit in memory, otherwise the cost of IOs[4] would be prohibitive. Thus, the number of joins that can be executed in pipeline in a right-deep tree, or using independent parallelism in a bushy tree, directly depends on the amount of available memory. Since it is not likely that the hash tables of all the base relations will always fit in main memory, [30] proposed a scheduling strategy called Static Right Deep Scheduling.

This strategy consists of slicing a right-deep tree into phases, such that each resulting fragment is expected to fit in memory, and spooling to disk the temporary results between two phases. [40] proposed avoiding spooling the intermediate results to disk which means slicing the RD trees into more phases, possibly diminishing potential parallelism, to save IOs. It was shown that this technique can be improved by using zigzag trees (see Figure 2.2) [41] which consume less main memory than static right-deep trees. Left-deep, right-deep, and zigzag trees are linear trees whose scheduling is much simpler than that of bushy trees. However, [7] demonstrated that some form of bushy trees called segmented right-deep trees can be interesting. [34] also considered bushy trees and included memory resources and pipelining in an optimization model for symmetric multiprocessors.

2.4.2 Search Space Size

In this section we investigate the sizes of the different search spaces. The analysis uses standard combinatorial methods, so details are omitted. Given a query with n relations, the question is how many plans can be built within each type of search space, without considering several join methods or scheduling, that is, only plan (or tree) shape matters.[5] The results are summarized in Table 2.1.

First, consider a bushy space. The number, x_n, of possible tree shapes for a query of n relations, supposing that each tree root node has a left (respectively right) operand capturing k (respectively $n - k$) relations is,

$$x_n = \sum_{k=1}^{n-1} \binom{n}{k} x_k x_{n-k}, \text{where} \qquad x_1 = 1$$

The solution is proven to be $x_n = (2n - 2)!/(n - 1)!$ in [37], which computes the maximum number of tree shapes obtained when the Cartesian product is permitted or all relations are pairwise joinable.

For chain queries (each relation can join with at most two others, and the two "ends" can join with only one) without the Cartesian product, there are fewer bushy trees, computed

---

[4]Reading and/or writing to disks.

[5][37] computes upper and lower bounds for the search space, supposing that the optimizer produces many trees with the same shape, considering the home of the intermediate relations and the scheduling.

Search Space	Min.[a] # of tree shapes	Max.[b] # of tree shapes	Max. # of tree shapes for 5 relations	Max. # of tree shapes for 10 relations
Left- or Right-deep	2^{n-1}	$n!$	120	3,628,800
Zigzag	$2^{n-2} \cdot 2^{n-1}$	$2^{n-2} \cdot n!$	920	232,243,200
Bushy	$\frac{2^{n-1}}{n}\binom{2n-2}{n-1}$	$\frac{(2n-2)!}{(n-1)!}$	1,680	17,643,225,600

[a]Chain queries, trees without Cartesian products.
[b]Queries where all relations are pairwise joinable or trees with Cartesian products.

Table 2.1: Maximum and minimum number of tree shapes in different search spaces.

by y_n below,

$$y_n = \sum_{k=1}^{n-1} 2 y_k y_{n-k}, \text{where} \qquad y_1 = 1$$

as the chain can be partitioned in $n - 1$ places, but either partition may be the left child. The relationship $y_n = 2^{n-1} x_n / n!$ may be verified by substitution in the recurrence. Chain queries have the fewest possible plans, so y_n gives the minimum number of bushy tree shapes.

Now consider a space of linear trees. If all relations are joinable or the Cartesian product is permitted, we have $n!$ as the maximum number of tree shapes in the left- or right-deep space, because all permutations of the n relations are considered. In a zigzag search space, the maximum number is multiplied by 2^{n-2}, because, in each point of a permutation, except the first and second points, the base relations can be joined as the left or right operand. What is a little surprising is that the number, z_n, of linear trees is exponential even for chain queries. If there are k operations to the left of the one chosen to be performed first, then there are $\binom{n-2}{k}$ ways to complete the plan (and there are two choices for the chosen first join). This gives the formula:

$$z_n = \sum_{k=0}^{n-2} 2\binom{n-2}{k} = 2^{n-1}$$

which is the minimum number of left- or right-deep tree shapes. The minimum number of zigzag tree shapes is obtained by multiplying by 2^{n-2}, as for the maximum number.

2.4.3 Heuristics

One reason why the search space for parallel execution is especially large is that it seems quite difficult to find heuristics that are good for all parallel architectures and execution systems. Even for a specific architecture it is not easy to find heuristics that are independent of the execution model or the available algorithms. We will, however, try to shed some light on the advantages and drawbacks of the shapes of trees that we presented above, with respect to distributed and shared memory architectures.

When there are few processors in shared memory (SM), left-deep trees seem better than other tree formats, because a good speedup is obtained by assigning all processors to a given operation, that is, intraoperation parallelism is enough. Interoperation parallelism introduced by other tree formats (such as right-deep) incurs time-sharing, with its associated overhead. Interoperation parallelism becomes interesting for a higher number of processors, when intraoperation parallelism introduces too much overhead relative to the amount of work of each thread.

The difference between bushy, right-deep, and zigzag is merely in the ratio of the number of processors to the amount of parallelism allowed. When memory is a limited resource, zigzag trees seem to dominate other linear trees [40]. If data are stored on disks and that disk bandwidth is not sufficient to have many operations executing in parallel, then left-deep trees are preferable over right-deep and bushy trees.

In distributed memory (DM), if relations are fully partitioned on all nodes, left-deep trees seem to be better than other tree formats, for two reasons. First, if relations are not repartitioned, interoperation parallelism introduced by other tree formats incurs time-sharing which may be costly. Second, repartitioning relations to avoid time-sharing incurs communication overhead. However, if relations are partitioned on disjoint homes, right-deep trees seem to dominate other tree formats because they allow exploitation of all processors.

One drawback of bushy trees is that they introduce synchronization points which limit parallelism. On the other hand, when relations are small, bushy trees seem better than right-deep trees because the pipeline stages in a right-deep tree are not active at the same time (that is, it reduces to a left-deep tree), while several operations of a bushy tree may still execute concurrently. When relations are partially partitioned, that is, some relations share the same home and the homes are disjoint (there is no overlap between homes), bushy trees are probably better than right-deep trees because some pipeline stages share the same home (that is, execute in time-sharing).

2.4.4 The Two-Phase Heuristics

As we said above, the two-phase approach is both a simple way to implement an optimizer for parallel execution, and a way to drastically restrict the search space. In this section we shed some light on the question of deciding when to use it. Intuitively, if all the sequential plans got the same speedup when parallelized, then the two-phase hypothesis would always be valid.

More precisely, let SP be a sequential plan and PP its best parallelization. Suppose that the cost function of a sequential plan is its total resource consumption: $seqcost(SP) = W(SP)$. Suppose now, as it is done in several systems [18, 41], that the cost function of a parallel plan PP is given by $parcost(PP) = W(PP) + k * T(PP)$ where T is the response time and k is a weighting factor. Parallelizing a plan introduces some overhead, $W(PP) - W(SP)$, for starting and terminating the processes, for synchronization, and because of the communications between the processors (in distributed memory). If this overhead was proportional to $W(SP)$, if the load was always perfectly distributed among the processing elements (processors, disks, ...), and if a fixed number of processing elements was allocated to all the plans, then $T(PP)$ would be proportional to $W(SP)$. In such a case $parcost(PP)$ would be proportional to $seqcost(SP)$ and the two-phase hypothesis would be valid. When such a proportional relation does not hold, it is likely that among all the sequential execution plans, some might get more benefit from parallelization than others. It would then be unlikely that sequential optimization and parallelization are independent.

It is interesting to note that the system in which the two-phase approach was first introduced (XPRS) is not very far from this situation. Its architecture is shared memory so that all the processors can be assigned to any join, and load balancing is much easier to achieve than in distributed memory. Moreover, the search space is restricted to left-deep trees which only allows intraoperation parallelism and thus load balancing (of a single query) is easily achieved if data are uniformly fragmented. Since data are partitioned on all the disks in a round-robin fashion, selections that do not use indices always use all the disks.

Suppose that the two-phase hypothesis is not valid for some query to be run on some systems. This means that the best join ordering, say SP_0, cannot be parallelized into the best parallel plan, which is in fact a parallelization of another join ordering, say SP_1. How is it possible that the parallel cost of SP_0 (that is, the parallel cost of its best parallelization) is worse than the parallel cost of SP_1 while its sequential cost is better?

From the formulas we gave above, we can deduce two cases which can lead to a violation of the two-phase hypothesis: either the overhead of parallelism is greater for SP_0, or the overhead is not greater but SP_0's response time is still greater than SP_1's.

In distributed memory it is not very difficult to produce an instance of the first case. In a two-phase optimizer, join ordering does not take into account the communication cost associated with data repartitioning. Then, a cost estimate based on the cardinality of intermediate results could eventually lead to a suboptimal parallel plan. Consider for example the following query in a system in which communication cost would be expensive:

Example 2.4.2

```
Select * from R₁, R₂, R₃
where    R₁.A=R₂.A and R₁.B=R₃.B and R₂.C=R₃.C
```

where R_1 has N tuples while R_2 and R_3 have $2*N$ tuples. Suppose that the three relations are hashed with the same function on all the processing nodes, and R_1, R_2, and R_3 are partitioned on $R_1.A$, $R_2.A$, and $R_3.C$, respectively.

For simplicity, suppose that the optimizer has additional information to deduce that $R_1 \bowtie R_3$ has N tuples while $R_1 \bowtie R_2$ has $2*N$ tuples. Then the following join ordering $(R_1 \bowtie R_3) \bowtie R2$ (denoted SP_0) would be chosen rather than $(R_1 \bowtie R_2) \bowtie R_3$ (denoted SP_1). However, for $R_1 \bowtie R_3$, R_1 and R_3 have to be repartitioned on attribute B while for $R_1 \bowtie R_2$, both R_1 and R_2 are ready to be joined. In both cases another repartitioning is necessary for the second join, and the smaller intermediate result of $R_1 \bowtie R_3$ does not compensate for the very poor choice of the first join.

In the second case, the worse response time for SP_0 is not due to the overhead of parallelism. Then, the reason must be that the parallelization phase was not able to use resources for SP_0 as well as for SP_1. In shared memory, these resources cannot be the processors, but it is possible that accessing some relations involves more disks than accessing other relations. This depends on the access methods used (indices, clustering or partitioning strategies) and on the form of the selection predicates. In distributed memory, relations might be partitioned on different sets of nodes.

As we said above, in the latter case interoperation parallelism can take advantage of more processing nodes and reduce response time. In a system taking advantage only of intraoperation parallelism, a dissymmetry in the possibility to use resources would be a serious problem: some operations could not fully use the resources. This can, however, be overcome in a multiuser environment. For example, the fact that some tasks can be IO-bound and others CPU-bound can be solved using interoperation parallelism and a multiquery scheduler [17]. [42] reports the results of experiments which confirm some of the conclusions of this section.

2.5 Cost Model

In this section, we first show the difficulties of modeling cost in a parallel execution environment and capturing the important aspects of parallelism and scheduling. Then, we present some solutions to these problems.

2.5.1 Exceptions to the Principle of Optimality

Some search strategies such as dynamic programming (DP) [1] build plans by assembling subplans rather than by transforming complete plans (that is, equivalent to the whole query being optimized) into other complete plans. Dynamic programming does not keep all the possible subplans, but keeps the best subplan among the set of equivalent subplans. This pruning process guarantees the optimality of the final (or complete) plan provided that the *principle of optimality* holds [1]. This principle says that the best plan has the best subplans. In the context of join ordering, this means that for any subset S of the relations to be joined, the best complete plan (that is, joining all the relations) would necessarily join the relations of S in the less expensive way. As pointed out by [31], this is not quite true, even in a sequential system, since the order of the tuples of the result of joining the relations of S can influence the quality of the overall plan: depending on this order a sort operation could be necessary or not. If optimality is to be guaranteed, the principle of optimality has to be adapted to cope with exceptions of this kind [31]. The principle of optimality can be formally stated as follows. Let $\mathcal{A}$ denote the set of all the relations in the query and S a subset of $\mathcal{A}$. We denote by $plan_{[S]}$ the plan built from relations in set S and $best_{[S]}$ the best of all plans built from S. The principle of optimality is guaranteed if the following formula is true:

$$\forall\,(plan, S)\;:\; cost(best_{[\mathcal{A}]}) < cost(plan_{[\mathcal{A}]})\;\Rightarrow\; cost(best_{[S]}) < cost(plan_{[S]})$$

Parallelism introduces new exceptions and thus forces us to further adapt dynamic programming. The first paper to point this out and to propose a general solution was [11]. The home of the result, and more generally the way this result is fragmented [41], or the scheduling of subplans [24] are some of the exceptions to take into account. This is illustrated in the following example, which is an extension of Example 2.4.1 by adding relation R_5.

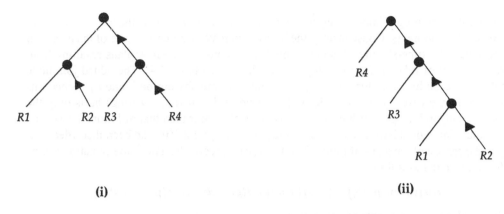

Figure 2.3: Bushy and right-deep trees with four relations.

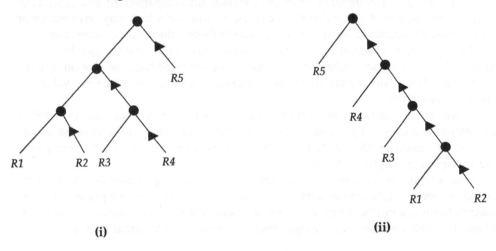

Figure 2.4: Bushy and right-deep trees with five relations.

Example 2.5.1

```
Select R₂.* from R₁, R₂, R₃, R₄, R₅
where   R₁.A=R₂.A and R₂.B=R₃.B and R₃.C=R₄.C and R₄.D=R₅.D
```

We assume a DM environment, where R_1, R_2, and R_5 are partitioned on home h_1, and R_3 and R_4 are partitioned on home h_2. Suppose that DP explores a bushy search space and that at a given stage it has to compare the plans of Figure 2.3 in order to discard the most costly plan. Figure 2.3(i) shows a bushy plan whose execution is split in two phases. R_3 and R_4 are joined in phase one, on home h_2. In the second phase, R_1 and R_2 are joined on home h_1 and the result is pipelined to home h_2, where it is joined with the result of $R_1 \bowtie R_2$ in parallel. Figure 2.3(ii) shows a right-deep plan whose nodes are executed in pipeline, that is, R_1 is joined with R_2 on h_1 and the result is pipelined to home h_2, where it is joined with R_3, whose result is joined with R_4. The two plans have the same set of involved relations and the result is produced on the same home (h_2), however, they have a different scheduling. Time-sharing occurs only in the second plan, as the last two joins are executed on home h_2. Consequently, the bushy plan may be better because of the overhead introduced by time-sharing. Assuming this is true, consider the new plans resulting from the addition of relation R_5 to both plans, as shown in Figure 2.4. The added join node takes place on home h_1 for both plans, resulting in time-sharing on home h_1. Since this is already the case for the right-deep plan on home h_2, it (time-sharing) hurts only the bushy plan, and the plan of Figure 2.4(ii) is probably better than that of Figure 2.4(i). The optimal plan would have been missed if the plan of Figure 2.3(ii) had been discarded. Let p and q represent the plans of Figure 2.3(i) and (ii) respectively. The above situation can be formally stated as follows:

$$cost(Join(p, R_5)) < cost(Join(q, R_5)) \;\; \not\Rightarrow \;\; cost(p) < cost(q),$$

thus violating the principle of optimality.

Therefore, the equivalence criterion must include the comparison of plan scheduling [24]. All the aspects of a plan that affect cost estimation, and which may favor successor nodes, must be considered when comparing plans to discard the most expensive ones.

The equivalence criterion abstracts all the properties of a plan that are used by the cost model: the set of captured relations, the home of the produced transient relation, and the scheduling. Thus, two subplans are considered equivalent if they have the same values for the above properties.

Based on this definition, linear plans scheduled as right-deep trees (thus executed in one phase) and consuming the same resources (that is, executed on the same home) are considered equivalent. On the other hand, bushy plans, scheduled in more than one phase, are not equivalent to plans scheduled as right-deep trees.

This solution can be seen as an extension to [11] by adding another dimension to the resource vector to take into account the execution over more than one phase. The cost metrics become a matrix, where each row represents the resource consumption over one phase. If the plan is scheduled as a right-deep tree, we obtain a vector as in [11].

2.5.2 Resources

In traditional query optimizers, typically of commercial DBMSs, the cost of an execution plan measures the number of disk accesses (or IOs) the execution plan is expected to perform at runtime. The reason for measuring only IOs is mainly because it is assumed that the time spent on disk accesses is more important than the computation time, that is, CPU time. While this is true for OLTP (on-line transaction processing) applications it is not true for DS (decision support) applications. [16] contains examples of OLTP and DS applications, called TPC-C and TPC-D, respectively.

An OLTP application is generally characterized by a large number of short, that is, access is limited to few tuples, and independent queries. The access pattern is thus random, resulting in incessant movement of the disk arms. On the contrary, a DS application is characterized by a small number of large queries, often submitted one at a time. A DS query involves a large number of tables, for example, six, and accesses large fractions of tuples from each table, often making a full table scan. Consequently, using the same hardware configuration, the IO bandwidth is much larger when running a DS application than an OLTP application, that is, an OLTP application generates a higher load on the disks while a DS application generates a higher load on the CPUs. It is thus legitimate (or understandable) to try to reduce IOs in an OLTP environment. Applying the same standard in a DS environment will lead to generating CPU-bound execution plans while a better plan would have a balance of CPU and IO activities.

Similarly, communication must also be considered in cost models for parallel execution environments. In effect, the parallel execution of a plan may incur redistribution (partitioning or broadcasting) of intermediate results between the nodes of the execution tree. This translates to message passing between processors across an interconnect in a distributed memory architecture. Redistribution is not free in a shared memory architecture because delays may result from contentions when multiple processors access shared data. Not considering communication in the cost model may lead to generating an execution plan which creates a heavy communication load.

2.5.3 Skew and Size Model

The cost model provides an abstraction of the parallel execution system in terms of operator cost functions and of the database in terms of physical schema information (that is, data placement, access paths, and statistics). Database statistics include distribution of attribute values in a relation. Attribute distribution is used to perform the most fundamental operation in a cost model, that is, computing the selectivity of predicates that appear in a query, which in turn helps determine the number of tuples satisfying the predicates. These estimates are particularly useful in determining the resource allocation necessary to balance workloads in parallel or distributed databases.

In real database applications, the distribution of attribute values in a relation is rarely uniform and the independence between the values of attributes in the same relation is more the exception than the norm.

Several pieces of work have demonstrated the need to maintain detailed attribute statistics for an optimizer to work properly [23, 8, 28]. However, it may be very expensive to store and maintain detailed and precise statistics on the database content, for at least two reasons. First, they need regular and frequent refresh in order to keep them up-to-date in an environment where DML queries (insert, delete, and update) flow is constant. Second, the storage requirement may be intractable if we want to store all correlations between attributes. For a relation with n attributes, the number of possible correlations is:

$$\sum_{k=2}^{n} \binom{n}{k}$$

whose development leads to 2^n, which is very high considering the fact that a relation may easily have more than 10 attributes, resulting in 1000 correlations.

Distributions of attribute values are typically stored in height-balanced histograms. Each bucket in a height-balanced histogram has the same number of values, except for the last one which may contain fewer values. Height-balanced histograms are considered more appropriate for the purpose of selectivity estimation than width-balanced histograms. The interested reader may find more details in [8, 26].

Database statistics are provided for base relations only. Statistics on intermediate relations are needed when an execution tree contains more than one operation. Several techniques have been proposed to derive statistics on intermediate relations. [27] wrote a survey on techniques to derive statistics on relations produced by selection, projection, and join operations. [12] studied the size of derived relations in relational algebra, particularly for projection and join, using probabilistic models. [13] proposed a technique to estimate the size of intermediate relations produced by large relational algebra expressions, in particular, those containing several equi-joins. It overcomes the problem posed by the independence assumption, using "virtual domains," and does not require extensive statistics about the database. The independence assumption may lead to unrealistic estimates. Finally, a more radical approach is based on sampling. Sampling-based techniques do not rely on storing and maintaining statistics about the data, rather they access a fraction of the actual data. It is argued that the time taken to compute the estimate is a small fraction of the time taken to compute the actual query. [10] provides a short survey of existing sampling-based techniques and proposes a new one.

2.5.4 The Cost Function

We define the cost of a plan as three components: total work (TW), response time (RT), expressed in *seconds*, and memory consumption (MC), expressed in *Kbytes*. The first two components are used to express a trade-off between minimizing the response time and maximizing the throughput. The third component represents the maximum size of memory needed to execute the plan. The cost function is a combination of the first two components, and plans that need more memory than available are discarded. Another approach [11] consists of using a parameter, specified by the system administrator, by which the maximum throughput is degraded in order to decrease response time. Given a plan p, its cost is computed by a parameterized function, $cost_{(W_{RT}, W_{TW})}()$, defined as follows:

$$
cost_{(W_{RT}, W_{TW})}(p) = \begin{cases} W_{RT} * RT + W_{TW} * TW & \text{if } MC \text{ of plan } p \text{ does not exceed} \\ & \text{the available memory} \\ \infty & \text{otherwise} \end{cases}
$$

where W_{RT} and W_{TW} are weight factors between 0 and 1, such that $W_{RT} + W_{TW} = 1$.

As stated in Section 2.3.2, pipelining and storing indications split the plan into nonoverlapping subtrees, called *phases*. Pipelined operations are executed in the same phase, whereas a storing indication establishes the boundary between one phase and a subsequent phase. Thus, the execution *scheduling* of a plan can be deterministically derived. The reasons for splitting the plan into phases are twofold. First, the algorithm that implements a plan operation may require the complete storage of one of its operands (such as the building operand of the hash join algorithm). For example, the bushy plan of Figure 2.4 is split into three phases according to the synchronization points imposed by the join algorithm. Indeed, suppose that the joins in the plan are implemented using the hash join algorithm and that the build operand is the left input of a node, then $J3 < J6$ and $J1 < J5 < J7$, where "$I < J$" means that operation J starts only after I is completed. Second, if a sequence of operations requires more memory than available to execute simultaneously, it is split into two or more phases, such that the memory requirement of each phase is below the available memory space. Note that we adopted the strategy of limiting interoperation parallelism, when available memory is not enough to hold all data needed by operations executed in parallel, in order to avoid disk accesses.

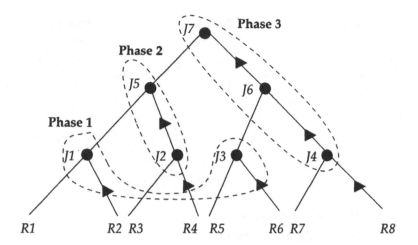

Figure 2.5: Bushy tree with eight relations.

Computing response time in a parallel execution environment poses three problems, each being tied to one kind of parallelism. First, computing the response time of an operation reduces to computing the response time of the slowest node to process the fragments assigned to it. When there is no data skew, all nodes process the same amount of data which is easy to compute: the operand's size is divided by the number of nodes. However, in presence of data skew, the cost model must know the size of fragments assigned to each node, which requires a significant amount of storage space and overhead to store and maintain the distributions of the data. Instead, we take advantage of the dynamic load balancing of SM, where fragments are assigned to processors at runtime depending on the load of each processor by using "fine grain" partitioning. Indeed, making fragments smaller increases load balancing. Thus, albeit not absolutely accurate, the assumption of uniform distribution may be used.

Second, unlike linear plans, bushy plans still tolerate nondeterminism in the execution order of operations once pipeline and stored operands are specified. This is due to the causal independence between some operations. However, the optimizer, in particular the cost model, works on plans where the execution order between nodes is completely determined, because it needs to know which operation consumes which resource. Thus, we indicate the phase number as annotation to the plan node. The optimizer can then explore all the possible ways of attaching a node to a phase when such freedom exists. Figure 2.6 shows a possible scheduling of the bushy plan of Figure 2.5, where node J_3 is executed in the first phase. A second scheduling is obtained by moving node J_3 to $phase_2$ as no **store** link exists between J_3 and any node of $phase_2$.

The optimizer uses an algorithm based on pipelining and storing annotations to produce all possible schedulings of a bushy plan, evaluate their cost, and retain the one with least cost. The algorithm principle is to produce all possible schedulings by moving nodes among phases using the two following rules: (1) a node can be moved from its actual phase to another phase if no **store** link exists between that node and any node of the next phase, and (2) no **pipeline** link exists between that node and another node of the same phase. For

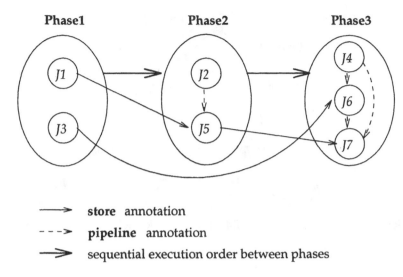

——————▶	**store** annotation
- - -▶	**pipeline** annotation
═══════▶	sequential execution order between phases

Figure 2.6: Scheduling of a bushy tree with eight relations.

example, consider a DM architecture where nodes J_1 and J_3 have the same home, and J_3 has a different home than nodes J_2 and J_5. The scheduling obtained by moving J_3 from $phase_1$ to $phase_3$ is better than the original one because no time-sharing occurs, contrary to the first scheduling where J_1 and J_3 execute in time-sharing on the same home. However, these decisions cannot be expressed in the output language of our optimizer. Thus, we adopted a default strategy to slice bushy plans into phases: operations are executed in the first possible phase, that is, the scheduling of Figure 2.6 is retained.

The third problem is caused by the pipeline execution of two operations. In order to compute response time of the subplan that includes the two operations, the cost model must know the starting time of each operation and its relative speed. [39] proposed a pipeline execution model and the associated cost functions.

2.6   Search Strategies

Given an input query, the optimizer search strategy explores the space of possible execution plans which implement the input query and seeks one that minimizes a cost function. The crucial issue in terms of search strategy is the join ordering problem, that is, NP-complete on the number of relations [19]. A typical approach to solve the problem is to use dynamic programming [31], which is a standard optimization technique. It is almost exhaustive and assures that the best of all plans is found. It incurs an acceptable optimization cost (time and space) when the number of relations in the query is small. However, this approach becomes too expensive when the number of relations is greater than five or six. For this reason, there has been recent interest in *randomized* strategies, which reduce the optimization complexity but do not guarantee the best of all plans. Another way to cut off the optimization complexity would consist of adopting a heuristic approach [33].

2.6.1 Deterministic Search Strategies

Deterministic strategies always choose the same plan for a given query in a given search space. Examples of such strategies are *Greedy* and Dynamic Programming (DP). DP-like strategies proceed by *building* plans, starting from base relations, joining one more relations at each step until complete plans are obtained. A Greedy strategy builds only one such plan, by depth-first search, while DP builds all possible plans breadth-first. To reduce the optimization cost, partial plans that are not likely to lead to the optimal plan are *pruned* (that is, discarded) as soon as possible.

Greedy

Greedy strategies are the faster ones because they investigate very few plans. They proceed depth-first, starting from the relation with the least cardinality. After each expansion, all the produced plans are pruned but one. Different heuristics may be used in conjunction with a Greedy strategy. In Augmentation Heuristic [36], the plan starts at the relation with the least cardinality and, at each expansion, the plan with the least cost is retained. [24] implemented a Greedy strategy with the least cardinality heuristic, that is, at each expansion, the plan with least cardinality is retained. Greedy strategies are also used to generate start solutions for randomized strategies.

[24] studied a variant that produces what is called the *Uniform Greedy* solution. This strategy produces one complete plan starting from each base relation via the Augmentation Heuristic, then chooses the least costly among these complete plans as the solution. It has been shown that this is a very effective strategy to find a start solution for Simulated Annealing in linear spaces.

Dynamic Programming

DP proceeds breadth-first, selecting the least recently generated plan to be expanded at each step. The strategy is almost exhaustive because heuristics are used to prune *bad* plans as soon as possible. Pruning discards expensive plans which are "equivalent" to a cheaper one.

In Section 2.5.1 we discussed the issues related to the equivalence criterion in a parallel execution environment and showed the criterion must include more properties thus reducing its effectiveness for pruning plans. As a consequence, many more plans are retained during the search than in a sequential environment, considerably increasing the optimization cost. Thus, running dynamic programming on reasonable queries (such as seven relations or more) in a parallel bushy search space often caused the optimizer to run out of space as shown in [24].

2.6.2 Randomized Strategies

Randomized strategies concentrate on searching for the optimal solution around some particular points. They do not guarantee that the best solution is obtained, but they avoid the high cost of optimization, in terms of memory size and CPU time. First, one or more *start* plans are built by a Greedy strategy. Then, the algorithm tries to improve the start plan by visiting its *neighbors*. A neighbor is obtained by applying a random *transformation* to the current plan. An example of a typical transformation consists of exchanging two randomly chosen relations of the plan, for example, swapping left and right inputs of a join node.

A plan is a *local minimum* if it has the least cost among all its neighbors. A plan is a *global minimum* if it has the least cost among all the local minima. The effectiveness of a randomized strategy is related to its ability to reach the global minimum.

Iterative Improvement (II) [36] and Simulated Annealing (SA) [21] are the most well-known randomized strategies. They differ on the criteria for replacing the "current" plan by the transformed one and on the stopping criteria.

Randomized Strategies versus Cost Metrics

The number of local minima depends on the execution space as captured by the cost model. Thus, the behavior of randomized strategies is significantly affected by the properties of the cost metrics. [20] stated that in search spaces following the ASI property, there is a unique local minimum, which is the global minimum. This enables very effective optimization. After choosing a randomly generated start plan, apply transformations until no less costly neighbor plan is generated. In sequential optimizers, cost functions corresponding to some join algorithms (such as merge join, hash join) do not follow the ASI property. Nevertheless, [20] observed that many subspaces follow ASI, leading to many local minima. This causes randomized strategies investigating many such subspaces to increase the opportunities of finding the global minimum. Each strategy implements this investigation of several subspaces in a different way.

When comparing the cost metrics of a sequential and a parallel optimizer, two observations can be drawn. First, the cost distribution in the parallel case is much more scattered, implying the need to look into more subspaces than in the sequential case. Second, the cost of a neighbor plan can be radically different (up to a factor of 10) from that of the starting plan.[6] This implies that, in a given subspace, the optimizer may be able to reach a local minimum earlier, with less transformations than in the sequential case. Both factors are more prevailing in bushy execution spaces, where there are more choices for scheduling, than in a linear one.

These observations lead to an important conclusion. A parallel optimizer acting in a bushy space should investigate more subspaces than a sequential one, spending less time in the exploration of each subspace.

Iterative Improvement

II [36] performs several *runs*. Each run consists of improving one start plan by applying *transforms*, until a local minimum is reached. Thus, only transformations that generate plans which are less costly than the original one are accepted. The number of runs is equal to the number of relations in the query, that is, each start plan is greedily generated from a different base relation. As the strategy is not exhaustive, not all the neighbors are visited and it is difficult to recognize a local minimum. A bound on the number of visited neighbors is typically accepted as a criterion for reaching the local minimum. This bound is proportional to the query size: a parameter *localBudget* times the number of relations in the query.

---

[6]This is not the case in sequential bushy spaces [20].

II visits as many subspaces as the number of relations in the query, due to the choice of several start plans. This has been proved effective in sequential optimizers [36] as well as linear parallel execution spaces [24]. However, the number of visited local minima is insufficient in a parallel bushy space due to the excessive scattering of the cost distribution resulting in the low quality of the plans chosen by II running in a bushy space. The local-Budget parameter may be smaller in bushy spaces. II converges very quickly to each local minimum. The reason is that, in bushy spaces, a single *transform* may generate a neighbor plan with a very low cost, compared to that of the original plan.

Simulated Annealing

Contrary to II, all the runs of SA are performed over a single start plan. However, the system has a temperature property *temp*, which is reduced at each run. Optimizer parameters allow specifying the initial temperature (a factor multiplied by the cost of the start plan, typically 2.0) and the decreasing ratio. The algorithm stops when temp $\leq$ the "freezing" temperature, or when a "stable" solution has been found (that is, it stays unchanged during four runs, as proposed in [20]). As in II, the local budget for each run is related to the size of the problem. The criterion for accepting a transformation, however, is different because transformed plans with a higher cost than the original plan are accepted with some probability that decreases with the temperature. Accepting *bad* moves corresponds to "hill climbing" [20]: on the other side of the hill there may exist a better solution. In [36] and [25] the start solution is obtained using Uniform Greedy strategy.

[24] observed that SA performed very well in linear spaces, but often failed to choose the optimal solution in bushy spaces. The reason is that a single start solution provides too few chances for exploring a large search space, for example, with bushy trees. Accepting "bad" moves proved to be not sufficient in a parallel bushy execution space. [24] proposed an enhancement which consists of running SA n times (n being the number of relations in the query), each time using a different start solution obtained by Greedy strategy. The final plan is the best of all runs.

To keep the optimization cost comparable to SA, each run is given $1/n$th of the optimization budget and a very low ratio for the initial temperature (0.1 instead of 2.0), impelling the system to accept bad moves less often. This is somewhat analogous to the 2-Phase Optimization strategy proposed in [20]. It was shown that this enhancement helps in picking better plans.

[24] reports the results of experiments using the above search strategies in a parallel execution environment and compares them using a formula that combines the optimization time and the cost of the produced plan.

2.7   Conclusion

In this chapter we have reformulated the problem of query optimization in the context of a multiprocessor system. First, we showed that the parallelization of sequential plans could be defined in terms of addition of information rather than as an arbitrary transformation. This simplification which considers algorithms as black boxes, is of course not to be taken as a dogma but simply as a very convenient heuristic which makes optimization for parallel execution tractable.

Then we discussed the interest in different kinds of heuristics commonly used to restrict the huge search space of parallel query optimization. Many of these heuristics are related to the shape of the execution trees (linear, bushy, ...) and a lot of literature has been published to exhibit the merits of each of them. A very important heuristic, namely the two-phase approach of XPRS, has been discussed and we showed why in distributed memory systems it was certainly not as interesting as in shared memory systems.

Later, we presented the problems related to the design of a cost model in a parallel environment. One important problem is the new exceptions to the principle of optimality which complicate some search strategies such as dynamic programming. Other problems include the specification of the scheduling of bushy trees and load balancing.

Finally, we introduced some known search strategies and discussed their effectiveness for searching a search space of parallel execution plans.

Bibliography

[1] R.E. Bellman, *Dynamic Programing*, Princeton University Press, 1957.

[2] B. Bergsten et al., "Language Levels and Computational Model for a Parallel Database Accelerator," *6th Int'l Workshop on Database Machines*, June 1989.

[3] B. Bergsten, M. Couprie, and P. Valduriez, "Prototyping DBS3, A Shared Memory Parallel Database System," *Proc. Int'l Conf. on Parallel and Distributed Information Systems*, 1991, pp. 226–234.

[4] H. Boral et al., "Prototyping Bubba, A Highly Parallel Database System," *IEEE Trans. Knowledge and Data Eng.*, Vol. 2, No. 1, Mar. 1990, pp. 4–24.

[5] L. Bouganim, D. Florescu, and B. Dageville, "Skew Handling in the DBS3 Parallel Database System," *Proc. Int'l Conf. of the Austrian Center for Parallel Computation*, 1996.

[6] L. Bouganim, D. Florescu, and P. Valduriez, "Dynamic Load Balancing in Hierarchical Parallel Database Systems," *Proc. Int'l Conf. on Very Large Data Bases*, 1996.

[7] M-S Chen et al., "Using Segmented Right-Deep Trees for the Execution of Pipelined Hash Joins," *Proc. Int'l Conf. on Very Large Data Bases*, 1992.

[8] S. Christodoulakis, *Estimating Selectivities in Data Bases*, Technical Report CSRG-136, Computer Science Research Group, Univ. of Toronto, Dec. 1981.

[9] R.L. Cole and G. Graefe, "Optimization of Dynamic Query Evaluation Plans," *Proc. ACM SIGMOD Int'l Conf. on Management of Data*, 1994.

[10] S. Ganguly et al., "Bifocal Sampling for Skew-Resistant Join Size Estimation," *Proc. ACM SIGMOD Int'l Conf. on Management of Data*, 1996, pp. 271–281.

[11] S. Ganguly, W. Hasan, and R. Krishnamurty, "Query Optimization for Parallel Execution," *Proc. ACM SIGMOD Int'l Conf. on Management of Data*, 1992, pp. 9–18.

[12] D. Gardy, *Bases de Données, Allocations Aléatoires: Quelques Analyses de Performances*, Doctorat d'Etat, Université de Paris-Sud-Centre d'Orsay, 1989.

[13] A. Van Gelder, "Multiple Join Size Estimation by Virtual Domains," *Proc. Int'l Conf. on Principles of Database Systems*, 1993, pp. 180–189.

[14] G. Graefe, "Encapsulation of Parallelism in the Volcano Query Processing System," *Proc. ACM SIGMOD Int'l Conf. on Management of Data*, 1990, pp. 102–111.

[15] G. Graefe and K. Ward, "Dynamic Query Evaluation Plans," *Proc. ACM SIGMOD Int'l Conf. on Management of Data*, 1989, pp. 358–366.

[16] Jim Gray, ed., *The Benchmark Handbook, 2nd ed.*. Morgan Kaufmann, 1993.

[17] W. Hong, "Exploiting Inter-Operation Parallelism in XPRS," *Proc. ACM SIGMOD Int'l Conf. on Management of Data*, 1992.

[18] W. Hong and M. Stonebraker, "Optimization of Parallelism Query Execution Plans in XPRS," *Proc. Int'l Conf. on Parallel and Distributed Information Systems*, 1991, pp. 218–225.

[19] T. Ibaraki and T. Kameda, "Optimal Nesting for Computing n-Relational Joins," *ACM Trans. Database Systems*, Vol. 9, No. 3, 1984, pp. 482–502.

[20] Y.E. Ioannidis and Y. Cha Kang, "Left-Deep vs. Bushy Trees: An Analysis of Strategy Spaces and its Implications for Query Optimization," *Proc. ACM SIGMOD Int'l Conf. on Management of Data*, 1991, pp. 168–177.

[21] Y.E. Ioannidis and E. Wong, "Query Optimization by Simulated Annealing," *Proc. ACM SIGMOD Int'l Conf. on Management of Data*, 1987, pp. 9–22.

[22] M. Jarke and J. Koch, "Query Optimization in Database Systems," *ACM Computing Surveys*, Vol. 16, No. 2, 1984.

[23] R-P. Kooi, *The Optimization of Queries in Relational Databases*, Ph.D. thesis, Case Western Reserve Univ., Dept. Computer and Information Sciences, 1980.

[24] R.S.G. Lanzelotte, P. Valduriez, and M. Zaït, "On the Effectiveness of Optimization Search Strategies for Parallel Execution Spaces," *Proc. Int'l Conf. on Very Large Data Bases*, 1993, pp. 493–504.

[25] R.S.G. Lanzelotte et al., "Industrial-Strength Parallel Query Optimization: Issues and Lessons," *Information Systems*, Vol. 19, No. 4, 1994, pp. 311–330.

[26] C.A. Lynch, "Selectivity Estimation and Query Optimization in Large Databases with Highly Skewed Distributions of Column Values," *Proc. Int'l Conf. on Very Large Data Bases*, 1988.

[27] M.V. Mannino, P. Chu, and T. Sager, "Statistical Profile Estimation in Database Systems," *ACM Computing Surveys*, Vol. 20, No. 3, Sep. 1988, pp. 191–221.

[28] G. Piatetsky-Shapiro and C. Connell, "Accurate Estimation of the Number of Tuples Satisfying a Condition," *Proc. ACM SIGMOD Int'l Conf. on Management of Data*, 1984.

[29] H. Pirahesh et al., "Parallelism in Relational Data Base Systems: Architectural Issues and Design Approaches," *Proc. 2nd Int'l Symp. on Databases in Parallel and Distributed Systems*, July 1990.

[30] D.A. Schneider and D.J. DeWitt, "Tradeoffs in Processing Complex Join Queries via Hashing in Multiprocessor Database Machines," *Proc. Int'l Conf. on Very Large Data Bases*, 1990, pp. 469–480.

[31] P.G. Selinger et al., "Access Path Selection in a Relational Database Management System," *Proc. ACM SIGMOD Int'l Conf. on Management of Data*, 1979, pp. 23–34.

[32] L. Shapiro, "Join Processing in Database Systems with Large Main Memories," *ACM Trans. Database Systems*, Sep. 1986.

[33] D. Shasha and T. Wang, "Optimizing Equijoin queries in Distributed Databases Where Relations are Hash Partitioned," *ACM Trans. Database Systems*, Vol. 16, No. 2, 1991, pp. 279–308.

[34] E. Shekita and K. Tan. "Multi-Join Optimization for Symetric Multiprocessors," *Proc. Int'l Conf. on Very Large Data Bases*, 1993.

[35] M. Stonebraker and L.A. Rowe, "The Design of POSTGRES," *Proc. ACM SIGMOD Int'l Conf. on Management of Data*, May 1986, pp. 340–355.

[36] A. Swami, "Optimization of Large Join Queries: Combining Heuristics and Combinatorial Techniques," *Proc. ACM SIGMOD Int'l Conf. on Management of Data*, 1989, pp. 367–376.

[37] K-L. Tan and H. Lu, "A Note on the Strategy Space of Multiway Join Query Optimization Problem," *Proc. ACM SIGMOD Int'l Conf. on Management of Data*, 1991.

[38] A.N. Wilschut and P.M.G. Apers, "Dataflow Query Execution in a Parallel Main-Memory Environment," *Proc. Int'l Conf. on Parallel and Distributed Information Systems*, 1991.

[39] M. Zaït, P. Valduriez, and D. Florescu, "Benchmarking the DBS3 Parallel Query Optimizer," *IEEE Parallel and Distributed Technology*, Vol. 4, No. 2, 1996.

[40] M. Ziane, M. Zaït, and P. Borla-Salamet, "Parallel Query Processing in DBS3," *Proc. Int'l Conf. on Parallel and Distributed Information Systems*, 1993.

[41] M. Ziane, M. Zaït, and P. Borla-Salamet, "Parallel Query Processing with Zigzag Trees," *VLDB Journal*, Vol. 2, No. 3, July 1993, pp. 277–301.

[42] M. Ziane, M. Zaït, and H.H. Quang, "Parallelism and Query Optimization," *Computer Systems Science and Engineering Journal*, Vol. 10, No. 1, Jan. 1995, pp. 50–56.

Chapter 3

New Approaches to Parallel Join Utilizing Page Connectivity Information

Chiang Lee

Abstract. *Due to the continuous increase of CPU MIPS and the decrease in hardware cost, parallel database computers have become one of the most promising research and development areas in years. A number of research prototypes and a few commercial systems have been built in the past decades. The key reason to have a parallel database computer is that the join operation is a very time-consuming yet frequently used operation in database systems. Design of algorithms to speed up the processing of a join operation has attracted enormous attention from researchers. Methods proposed in the past, however, have reached a barrier to providing a major improvement in the performance of a parallel system.*

In this chapter, we first design a new classification scheme that categorizes the approaches based on three dimensions. Then, we propose a new method found in our classification scheme that optimizes certain steps in the parallel join execution. In this manner, join performance in a parallel system is drastically improved.

Keywords: parallel join execution, page connectivity information, workload balance, join index, bipartite graph

3.1 Introduction

The join operation has attracted great attention from researchers because it is one of the most time-consuming database operations and its execution algorithms are, in general, applicable to the execution of the other complex database operations (such as union, difference, and intersection). Various algorithms have been proposed to shorten its execution time. Due to the decrease in hardware cost, multiprocessor-based architectures have become the design trend for the support of the execution of join queries.

We surveyed the past solutions and designed a new classification scheme to classify the parallel algorithms proposed previously. Figure 3.1 shows the scheme which characterizes parallel join algorithms from three dimensions: the *Query/Operation Parallelism*, the *Multiprocessor Architecture*, and the *Relevance of Data*. The query/operation parallelism is divided into *interquery parallelism* and *intraquery parallelism*. Interquery parallelism [20] represents the execution of multiple queries in parallel, and intraquery parallelism [22, 30, 12] indicates that each query is performed in parallel but one query at a time. In our classification scheme, intraquery parallelism is further divided into *horizontal parallelism*, meaning that all processors execute one operation at a time [1, 17, 13, 33, 34], and *vertical parallelism*, indicating that several operations are executed in a pipelined fashion. In such an execution method, intermediate results are generated block by block from a processor and sent to another to perform a different operation [4, 5, 9, 14, 21, 29]. Multiprocessor architectures of past parallel database servers can be classified into *shared nothing* (SN), *shared disk* (SD), and *shared everything* (SE) architectures [15, 7, 31, 2, 17, 13]. The third dimension, relevance of data, is, in general, representable as *join connectivity* information, describing whether one piece of data is joinable with another. Dependent on the granularity, join connectivity can be further classified into *bucket connectivity* (the coarsest level), *page connectivity*, and *tuple connectivity* (the finest level). Join connectivity at bucket level is normally used in hash-based join algorithms, in which join relations are partitioned into buckets and only corresponding buckets need to be joined (indicating some connectivity between buckets). Tuple connectivity, represented as join index [32] of tuples, stands for the other extreme of this dimension. Joinable tuples are normally linked through the use of tuple IDs (surrogates). Page connectivity is the same as tuple connectivity except that joinable pages (that is, those pages containing at least one tuple that can be joined with a tuple of another page), rather than joinable tuples, are linked. All together, this classification scheme represents at least 3*3*3=27 different types of parallel join algorithms. Many new designs, including those that perhaps have never been investigated, can be found from this scheme. (The dotted line in the figure does not have any special meaning. It is simply used to make the figure more readable.) If hybrid designs are considered (for example, a strategy that has both interquery and intraquery parallelism, an architecture that has an SN architecture at its top level and each processor has an SE architecture, and so on), then even more types of parallel algorithms can be represented.

This chapter studies issues pertaining to the dimension of relevance of data. In the past, approaches based on bucket connectivity (representing hash-based algorithms) dominated the design of join algorithms. However, a requirement of these algorithms is that join relations must be partitioned before a join can be performed. On the other hand, the advantages of using the tuple/page connectivity information are as follows:

- The joining relations need not be hashed as in the hash-based join algorithms to find the possibly matched data buckets. This reduces a significant amount of time spent on accessing relations for hashing.

- Nonjoinable tuples/pages need not be accessed. Whereas in partition-based (such as hash join) algorithms each tuple of an entire bucket needs to be compared with some tuples in another bucket. Thus it reduces unnecessary data accesses and comparisons.

- The tuples/pages to be joined (or more accurately, concatenated) are known before-

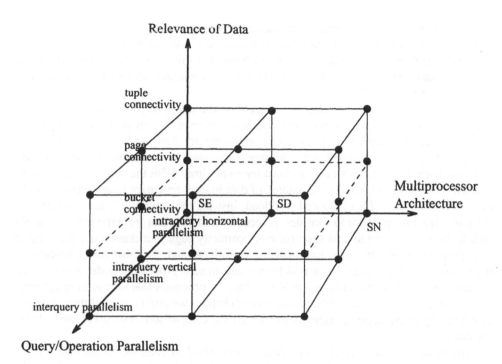

Figure 3.1: A classification scheme for parallel join algorithms.

hand. The processors can be scheduled in advance (in accessing and processing them) to optimize the utilization of computation resources. This is not possible in a hash-based join algorithm.

Comparing algorithms based on tuple connectivity and page connectivity, one can find that although join can be more efficiently executed by having tuple connectivity (as the IDs of joinable tuples are already available), a high maintenance cost of the ID tables is the price to pay in this approach. Page connectivity is a compromise between the two extremes. It eliminates the partition (hash) phase required in the bucket connectivity approach without incurring a high maintenance cost as in the tuple connectivity approach. Interestingly enough, very few past algorithms take an approach based on page connectivity. Pramanik and Ittner [27] were the first who seriously considered how to utilize page connectivity information in the optimization of a join operation. They studied how to use the least amount of memory to perform a join with the support of page connectivity information. Later, [10] and [24, 25] studied the same issue in a shared everything multiprocessor environment. Their goal was to minimize the processor idle time so as to optimize the overall performance.

All these proposals studied the optimization issues of utilizing page connectivity information in either a single processor or a shared everything (SE) environment. From an architecture point of view, the SE architecture is not the most suitable architecture for using page-connectivity information for the support of join operation. Generally speaking, a shared nothing (SN) architecture has more advantages than an SE system. The most attractive feature of this architecture is its scalability. Scaling an SE system into the range of several dozens or hundreds of processors is impractical, whereas an SN system of such a scale is normal in very large database applications. For this reason, the design of a commercial product, DBC/1012 by Teradata [31], and many research prototypes were based on this architecture [2, 8, 17, 20, 30, 12].

In this chapter, we will discuss our research on the issues of join based on page connectivity information under an SN architectural environment. Many more issues appear in this new environment than existed in an SE environment. First, in hash-based join algorithms, it is generally assumed that if all processors own the same amount of data, then they will complete their join tasks at about the same time. With the support of page connectivity information, however, the amount of data in each processor is not necessarily the most important factor for a balanced workload. Instead, the number of page joins (that is, the join edges) is the factor to consider. A second problem arises from the fact that an SN architecture is sensitive to data skew (or more correctly page join skew, since the number of page joins is the key factor for balancing considerations). Another major problem is the scheduling of data pages to be read from a disk in each processing node. A page fetch scheduling algorithm should be designed to reduce the processor idle time so as to optimize the overall performance of an SN system. In this chapter, we discuss our solutions to these problems. In addition, performance of the design and comparisons with other methods are studied.

The remaining sections of this chapter are organized as follows. In Section 3.2, we will give a motivating example to show how a read schedule for data pages affects the CPU utilization (and the performance). The methodology of our design, including the load balancing algorithm and the page fetch scheduling algorithm, is presented in Section 3.3. In Section 3.4, we give a simulation model and discuss the results of the experiments. Finally in Section 3.5, we give a brief conclusion of our research. Some future work is also discussed.

3.2   The Environment and a Motivating Example

In this section, we will set up an environment for the study of the issues. Also, we will give an example to illustrate the importance of balancing workload of PNs and of scheduling the page read sequence.

For ease of illustration, we assume that the duration of a join between two data pages (or a page join) is roughly equal to the time required to load one page of data from secondary storage into main memory [27, 24, 25]. Our method can be easily adjusted if the access time of a disk page is equal to p page joins. In the rest of the chapter, we will refer to the time required to load one page (equivalent to the time of performing a join on two pages) as one unit of time.

The environment under study is an SN system with tightly coupled PNs. Communication between the PNs is through a very fast communication channel (such as optical fiber). As this type of communication channel (providing a bandwidth as wide as a few hundreds of megabits per second) has a bandwidth of about two orders of magnitude higher than the bandwidth of disk access, we will not consider communication contention a problem in our design.

Page connectivity information in this environment can be created in several ways. One of them is based on the join index proposed in [32]. Another way is to utilize spatial file structures, such as the grid file [26] partitioning scheme and k-d tree [16], in a multiprocessor environment [12] for join execution. A recent paper [28] gave a complete discussion on the process of generating a bipartite join graph (that is, page connectivity graph) from two grid-partitioned relations. Any of these schemes can be used as a preprocessing phase additional to our work to generate bipartite join graphs.

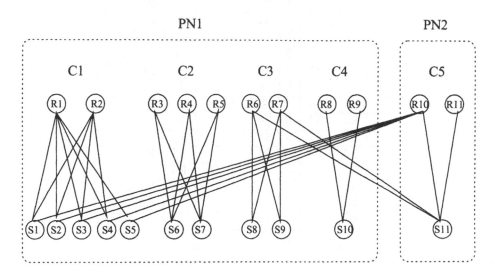

Figure 3.2: Example bipartite join graphs in an SN system.

Now, let us use an example to illustrate the issues in this research. Assume that there are two PNs in an SN system as shown in Figure 3.2. Each PN has a number of pages that may connect to other pages within the same PN or in a different PN. If both of the pages connected by an edge are located in the same PN, then the edge will be called a local join edge (or simply a local edge). The join is called a local join. Otherwise, the edge is called a remote join edge (or remote edge). The join is a remote join. A set of pages of a PN forms a join component if all these pages are connected (through local edges). In the example, PN1 has four join components (that is, C1, C2, C3, and C4) and PN2 has one join component (that is, C5). It is obvious that the workloads of the PNs are skewed. To balance their workloads, some pages must be transferred from PN1 to PN2, and the joins on those transferred pages should be performed by PN2. Figure 3.3 shows a result of executing the joins in this example. The schedule of reading R and S pages is shown in the figure. In total, it takes 20 units of time to perform the task. The column "PNi" indicates the join that is performed by the PN in each time unit. Within each processor, the column "R" indicates the page to be read in each time unit, and the column "T" shows the page that is sent/received by the PN in each time unit. In this example, we balance their workloads by assigning all remote joins to PN2 (that is, executed in PN2). Also, we assign the local joins of C2 to PN2. Hence, the pages of C2 (including R3, R4, R5, S6, and S7) are transferred to PN2 and the joins of C2 pages are performed in PN2.

Time	PN1			PN2		
	R	T	Processor	R	T	Processor
1	R1		-	R10		-
2	S1	S1	-	S11		-
3	R2		R1-S1	R11	S1	R10-S11
4	S2	S2	R2-S1			R11-S11
5	S3	S3	R2-S2		S2	R10-S1
6	S4	S4	R2-S3		S3	R10-S2
7	S5	S5	R2-S4		S4	R10-S3
8	R6	R6	R1-S2		S5	R10-S4
9	S8		R1-S3		R6	R10-S5
10	R7	R7	R1-S4			R6-S11
11	S9		R1-S5		R7	-
12	S6	S6	R6-S8			R7-S11
13	R3	R3	R6-S9		S6	-
14	S7	S7	R7-S8		R3	-
15	R4	R4	R7-S9		S7	R3-S6
16	R5	R5	-		R4	R3-S7
17	S10		-		R5	R4-S7
18	R8		-			R5-S7
19	R9		R8-S10			R4-S6
20			R9-S10			R5-S6

Figure 3.3: Read schedule for both PNs in the example.

It should be noted that how to balance the workload and how to schedule the accesses to the pages are important issues which determine the system's overall performance. In this example, only two PNs are assumed to exist in the system. If tens or even hundreds of PNs are involved, the complexity of the issue is much higher than that shown in this example. Also, we have carefully used a balancing algorithm and a scheduling algorithm to minimize the idle time in each PN. However, since C2 needs to be transferred from PN1 to PN2, reading its pages without performing joins on them keeps the disk busy but the CPU idle. As a result, the performance of an algorithm can be much worse than the one presented in Figure 3.2 if those CPU time units are not well utilized.

3.3   The Methodology

In this section, we present a method to resolve the previously mentioned problems. Our scheme takes join components (represented as bipartite join graphs) of all PNs as input, and outputs a schedule of reading and transferring data pages. To generate a schedule, two tasks are involved and each of them is treated as an execution phase in our scheme. The first phase is a Balancing Phase which considers the balance of workload. The second phase is a Scheduling Phase which determines the sequence of reading data pages.

As mentioned in [22], data skew is typically found in textual databases. This data skew presents nonuniformly distributed attribute values when some values occur more frequently than others. In our method, the balancing phase is used to resolve this problem and balance the workload of PNs. This phase proceeds in two stages. The first stage, termed the Remote Join Balancing (RJB) stage, balances the workload for executing remote joins between pages in different PNs. Since the execution of a remote join involves a page transfer from one PN to another, which PN will perform the task has to be determined. An algorithm, to be presented later, is designed to resolve the issues involved in this problem. The second stage, termed the Local Join Balancing (LJB) stage, balances the workload by assigning local joins of each component to a proper PN. In this stage, the still unbalanced workload resulting from the first stage is taken into account in the assignment of local joins to the PNs.

The scheduling phase mainly considers the sequence of reading data pages into memory. Whether a high connectivity data page should be read first is the major issue considered in this phase. In addition, when a data page that needs to be transferred to another PN is read should also be considered. We design a Scheduling Algorithm to manage these issues.

We note here that in the balancing phase, only a "plan" is made to balance the workload. Designing the plan only requires some simple computation that can be done in a preassigned coordinator (one of the PNs). Thus, the balancing phase does not incur any data movement. The real movement of data pages is performed in the scheduling phase when those data pages are loaded into memory for join execution.

In Section 3.3.1, we give a list of parameters used in the algorithms presented in later subsections. In Section 3.3.2, the balancing phase algorithms are presented. Then, in Section 3.3.3, the schedule for reading data pages in our method is described.

3.3.1 Definition of Parameters

The following list of parameters will be used in presenting the algorithms in our methodology.

n Number of PNs in the system.

α_i Number of join components in PN_i, where $1 \leq i \leq n$.

$C_{i,j}$ The jth join component of PN_i.

$L(C_{i,j})$ Number of local join edges of $C_{i,j}$.

$\mathcal{L}_i$ Number of local joins of all components in $PN_i = L(C_{i,1}) + L(C_{i,2}) + \ldots$
         $+L(C_{i,\alpha_i})$.

$N(C_{i,j})$ Number of nodes (data pages) within $C_{i,j}$.

$P_{i,j,k}$ The kth page of the jth join component of PN_i.

$r(P_{i,j,k}, h)$ Number of remote joins of the page $P_{i,j,k}$ with pages of PN_h.

$R(C_{i,j}, h)$ Number of remote join edges between $C_{i,j}$ and the pages of PN_h.
         $= r(P_{i,j,1}, h) + r(P_{i,j,2}, h) + \ldots + r(P_{i,j,N(C_{i,j})}, h)$.

$E(C_{i,j})$ Number of edges of the jth join components in PN_i.
         $= L(C_{i,j}) + \{R(C_{i,j}, 1) + R(C_{i,j}, 2) + \ldots + R(C_{i,j}, n)\}$.

$\mathcal{R}_{ih}$ Number of remote join edges between PN_i and PN_h.
         $= R(C_{i,1}, h) + R(C_{i,2}, h) + \ldots + R(C_{i,\alpha_i}, h)$.

$O(C_{i,j})$ Number of pages of $C_{i,j}$ that need to be output to other PNs.

$I(C_{i,j})$ Number of remote pages that $C_{i,j}$ has to receive from other PNs in order to complete all joins that $C_{i,j}$ involves.

J_i Number of total (that is, remote and local) joins to be performed in PN_i.

$\mathcal{C}_i$ The set $\{C_{i,1}, C_{i,2}, \ldots, C_{i,\alpha_i}\}$.

$D(p)$ Degree of connectivity of the page p.

$W(p)$ Weight of the page p. To be explained in the algorithm.

BW Bandwidth of the network channel in pages per unit of time.

OPT The optimal number of joins to be executed in each

$$PN = (\sum_{i=1}^{n} \mathcal{L}_i + \sum_{i=2}^{n} \sum_{h=1}^{i-1} \mathcal{R}_{ih})/n.$$

BF Balancing Flag.

T Buffer for data pages to be transferred to other PNs.

3.3.2   The Balancing Algorithm

In this section, we present the Balancing Algorithm for join operation in a multiple PNs environment. The algorithm contains two stages: the Remote Join Balancing (RJB) stage and the Local Join Balancing (LJB) stage. In both stages, we use a best-fit-first algorithm to perform the task. Our adopting this best-fit-first algorithm is based on our past experience [12, 13] that the algorithm is simple to implement and yet results in quite balanced workload.

The RJB Stage

The RJB stage essentially counts the number of remote joins and assigns them evenly among the PNs. There are two cases (representing two granularities) of transferring data between PNs in order to balance the workload.

1. let PN_i perform the remote joins $\mathcal{R}_{ih}$, if $\mathcal{L}_i < \mathcal{L}_h$, by transferring the remote join pages of PN_h to PN_i; and

2. let PN_k perform the remote joins $\mathcal{R}_{ih}$ by transferring the remote join pages of PN_i and PN_h to PN_k.

In the above cases, assigning a global join edge of $\mathcal{R}_{ih}$ to PN_h indicates that a page of PN_i will be copied and transferred to PN_h, and the join for this pair of pages is performed in PN_h. We found that Case 1 is a more practical and viable solution than Case 2. The reason is that Case 2 requires two page transfers (instead of one) for each remote join. This extra communication causes the problems that not only is extra communication cost needed, but the join process can also be delayed since a remote join can only be performed when both data pages are available in a PN. Although letting a third PN (say PN_k) perform a remote join on pages belonging to PN_i and PN_h could result in a slightly more balanced workload, this insignificant benefit can be overplayed by the extra costs in communication and in waiting for the arrival of both pages to execute the join. In the following, we present the RJB scheme.

Remote Join Balancing Scheme

{ /* The coordinator assigns the global joins $\mathcal{R}_{ih}$ to the processing node with SMALLER($\mathcal{L}_i$, $\mathcal{L}_h$) */
Sort the number of local joins of the PNs in descending order such that $\mathcal{L}_1 \geq \mathcal{L}_2 \geq \ldots \geq \mathcal{L}_n$;
/* Note that this is not necessary. We give this statement here only for the ease of understanding our algorithm. */

```
FOR i=1 TO n DO
    J_i = L_i;
ENDFOR
FOR i =1 TO n DO
    FOR h = i + 1 TO n DO
        /* Now L_i must be greater than or equal to L_h. */
        trans_load = ((J_i - J_h) + R_ih)/2;
        IF trans_load > R_ih
            THEN /* assign all (R_ih) remote joins between PN_i and PN_h to PN_h; */
                Assign all R_ih remote joins to PN_h;
                J_h = J_h +    α_i Σ_{j=1} R(C_i,j, h);
            ELSE /* assign some remote joins to PN_h */
                Find the components C_i,j for 1 ≤ j ≤ α_i such that the summation of
                    R(C_i,j, h) of these components is the closest to the value trans_load;
                Let Γ = {C_i,1, C_i,2, ... , C_i,f} be the set of these components;
                Assign the remote joins of the components in Γ to PN_h;
                /* Those components need not be moved. Only the pages that involve a
                    remote join are transferred to PN_h. */
                J_i = J_i +    α_i Σ_{j=f+1} R(C_i,j, h);
                J_h = J_h +    f Σ_{j=1} R(C_i,j, h);
        ENDIF
    ENDFOR
ENDFOR
}
```

In this scheme, the assignment of remote joins is at the component level. In other words, when there exists imbalance between PN_i and PN_h, all the pages of component $C_{i,j}$ that involve the $R(C_{i,j}, h)$ remote joins are assigned to either PN_i or PN_h. (Note that not all the pages of $C_{i,j}$ are assigned.) Correspondingly, there can be two other ways to assign the remote joins: a (coarser) PN-level assignment, in which all $\mathcal{R}_{ih}$ remote joins are assigned to one of the two PNs, and a (finer) page-level assignment, in which a page involving a remote join can be assigned during the balancing stage. The coarser level assignment will not be able to provide a satisfactory result when $\mathcal{L}_i$ is close to $\mathcal{L}_h$ and $\mathcal{R}_{ih}$ is a large number. On the other hand, the page-level assignment can give a better balanced workload for PNs. However, the complexity of this algorithm is higher than that at the component level. For complexity reasons, we adopt the component-level assignment. Also note that in this scheme we consider the balance of workload for two PNs (that is, PN_i and PN_h) at a time. The scheme can be further improved by considering more than two PNs at a time in balancing the workload. We use a simpler algorithm in the presentation due to the consideration of algorithm complexity and also for ease of understanding. However, the algorithm can be modified to work at other granule levels.

Note that the two FOR statements in the RJB algorithm are necessary, since with these two FOR loops, each PN (for example, PN_i) has a chance to check every other PN (for example, PN_h) to see whether the balance condition can be improved by using the $\mathcal{R}_{ih}$. However, it is still possible that loads among PNs are not satisfactorily balanced. In that case, we use the LJB algorithm presented next for further balance.

The LJB Stage

The RJB process does not guarantee a balanced workload distribution. The still unbalanced workload is further balanced in the LJB stage. In this stage, there are also two cases (representing two granularities) of moving local joins among PNs in order to balance the workload.

1. transfer all the local joins of a component from PN_i to PN_h, if $\mathcal{L}_i > \mathcal{L}_h$;

2. transfer only part of the local joins of a component from PN_i to PN_h, if $\mathcal{L}_i > \mathcal{L}_h$, and assign either PN_i or PN_h to perform the remote joins that are caused by splitting a local join component into two.

It is apparent that Case 1 is more practical and viable than Case 2, as Case 2 creates remote joins (originally being local joins) which result in extra communication cost and slow down the join process.

At the end of this stage, the workload balance phase is complete. The rationale behind this scheme is that workload is balanced by transferring local joins of a component from a heavily loaded PN to a lightly loaded one. However, there is an issue that needs further consideration. Note that in the load balancing phase we first consider the balance of remote joins (in the RJB stage) and then the balance of the local joins (in the LJB stage). In the RJB stage, a remote join between page $P_{i,j,k}$ and page $P_{l,m,n}$ is either assigned to PN_i or PN_l. Let us assume that PN_i is assigned to perform the task. In the LJB stage, due to the movement of join component among PNs, these two join pages can eventually be moved to any PNs. Six possible cases arise in this situation:

1. both $P_{l,m,n}$ and $P_{i,j,k}$ are transferred to PN_h (where $h \neq i$),

2. $P_{l,m,n}$ and $P_{i,j,k}$ are moved to PN_g and PN_h (where $g \neq l$ and $h \neq i$), respectively,

3. $P_{l,m,n}$ is transferred to PN_i and $P_{i,j,k}$ is not moved,

4. $P_{l,m,n}$ is not moved and $P_{i,j,k}$ is transferred to PN_l,

5. $P_{l,m,n}$ is transferred to PN_h (where $h \neq i$) and $P_{i,j,k}$ is not moved, and

6. $P_{i,j,k}$ is transferred to PN_h (where $h \neq l$) and $P_{l,m,n}$ is not moved.

Since reassigning the remote join to any PN_h other than PN_i will disrupt the already balanced workload, the execution of the remote join must remain in PN_i. Our solution to this problem is that PN_i keeps a copy of the page $P_{i,j,k}$ if that page has to be moved to another PN for balance reasons. Meanwhile, if $P_{l,m,n}$ has to be moved to PN_h (where $h \neq i$), then PN_l will also send a copy of $P_{l,m,n}$ to PN_i such that the remote join between $P_{i,j,k}$ and

$P_{l,m,n}$ is still performed in PN$_i$. The local joins of $P_{l,m,n}$ with other pages belonging in its join component are performed in PN$_h$. For simplicity, this general method can be used in any of the above six cases.

Local Join Balancing Scheme

{ /* The workload is further balanced by moving PN's local join components. */
OPT = the optimal number of joins to be executed in each PN;

```
REPEAT
     BF = 1;
     J_p = max(J_1, J_2, ... , J_n); /* Find the PNs with the maximum and minimum join loads; */
     J_q = min(J_1, J_2, ... , J_n);
     Place | C_{p,i} | in descending order such that | C_{p,1} |>| C_{p,2} |> ... >| C_{p,α_p} |;
     FOR m = 1 TO α_p DO
          J_{p'} = J_p - | C_{p,m} |;
          J_{q'} = J_q + | C_{p,m} |;
          IF (| J_p - OPT | + | J_q - OPT |) - (| J_{p'} - OPT | + | J_{q'} - OPT |) > ξ
          /* ξ is a preassigned small value used as a threshold */
          /* "> ξ" means that moving C_{p,m} to PN_q will result in a more balanced
          workload distribution. */
          THEN
                    J_p = J_p | C_{p,m} |;
                    J_q = J_q + | C_{p,m} |;
                    SET BF = 0;
          ENDIF
     ENDFOR
UNTIL (BF = 1)
}
```

A relevant issue may arise in this circumstance: Should the sender keep a copy of the data page (that is sent to the receiver) during data movement? There are some advantages if data are allowed to be replicated in PNs since joins can be assigned to a PN without having to move data around. However, this approach is infeasible if the cost for a huge storage is a major concern. Also, there can be an associated high maintenance cost for the replicated data if concurrency control issues are considered. For these reasons, most of the past proposals using a hash join or a sort-merge join algorithm keep only one copy of the data throughout the join process [15, 7, 31]. (Note that [11] proposed a multicopy approach for query processing in multiprocessor database machines. However, their key issue is to consider the availability (recovery) of the system. We do not consider that issue in this chapter.) In order to maintain only one copy of the data in the system, a simple solution is to periodically delete unnecessary copies of the relation pages in PNs. Hence, similar to many other works, we assume that at the beginning of processing every query, each relation has only one copy in the system.

Finally, we note that the above two stages may alternatively be performed in reverse order. In other words, the LJB scheme can be executed ahead of the RJB scheme. We did not use this execution order because we believe that, in general, the number of remote joins to be executed in each PN is much fewer than the number of local joins [3]. Thus, if the workload is still unbalanced after the local join balancing stage, the amount of remote joins may not be large enough to even up the workload for underloaded PNs.

At the end of the process, the coordinator sends the local join assignment information (containing the IDs of the pages and of the components to be transferred) to the involved PNs. This information will be used in the scheduling algorithm.

3.3.3 Schedules for Reading Join Components and Data Pages

Even though the workload of PNs is balanced using the presented schemes, a system may still perform poorly if the schedule for reading data pages is not carefully designed. This can be seen by the example shown in Section 3.2. In this subsection, we present some high performance schedules for reading data from disk to memory. We will first present the join component reading strategy, and then the strategy of reading data pages within a join component. In our environment, join tasks are performed in parallel in all PNs. Since some data need to be moved from one PN to another, the components that read to memory in previous stages can affect the execution in later stages. For each component, three factors need to be considered to determine the reading sequence of join components: $O(C_{i,j})$, $E(C_{i,j}) - N(C_{i,j})$, and $I(C_{i,j})$ (refer to Section 3.3.1 for their definitions). For each factor, we should also consider whether a component having a large value or a small value of the factor is read first (more discussions are given shortly). These three factors result in various possible combinations of reading sequences.

To reduce the complexity of the problem, we choose from all combinations those easy to implement and heuristically more efficient than others. Our selection considerations are discussed in the following. Since we assume that the time to read a page is about equal to the time to perform a join over a pair of linked pages, there are at most[1] $N(C_{i,j})$ such joins performed during reading $N(C_{i,j})$ pages from disk. For a component of $E(C_{i,j})$ local join edges, there will be at least $E(C_{i,j}) - N(C_{i,j})$ time units that the CPU is busy and the disk is in an idle state. Those time units can be utilized by the disk to read other data pages. For these reasons, we understand that it is beneficial to read a component having a large $E(C_{i,j}) - N(C_{i,j})$ value earlier than the other components. The second factor, $O(C_{i,j})$, stands for the number of pages of a component that will be transferred to other PNs. If all the PNs read a component of large $O(C_{i,j})$ value early in the join process, then all the PNs will also receive transferred data pages in early stages, which could also be beneficial for the PNs since they may utilize the CPU idle time to process the joins involving the received data pages. If those components are read late, the chance of utilizing CPU idle time is diminished. Therefore, we envision that reading components of large $O(C_{i,j})$ early will benefit all PNs in later stages, which is helpful for upgrading the overall performance. As for $I(C_{i,j})$, a component having a large $I(C_{i,j})$ value should be read into memory as late as possible. The reason is that even if it is read into memory, the CPU may not be able to process all its data pages early in the join process since it is very likely that some of the needed remote pages are not yet received. If each PN reads a component of large $I(C_{i,j})$ late in the join process, then the chance of having received the needed remote pages is

---

[1] If the page reading order is not carefully designed, some of the loaded pages may not have a link in between them such that the CPU will be idle in certain time units (see the example in Section 3.2).

much higher such that the PN will not waste much time in waiting pages for remote joins. From the above analysis, we conclude that the following three reading strategies are valid strategies. For all the components that are still in disk,

S1: is to read first a component currently having the $\max(E(C_{i,j}) - N(C_{i,j}))$ value,

S2: is to read first a component currently having the $\max(O(C_{i,j}))$ value,

S3: is to read first a component currently having the $\min(I(C_{i,j}))$ value.

Although the above analysis gives us a clue in determining the order of reading a PN's components, it is still unclear which one can give the best performance under various conditions. Later in Section 3.4, we will compare the performance of these strategies.

In the following, we present an algorithm that schedules the sequence of reading components and data pages. We do not consider the case that two components have the same value on the determining factor since that chance is very low. Also, it is noted that there can be some other ways to determine the sequence, although they will not be as simple and effective as the ones discussed above. Extensions of the research in this respect are possible. However, we will not continue on this subject in this chapter.

Scheduling Algorithm(S_i)

{ /* Schedule the sequence of reading and transferring data pages;
S_i can be S_1, S_2, or S_3; Each PN does the following. */
Initialize Buffer T;
$C_i = \{C_{i,1}, C_{i,2}, \ldots, C_{i,\alpha_i}\}$;
/* Initially, C_i contains all join components of PN_i in disk */

WHILE ($C_i \neq \phi$) DO
    SWITCH (S_i)
    {
    CASE 'S_1': Find the component with $\max(E(C_{i,j}) - N(C_{i,j}))$, where $1 \leq j \leq \alpha_i$;
        Let $\mathcal{F} = \{C \mid C \in C_i, C$ satisfy $\max(E(C_{i,j}) - N(C_{i,j}))\}$;
    CASE 'S_2': Find the component with $\max(O(C_{i,j}))$, where $1 \leq j \leq \alpha_i$;
        Let $\mathcal{F} = \{C \mid C \in C_i, C$ satisfy $\max(O(C_{i,j}))\}$;
    CASE 'S_3': Find the component with $\min(I(C_{i,j}))$, where $1 \leq j \leq \alpha_i$;
        Let $\mathcal{F} = \{C \mid C \in C_i, C$ satisfy $\min(I(C_{i,j}))\}$;
    }
    Arbitrarily select a component from $\mathcal{F}$. Let $C_{l,m}$ be the component.
    Execute Read_Scheduling($C_{l,m}$); /* to be presented */
    $C_i = C_i - \{C_{l,m}\}$;
ENDWHILE
}

The Read_Scheduling() procedure in the algorithm is to be presented shortly. Note that in the Scheduling algorithm, the FIND process does not take much time since there is no need to retrieve all components and make the MAX/MIN comparison select the proper one. A small in-memory table that keeps the size information of the components will be sufficient for the process.

In the following, we present the Read_Scheduling procedure. The purpose of this procedure is to determine the order of reading data pages of the selected component in the

Scheduling algorithm. The key idea is to read the page with a high degree of connectivity. The reason is that once such a page is in memory, it can be joined with many other pages so that the CPU can be kept busy. More specifically, the algorithm is to read from disk a data page with the highest degree of connectivity (among the pages that are still on disk). Then, it is the page connected to the previously read pages and having the highest degree of connectivity that shall be read from disk, rather than the page with simply the next highest connectivity. This is because reading the page with the next highest connectivity (say page P) may still cause the CPU to be idle if the pages connected to page P are all on disk. In the algorithm, we use a weight function W(p) to place an order on the pages that should be read from disk. A similar design used in a shared memory environment was proposed in [24].

Procedure Read_Scheduling($C_{i,j}$)

{ Set $W(P_{i,j,k}) = 0$ for all $1 \leq k \leq N(C_{i,\alpha_i})$.
/* $W(\cdot)$ is a weight function whose value determines the priority of a data page in the read sequence. A larger weight value corresponds to a higher priority. */

$\Psi = \{p \mid p$ is a $P_{i,j,k}$, where $1 \leq k \leq N(C_{i,\alpha_i})\}$
/* the set of data pages of $C_{i,j}$ to be read from disk */
WHILE $\Psi \neq \phi$ DO /* not finish reading $P_{i,j,k}$ yet */
    Let $\varphi = \{p \mid p$ satisfy $\max(W(p))$ for all $p \in \Psi\}$;
    /* φ is a set since there may be more than one p satisfying $\max(W(p))$. $p \in \Psi$ is a page
       still on disk. */
    Let $\delta = \{p \mid p$ satisfy $\max(D(p))$ for all $p \in \varphi\}$;
    /* $D(p)$ represents the degree of connectivity (that is, number of links) of p */
    $p' =$ arbitrary one in δ;
    Read the data page p' from disk;
    $\Psi = \Psi - \{p'\}$;
    IF (1) p' has a remote join edge to some join component in PN$_h$ ($h \neq i$), and
        (2) this remote join is assigned to PN$_h$
        THEN copy p' to T too; /* This page is to be transferred to PN$_h$ */
    FOR all $p \in \Psi$ and p is connected to p' DO
        W(p) = W(p) + 1;
        /* that is, p satisfies the conditions
        (1) $p \in \Psi$
        (2) p is still on disk, and
        (3) p is connected to p'. */
ENDWHILE
}

In our method, when a PN receives a remote data page, the PN keeps the page until the remote join(s) on that page is (are) complete. The page can be discarded when all the joins on this page are complete. Although some memory space is required to retain those pages, our experimental results (to be presented next) show that it does not cause a serious problem to retain them in memory. In any case, if there is a need to swap the remote pages in and out, a reasonable extension of the algorithm is that the received pages with a high connectivity are retained in memory. Other pages shall be downloaded to disk and will be retrieved when needed.

For completeness in the presentation, we give in the following a simple procedure for transferring data pages from one PN to another. This procedure is executed whenever there is a data page in the T buffer of a PN.

Procedure Transfer()

{

REPEAT
    IF the network is busy
        THEN wait
        ELSE transfer BW pages in T to the target PN(s) within every time unit;
UNTIL T is empty;
}

3.4 Performance Analysis

We have designed and implemented a simulator to examine the performance of the proposed parallel join method. In this section, we will first present the model used in the simulation. Then, performance results obtained under varying parameter values are discussed.

3.4.1 The Evaluation Method

To examine the efficiency of our design, we implemented the proposed schemes (RBJ and LBJ) and the scheduling algorithms on a SUN-4 SPARC-II workstation [3]. We use the machine to work as a single PN and also use it to emulate a multiprocessor system in executing the join operation. Our choice of a single machine to emulate a multiprocessor environment was to avoid involvement in irrelevant works (such as networking details) and to avoid being limited by the configurations of the hardware.

In terms of data generation, a major difficulty we faced in the design of the model was that every bipartite join graph, when used in an evaluation, gives a result that only signifies the situation under that particular graph. In order to obtain average performance under any particular set of parameter values, many different graphs need to be tested. Evaluation on so many graphs makes that approach unrealistic. To overcome the problem, we need to have a flexible model that uses a set of representative join components and, when necessary, can be easily modified to represent different types of components. The key issues involve the determination of component sizes, the connection of the pages within a component, and connection of remote join pages. Details are presented in the following.

Component Sizes

In generating components of a PN, it is necessary to model the skewed distribution of data in the evaluation. We model the skew of data by using a generally acceptable function, the Zipf-like distribution function [34, 13, 22], to determine the component sizes. The function is defined as follows. Assume that R and S are the relations to be joined. Each relation is decomposable into B disjoint buckets, $R_1, R_2, \ldots, R_B$ and $S_1, S_2, \ldots, S_B$, where

$$|R_i| = \frac{|R|}{i^{1-Z} \sum_{j=1}^{B} \frac{1}{j^{1-Z}}}$$

and $|X|$ stands for the size of X in pages. In the expressions, Z is referred to as the degree of skew. The distribution with $Z = 0$ corresponds to a pure Zipf distribution, which is highly skewed, and $Z = 1$ corresponds to a uniform distribution. For a more detailed discussion on Zipf distributions, we refer the reader to [34, 35]. Each pair of corresponding buckets, R_i and S_i, in Zipf distributions forms a join component. The tuples in a component are divided into pages. The joinable pages are connected by a created join edge (to be discussed next). The components of different sizes are randomly assigned to PNs. Due to the random assignment, the number of components in each PN is about the same (but their sizes are different). As a result, the total amounts of data in the PNs are skewed. In this manner, the skewed distribution of data is modeled.

Page Connection within a Component

We distinguish the connectivity of a component into three classes: high, medium, and low. The connectivity is the number of local join edges, not including the remote joins. For simplicity, we assume that $X/2$ pages of an X page component belong to one join relation and $X/2$ pages belong to another relation. We define the high, medium, and low connectivities of a component of size X as follows:

    High: min(#_join_edges) + (max(#_join_edges) − min(#_join_edges))*80%
    Medium: min(#_join_edges) + (max(#_join_edges) − min(#_join_edges))*50%
    Low: min(#_join_edges) + (max(#_join_edges) − min(#_join_edges))*20%

where min(#_join_edges)=$X - 1$ and max(#_join_edges)=$(X/2)^2$.

Each component that we obtained in Section 3.4.1 will be assigned randomly to have a high, medium, or low connectivity. Once the connectivity is selected, the number of local edges can be calculated by using one of the above formulae. The real connections among pages are again assigned randomly to pages of the component with the only constraint being that the component pages have to be connected as a connected bipartite graph.

Generation of Remote Join Edges

As for the remote join edges, each of them is created by randomly choosing two pages from different PNs and making the connection. The number of remote joins is a variable in the evaluation which is a certain percentage of the total local joins of all components in the PNs. Remote joins are created by randomly assigning a remote edge to two pages of different PNs until the number of remote joins is equal to Y percent of the total local joins. The effect of remote joins on the performance is inspected by varying this percentage in the evaluation.

3.4.2   Evaluation Results

The metrics to be measured are the execution time of the join operation and the degree of imbalance. The execution time in all the figures is measured in time units rather than in seconds or minutes (as is the case in many other papers). This is because we assumed in Section 3.3 that the time to access one disk page is a unit of time which is about equal to the time to join two such pages of data, and join execution is composed of these fundamental operations. The execution is performed in parallel in all PNs (by using a clock in each PN in the emulation). The execution time is measured from the beginning of a join execution until the last PN finishes its join task. The degree of imbalance is measured by the difference in execution time of different PNs. Its definition is:

$$\text{Degree of imbalance} = \frac{\max_{1 \leq i \leq n}(t_i) - \min_{1 \leq i \leq n}(t_i)}{\max_{1 \leq i \leq n}(t_i)} * 100\%$$

where n is the number of PNs in the experiments and t_i is the time at which PN_i completes its execution on the join operation. From this definition, the greater the difference between $\max_{1 \leq i \leq n}(t_i)$ and $\min_{1 \leq i \leq n}(t_i)$, the less balance in the workload of PNs (that is, the degree of imbalance is higher).

In the evaluation, we use up to 40 PNs to simulate the join. Each of the relations participating in a join is assumed to have 50,000 tuples. Each page contains 20 tuples. Simulation results are obtained by varying a number of parameters, including the number of remote joins, the skew parameter Z, the number of join components, the connectivity of a join component, and so forth. The default parameter values used in the evaluation are as follows:

- The number of join components (also represented by B in the following discussion) = 900.

- Each join component is randomly assigned as one of the low (20 percent), medium (50 percent), and high (80 percent) connectivities for its pages.

- The number of remote join edges = 20 percent of the total local join edges in all PNs.

- The degree of skew Z = 1.

- The number of PNs = 20.

- The PN-to-PN communication bandwidth[2] = 50 pages/time-unit.

In the following, we present the results of the experiments.

The Execution Time of Different Reading Strategies

One experiment here is to compare the performance of the three reading strategies discussed in Section 3.3.3. The three strategies are listed again:

---

[2]This bandwidth is estimated based on the assumptions that a 80 Mbits/sec token ring network is used with each page being 4 Kbytes and each disk access being 20 ms.

S1: $\max(E(C_{i,j}) - N(C_{i,j}))$

S2: $\max(O(C_{i,j}))$

S3: $\min(I(C_{i,j}))$

It is hard to predict the performance of the strategies, since in S1, join components having high connectivity will be read first, and in S2 and S3, components having a greater number of pages to send to and having a smaller number of pages to receive from other PNs, respectively, are accessed early. Reading the components having a high connectivity first can certainly keep the processor as busy as possible at an early stage. However, if all the PNs only intend to keep their own processors busy, at a late stage when the components of low connectivities are read into memory, the processors may become idle later in certain time units since all the PNs did not prepare for remote joins (by accessing and sending data pages that are required to perform remote joins to other PNs). In S2, the same problem can be avoided since components having a large number of data pages to send to other PNs are read first. However, these components may not all have a high connectivity to keep the PNs as busy as possible in all stages. So the CPU can idle from time to time when the PN is loading a low connectivity component. As for S3, similar pros and cons can be summarized such that no affirmative clue can lead to a sure answer of which strategy is absolutely the best.

An experiment comparing the performance of these strategies is conducted and Figure 3.4 shows the result. Surprisingly, the three reading strategies present rather clear differences in their performance. We found the reason being that the performance is strongly influenced by the size distribution of the components. The Zipf distribution makes a small number of components very large and a large number of components having only medium and small sizes. Also we observe a fact that, in general, strategy S1 reads large components in the beginning of the join process, strategy S2 reads medium and large components in the early stages, and strategy S3 mainly accesses small components early in the execution. Since a large component of high percentage of connectivity has a much greater $E(C_{i,j})$ value than its $N(C_{i,j})$ value, a PN using the S1 strategy will have many page joins to perform after the component is loaded into memory. The join time will allow the disk to read some other medium and small components without letting its CPU idle. These medium and small components again give a number of local joins for the CPU to execute. Besides, since we assume that the remote join pages are randomly distributed over all data pages, a larger component is likely to have a larger number of such pages. Reading such pages first as in S1 means therefore automatically reading many remote join pages early, which is also helpful for minimizing CPU idle time. As a result, strategy S1 is ideal for minimizing the idle time units of the join process so as to achieve the best performance. For similar reasons, S3 gives the worst performance and S2 is in the middle.

Also, the figure shows that the higher the percentage of remote join edges, the higher the join execution time. This is because when more remote joins are involved, there will be more pages to be transferred between PNs. Since a remote join is not executable until the remote page is received, more remote joins directly reflect a longer processing time. For this reason, the execution time increases steadily with the increase of remote joins.

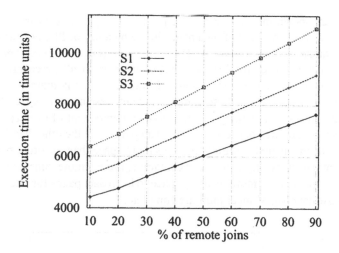

Figure 3.4: Execution time for different strategies.

The Peak Memory Size Required in Different Reading Strategies

In this section, we intend to find the peak size required in performing a join operation under different reading strategies. A basic assumption about the data pages in the evaluation is that a page will be retained in memory if any of the following is true.

For a sender PN:

1. A data page is read into memory and the local joins that the page involves are not all complete yet.

2. A data page involving a remote join is read into memory and waiting to be transferred to another PN.

3. A data page belonging to a join component that is going to be transferred entirely to another PN is read into memory and waiting to be transmitted.

For a receiver PN:

1. A data page is read into memory and the local joins that the page involves are not all complete yet.

2. A remote data page from another PN is received, but the page with which the remote data page is joined is not loaded yet, or is loaded but the remote join is not performed yet.

3. A data page involving a remote join is read into memory, and the remote data page from another PN has not arrived yet, or has arrived but the join is not performed yet.

4. Some or all pages of a join component are received, but their local joins are not executed by the receiver PN yet.

The results are shown in Figure 3.5. The peak memory size is measured as follows. Assume that $m_i(t)$ is the number of data pages in the memory of PN_i at time t. The peak memory size required is $\max(\max_{\forall t}(m_1(t)), \max_{\forall t}(m_2(t)), \ldots, \max_{\forall t}(m_n(t)))$. The results indicate that S3 needs the least amount of memory at all percentages of remote joins, and S1 uses more memory than both S2 and S3. This is mainly because in S3 small components are read first. These components take less memory space than a larger component does. In addition, strategy S3 first reads a component of $\min(I(C_{i,j}))$, which takes the least amount of memory to keep input data pages. On the other hand, strategy S1, reading large components first, naturally requires more space than the other two strategies. Also, a large component, having a chance of containing more remote join pages than a small component does, will acquire more memory space to keep data pages for later remote joins even though those data pages' local joins are complete.

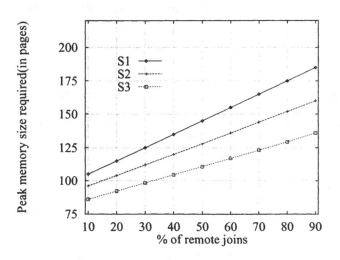

Figure 3.5: Peak memory sizes for different strategies.

We also notice that the peak memory size in this figure increases linearly with the increase in the percentage of remote joins. The reason is that the number of total local joins is a constant in the evaluation (that is, once a component and its page connections are generated, the local joins will remain the same for all percentages of remote joins). The increase in percentage of remote joins therefore only results in a linear increase in the total amount of joins.

Also, we found that when the percentage of remote joins decreases from a large value, the three lines in the figure get closer to each other. This can be explained by considering the extreme case that there do not exist any remote join edges. If this happens, only local joins need to be executed. Since remote joins do not exist, no pages need to be kept in memory to wait for a remote page to execute the join. For a component whose joins are executed locally, the size of memory required will be no more than the number of pages of the component, which is normally not very large. For a component that is to be transferred to other PNs, since they are normally transferred to other PNs in the same or consecutive time units (if the transfer within one unit of time is not enough), the receiving PN can also execute those joins in consecutive time units, shortening the average time duration that a page of data will stay in memory and thus lessening the required peak memory size.

Since S1 gives the shortest execution time (as indicated in Figure 3.4) and since the required peak memory size is not much different from that of the other strategies, we use S1 as the reading strategy in the following comparisons and assume that the available memory size is at the peak value for S1.

Zipf-Like Distribution and the Performance

Figure 3.6 shows the execution time for $Z = 1$ (uniform distribution), $Z = 0.5$, and $Z = 0$ (pure Zipf distribution) under various numbers of join components. The other parameters are at their default values. The curves show that the performances for the cases of $Z = 1$ and $Z = 0.5$ are very close, and they have much better performances than the $Z = 0$ case. The big difference tells the importance and necessity of load balance and optimization under a highly skewed data distribution. The reason for the big difference is that in a skewed distribution there are some large components. A large component inherently has many more join edges than a small component. The total number of local joins in the case of $Z = 0$ is therefore significantly greater than that of $Z = 1$. For a similar reason, the performance of a large number of join components (that is, B) is better than that of a small B, as shown in the figure.

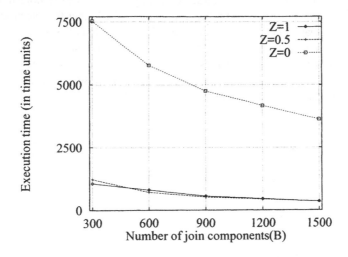

Figure 3.6: Zipf-like distribution and the execution time.

Figure 3.7 shows the degree of imbalance under the same environment as in Figure 3.6. But the $Z = 0.5$ curve is not displayed since it is very close to that of $Z = 1$. The $Z = 0$ curve shows that the degree of imbalance is within 10 percent for all the numbers of join components. This indicates that although data are highly skewed among the PNs, our balancing algorithms work well to keep the imbalance among the PNs within a satisfactory range, especially when the number of join components is more than 900 and the degree of imbalance is improved to within 5 percent.

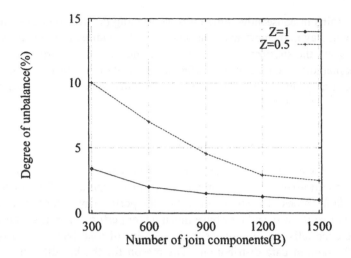

Figure 3.7: Zipf distribution and the degree of imbalance.

Effect of the Remote Joins on the Performance

Figure 3.8 shows the execution time under varying percentages of remote join edges. In general, the larger the percentage of remote join edges, the higher the execution time. For a small B, the increase in execution time is at a faster rate than that of a large B. This is mainly because when B is small, the size of each join component is large. As a result, not only the number of local join edges, but also the number of remote join edges of a component under a small B are, on average, greater than those of a large B (referring to Section 3.4.1), causing a faster increase in the execution time.

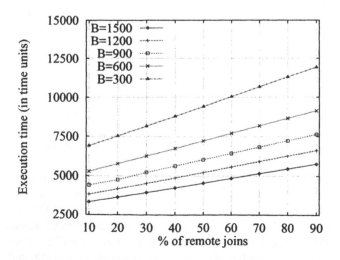

Figure 3.8: Execution time versus remote joins for different B values.

Again, the degree of imbalance in this situation is obtained and shown in Figure 3.9. For a small B, there exists noticeable unbalanced execution at very low percentages of remote join edges. But for a B greater than 600, the execution proceeds in a quite balanced condition at almost all the percentages of remote joins. The execution is especially balanced for curves of large B at high percentages of remote joins. The reason for a large B giving a more balanced execution has been previously explained. As for another scenario that the degree of imbalance is low at high percentages of remote joins, the reason is that remote joins are utilized in the balancing phase to balance the workload of PNs. Without them, the workload can only be balanced by moving join components among PNs. Thus, the more remote joins we have, the better we can balance the workload (although the execution time is longer due to more page joins).

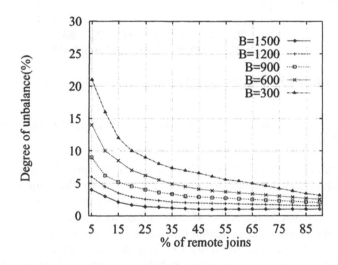

Figure 3.9: The degree of imbalance versus percentage of remote joins.

Effect of Local Join Edges on the Performance

Figure 3.10 and Figure 3.11 show the execution time and degree of imbalance, respectively, with respect to various percentages of local join edges. In this experiment, instead of randomly generating components of 20 percent, 50 percent, and 80 percent connectivities (refer to Section 3.4.1 for details), we fixed the amount of connection edges within each component at a constant value. For instance, a 20 percent local join edges means that the creation of the local joins of all components are based on the expression: MIN(#_join_edges) + (MAX(#_join_edges) − MIN(#_join_edges))*20%.

Comparing these two figures with Figure 3.8 and Figure 3.9, we find that they are somewhat similar except for the following differences:

1. the lines in Figure 3.10 start at a lower execution time (around 2,500 time units versus 5,000) and increase at a faster rate than those in Figure 3.8, and

2. the workload of PNs is balanced at a faster rate when varying the percentage of

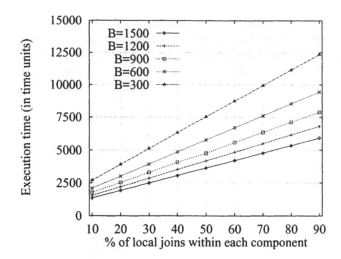

Figure 3.10: Execution time versus percentage of local joins.

remote joins (as shown in Figure 3.9) than when varying the percentage of local joins (as shown in Figure 3.11).

The first difference is due to the fact that the curves in Figure 3.8 are measured under mixed (including high, medium, and low) connectivities for the components, and the curves in Figure 3.10 are measured under the same connectivity for all components. In Figure 3.10, when the percentage is low, all components have a low connectivity for their pages, resulting in a much lower execution time for all Bs. For similar reasons, the lines rise up at a faster rate than those in Figure 3.8. The second difference indicates that the increase of remote joins gives a better effect in balancing the workload than the uniform increase of local joins in all components. This is mainly because in our methodology we first use the remote joins to balance the workload. The join components are used only when using the remote joins still falls short of balancing the workload. Another reason is that to perform a remote join only a one-page move is required. But a two-page move is required in order to let one PN perform a local join for another PN.

A Comparison with a Hash-Based Join Algorithm

In our experiments, we also performed comparisons with a hash-based join algorithm under varying percentages of remote joins and varying numbers of join components. Since in a hash-based join, data of two relations are hashed into buckets and each page in a bucket is joined with all the pages of a corresponding bucket of another relation, we assume that each component used in the hash join algorithm is a fully connected bipartite graph (corresponding to a 100 percent connectivity in our case). Also, in the hash join algorithm, since the hash phase hashes joinable tuples to the same bucket, no remote joins will be involved in the join phase. And since the hash cost is usually insignificant compared to the join cost, the cost of hash phase is ignored in the experiments. The hash join algorithm used in the comparison is similar to the previously proposed hash join algorithms (including simple-

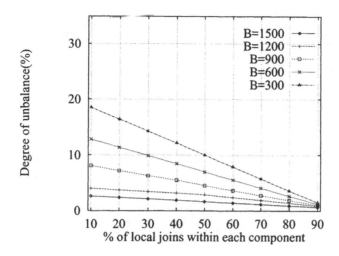

Figure 3.11: The degree of imbalance versus percentage of local joins.

hash, Grace-hash, hybrid-hash join algorithms, and so forth [6]), but some assumptions were made to simplify the process. We assume that our memory is large enough to retain any single bucket during the hash and the join phases. All buckets have to be unloaded to disk after a relation is hashed, and reloaded in the join phase. Also, we assume in the comparisons that the component and the bucket size distributions of the two methods are exactly the same. In the hash join case, the algorithms for balancing the load and scheduling the data access are also the same as in our case.

Figure 3.12 shows the execution time when the value of Z is 0 and Figure 3.13 shows the execution time when the value of Z is 1. Note that the execution times in these two figures are very different. As shown in the two figures, the performance of hash join is invariant to the number of remote joins. For a Z value of 0, even though remote joins exist in our case, the performance is still much better than that of a hash join algorithm. The main reason is that the total local joins in our case are less than those of a hash join case (since each page of a bucket has to be joined with all the pages in a corresponding bucket of another relation). The reduction of local joins in our case is caused by the use of the page-level join indices on the pages of two relations. By adopting this more detailed join information (than those from the simple partition of data based on hash), the number of page joins can be remarkably reduced.

Figure 3.13 shows that under uniform data distribution, the performance of the hash join algorithm is better at medium and large percentages of remote joins. This is mainly because for uniform data distribution, each component is much smaller than the size of a large component that is obtained under a Zipf distribution. Since the size is small, the number of local joins becomes much less than that of a Zipf distribution and the number is comparable to the number of remote joins. This causes the performance in our case to be worse than that of a hash join case at medium and high percentages of remote joins.

Figure 3.14 shows a similar comparison for varying numbers of join components. The curves show that for uniform distribution, the performance of the two cases are close and

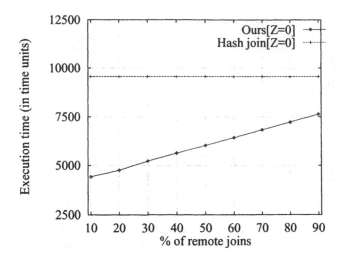

Figure 3.12: Comparing our method with a hash join algorithm at pure Zipf distribution ($Z = 0$).

much better than those of a pure Zipf distribution. Still, the hash join method gives much worse performance than our method when data are skewed. This again signifies the importance of workload balance and optimization in a join execution.

Finally, from the above results we conclude that a hash-based join algorithm performs well if the relations are hashed into a large number of buckets and data are close to a uniform distribution. Compared to the hash join algorithm, our method is inherently more tolerant of skewed data distribution.

Performance Comparison of the SN and SE Architectures

In a shared everything (SE) architecture, the processors are connected to each other through a communication channel. The storage devices including memory and disk are shared by all processors. The assumptions for both environments are about the same: they own the same size of data, the same Zipf distribution on component sizes, the same local join edges on the pages, the same number of processors, and so forth. In an SE architecture, each access by a processor is through the processor-to-memory channel, and we assume that no bottleneck will appear in the channel (similar to the assumption for the communication channel in the shared nothing (SN) architecture presented in Section 3.2).

However, some minor differences exist in the two environments. The past algorithms designed for an SE architecture use just one disk [24]. This uni-disk architecture has the advantage over an SN architecture that data skew problems and also the remote joins do not exist in that environment. Here we note that we can either generate the remote joins in a manner similar to the one used in an SN architecture (that is, random distribution over all data pages of different components), or use multiple disks in the SE architecture and generate remote joins on the data pages in different disks. However, there is not any algorithm proposed before for an SE environment that considers the possible performance degradation caused by remote joins and schedules the component reading priority to minimize the degradation. If we use the existing algorithms by allowing components to be accessed ran-

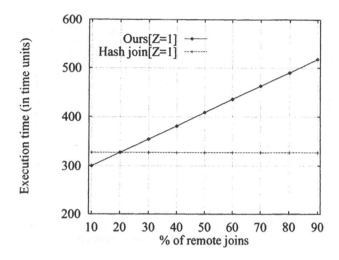

Figure 3.13: Comparing our method with a hash join algorithm at $Z = 1$.

domly, the performance becomes very poor since some "remote" joins may not be executed for a long time only because the participating data pages are not in memory yet. Due to these reasons, we simply eliminate the existence of remote joins in the SE environment. (This is an assumption in favor of the SE architecture.)

The algorithm used in the comparison is the one presented in [24] which runs in an SE architecture and satisfies all the above mentioned assumptions. Without data skew problems and the remote joins, the algorithm only needs to perform tasks similar to our Read_Scheduling() procedure to arrange the reading order of data pages.

The comparison results are shown in Figure 3.15. The percentages in the legend of the figure indicate the percentages of connectivity in each join component. As we can see, the performance of the SN system improves with the increase in the number of processors. But the performance of the SE system hardly improves after the number of processors exceeds 20. Also, we notice that when the number of processors is small (for example, five), the performance of an SE system is quite close to or even better than that of an SN system. All these phenomena are caused by the fact that in an SE system, reading a page from disk to memory may not invoke enough page joins to make all processors busy. For instance, a 10 page join component of 100 percent connectivity on its join pages, as shown in Figure 3.16, is processed by five processors. Assume that the reading order is page 1, page 2, page 3, ..., up to page 10, and in each time unit one page is read from disk. In other words, page 1 is read into memory at time $t(1)$, page 2 at $t(2)$, and so on. Then we can envision that at $t(i)$ (when page i is read into memory), $\lfloor i/2 \rfloor$ page joins will be invoked and executed by the processors, where $\lfloor \cdot \rfloor$ is a floor function. Therefore, only $\lfloor i/2 \rfloor$ processors are assigned a join task and others are idle there. For example, at $t(5)$ page 5 is read into memory resulting in two new joins to be executed: page 5 joins page 2 and page 5 joins page 4. At this time instance, two processors are assigned a task and the other three are idle. In this particular example, only at $t(10)$ will all five processors be used simultaneously. At each of the previous time instances (from $t(1)$ to $t(9)$), there are some processors in an idle

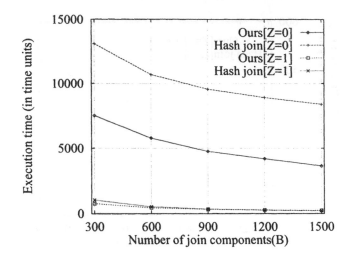

Figure 3.14: Comparing with a hash join algorithm under different number of join components.

state. For this reason, an increase in the number of processors will not be able to improve the overall performance. In the SN system, however, reading a data page in each PN can almost always result in some new page joins for the CPU to execute.

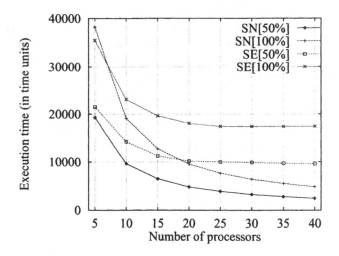

Figure 3.15: Comparison with SE environment.

We notice that when the number of processors is very low and the percentage of connectivity within a component is very high, the SE system outperforms the SN system as the upper-left portion of the curves show in Figure 3.15. This is mainly because in this comparison we did not consider remote joins in the SE environment. If the same assumption is made in the SN environment, then the two curves will have identical performance when the number of processors is equal to 1.

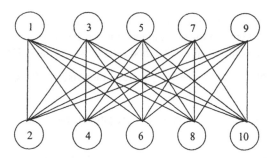

Figure 3.16: An example join component.

3.5   Concluding Remarks and Future Work

In this chapter, we addressed the problems of utilizing page connectivity information for the support of join execution in a shared nothing (SN) environment. Using this information, join can be executed more efficiently than hash-based join algorithms. However, the difficulties are twofold. First, the performance of an SN architecture is sensitive to data skew. Load of PNs must be balanced in order to achieve good overall performance. Second, since data are stored in the form of join components and the connectivity information indicates the necessity of one data page to be joined with others, the order that join components and data pages are read from disk determines the utilization of PNs. To resolve these problems altogether, we proposed new methods, including load balancing algorithms and page fetch scheduling algorithms, to optimize the execution of a join operation. Various issues in designing those methods were described and analyzed in detail in this chapter.

An evaluation model was designed to study the performance of the proposed algorithms. The proposed schemes and scheduling algorithms were implemented on a SUN-4 SPARC II workstation. We compared the performance of three component retrieving strategies. Among them, strategy S1 gives the best performance (in execution time). Our method was also compared with a hash-based join algorithm and the results showed a much better performance by using our method even when the degree of skew is high (such as pure Zipf distribution). This is because our method minimizes the degree of imbalance during fetching data pages and executing page joins. Also, we investigated the effect of remote joins and local joins on the performance. The results showed that with the increase of either of them, the total execution time increases but the degree of imbalance decreases. Finally, the comparison of an SN and an SE environment in executing the proposed algorithms showed that the SN environment performs consistently better than the SE environment when the number of PNs is greater than 10.

Two interesting extensions of this work are as follows:

When the size of memory is limited.   In a multiuser environment, the size of available memory may not always be large enough to hold the data. When the available memory size is large, we can use a fast algorithm that might take more memory space. When the available size is small, however, the process may need to shift to an algorithm which takes less memory space. The speed of the algorithm becomes the secondary consideration in this situation. Since in Section 3.4.2 the peak memory sizes required in different component reading strategies were obtained, an algorithm can be designed on the basis of those results. Roughly, the algorithm can be sketched as follows. In each PN,

Step 1: if (the available memory size $\geq \rho_1$ pages), then use the S1 strategy for the execution;

Step 2: if ($\rho_1 \geq$ the available memory size $\geq \rho_2$ pages), then use the S2 strategy for the execution;

Step 3: if ($\rho_2 \geq$ the available memory size), then use the S3 strategy;

Step 4: if the memory is full, then stop reading data until empty space is available;

where ρ_1 and ρ_2 are empirical values. This simple algorithm changes its reading strategies based on the size of available memory. The S1, S2, and S3 strategies are used in the above sequence since in the performance evaluation we learned that S1 is the fastest and also the most memory-taking algorithm, and S3 the slowest and the most memory-saving one.

A dynamic approach.   Another possible solution to the proposed problem is to allow each PN to individually and dynamically determine the most suitable reading strategy at its current state. This is due to the consideration that the amounts of local joins, remote joins, pages to send, and pages to receive are different in different PNs. A flavor of the issues in designing such an algorithm is given as follows.

We assume that the state of a PN during the join execution is represented by a 5-tuple $\langle \#\_P, \#\_P\_S, \#\_P\_R, \#\_LJ, \#\_RJ \rangle$, where $\#\_P$ stands for the number of pages in memory, $\#\_P\_S$ for the number of pages of a PN that are still in disk at this state and required to send to other PNs, $\#\_P\_R$ for the number of pages yet to receive (for executing remote joins), $\#\_LJ$ for the number of joins (including those components transmitted entirely to this PN), and $\#\_RJ$ for the number of remote joins to perform. The key point is to consider those constituent factors of a state altogether and try to achieve the optimal performance. For example, when the $\#\_P$ value of a state is high, the reading strategy should be changed to the one that will use the least amount of memory. Also for example, if the $\#\_P\_R$ value of a state is high, then the reading strategy will again be changed to a strategy opposed to S3 such that the system will move toward a state having a lower $\#\_P\_R$. In addition to this, if we assume that each PN can report its current state and its needs (such as the remote pages) to other PNs, then the optimization can be carefully designed and approached through a global point of view. For instance, if a PN, say PN_i, has a number of pages in memory waiting to be joined with the remote pages that will be sent from PN_j, then in PN_j the join component(s) owning those data pages should be loaded as soon as possible such that the data can be sent to PN_i early to speed up data processing in PN_i. However, this preemptive action can slow down the process in PN_j and maybe other PNs. Therefore, a global consideration on the status of all PNs and a judgement on the globally optimal move is possible for achieving high overall system performance.

Additionally, systems of different combinations of the three key factors: *relevance of data*, *query/operation parallelism*, and *multiprocessor architecture*, as mentioned in Section 3.1, especially for those that have never been investigated, may also be studied to find even better performing systems.

Bibliography

[1] D. Bitton et al., "Parallel Algorithms for the Execution of Relational Database Operations," *ACM Trans. Database Systems*, 1983, pp. 324–353.

[2] H. Boral et al., "Prototyping Bubba, A Highly Parallel Database System," *IEEE Trans. Knowledge and Data Eng.*, Vol. 2, No. 1, 1990, pp. 4–24.

[3] Z.A. Chang, *A Query Optimization Technique in Multi-Computer Database Systems*, M.S. Thesis, Inst. of Information Eng., National Cheng-Kung Univ., Tainan, Taiwan, 1992.

[4] M.S. Chen, P.S. Yu, and K.L. Wu, "Scheduling and Processor Allocation for Parallel Execution of Multi-Join Queries," *Proc. 8th Int'l Conf. Data Eng.*, IEEE CS Press, Los Alamitos, CA, 1992, pp. 58–67.

[5] M.S. Chen et al., "Applying Segmented Right-Deep Trees to Pipelining Multiple Hash Joins," *IEEE Trans. Knowledge and Data Eng.*, Vol. 7, No. 4, Aug. 1995, pp. 656–668.

[6] D. DeWitt et al., "Implementation Techniques for Main Memory Database Systems," *Proc. 1984 SIGMOD Conf.*, ACM Press, New York, NY, 1984.

[7] D. DeWitt et al., "GAMMA-A High Performance Dataflow Database Machine," *Proc. 12th Int'l Conf. Very Large Data Bases*, 1986, pp. 228–237.

[8] D. DeWitt et al., "The Gamma Database Machine Project," *IEEE Trans. Knowledge and Data Eng.*, 1990, pp. 44-62.

[9] S. Ganuly, W. Hasan, and R. Krishnamurthy, "Query Optimization for Parallel Execution," *Proc. ACM SIGMOD*, ACM Press, New York, NY, 1992, pp. 9–18.

[10] P. Goyal et al., "Scheduling of Page Fetches in Join Operations Using Bc-Trees," *Proc. 4th Int'l Conf. Data Eng.*, IEEE CS Press, Los Alamitos, CA, 1988, pp. 304–310.

[11] H.I. Hsiao and D.J. DeWitt, "Chained Declustering: A New Availability Strategy for Multiprocessor Database Machines," *Proc. Int'l Conf. Data Eng.*, IEEE CS Press, Los Alamitos, CA, 1990, pp. 456–465.

[12] K.A. Hua and C. Lee, "An Adaptive Data Placement Scheme for Parallel Database Computer Systems," *Proc. Int'l Conf. VLDB*, 1990.

[13] K.A. Hua and C. Lee, "Handling Data Skew in Multiprocessor Database Computers Using Partition Tuning," *Proc. Int'l Conf. VLDB*, 1991.

[14] Y.E. Ioannidis and Y.C. Kang, "Left-Deep vs. Bushy Trees: An Analysis of Strategy Spaces and its Implication for Query Optimization," *Proc. ACM SIGMOD*, ACM Press, New York, NY, 1991, pp. 168–177.

[15] M. Kitsuregawa, H. Tanaka, and T. Moto-oka, "Architecture and Performance of Relational Algebra Machine GRACE," *Proc. Int'l Conf. Parallel Processing*, IEEE CS Press, Los Alamitos, CA, 1984.

[16] M. Kitsuregawa, L. Harada, and M. Takagi, "Join Strategies on k-d Tree Indexed Relations," *Proc. Int'l Conf. Data Eng.*, IEEE CS Press, Los Alamitos, CA, 1989, pp. 85–93.

[17] M. Kitsuregawa and Y. Ogawa, "Bucket Spreading Parallel Hash: A New, Robust, Parallel Hash Join Method for Data Skew in the Super Database Computer (SDC)," *Proc. Int'l Conf. VLDB*, 1990, pp. 210–221.

[18] C. Lee and Z.A. Chang, "Workload Balance and Page Access Scheduling for Parallel Joins in Shared-Nothing Systems," *Proc. Int'l Conf. Data Eng.*, IEEE CS Press, Los Alamitos, CA, 1993, pp. 411–418.

[19] C. Lee and Z.A. Chang, "Utilizing Page-Level Join Index for Optimization in Parallel Join Execution," *IEEE Trans. Knowledge and Data Eng.*, Vol. 7, No. 6, Dec. 1995, pp. 900–914.

[20] R. Lorie et al., "Adding Intra-transaction Parallelism to an Existing DBMS: Early Experience," *IEEE Data Eng. Bulletin*, Vol. 12, No. 1, Mar. 1989, pp. 2–8.

[21] H. Lu, M.C. Shan, and K.L. Tan, "Optimization of Multi-way Join Queries for Parallel Execution," *Proc. 17th Int'l Conf. Very Large Data Bases*, Sep. 1991, pp. 549–560.

[22] C.A. Lynch, "Selectivity Estimation and Query Optimization in Large Databases with Highly Skewed Distributions of Column Values," *Proc. VLDB Conf.*, 1988, pp. 240–251.

[23] T.H. Merret, Y. Kambayashi, and H. Yasuura, "Scheduling of Page-Fetches in Join Operations," *Proc. 7th Int'l Conf. Very Large Data Bases*, 1981, pp. 488–498.

[24] M.C. Murphy and D. Rotem, "Processor Scheduling For Multiprocessor Joins," *Proc. 5th Int'l Conf. Data Eng.*, IEEE CS Press, Los Alamitos, CA, 1989, pp. 140–148.

[25] M.C. Murphy and D. Rotem, "Effective Resource Utilization For Multiprocessor Join Execution," *Proc. 15th Int'l Conf. Very Large Data Bases*, 1989, pp. 67–75.

[26] J. Nievergelt, H. Hinterberger, and K.C. Sevcik, "The Grid File: An Adaptable, Symmetric Multikey File Structure," *ACM Trans. Database Systems*, 1984, pp. 38–71.

[27] S. Pramanik and D. Ittner, "Use of Graph-Theoretic Models for Optimal Relational Database Accesses to Perform Join," *ACM Trans. Database Systems*, 1985, pp. 57–74.

[28] D. Rotem, "Spatial Join Indices," *Proc. 7th Int'l Conf. Data Eng.*, IEEE CS Press, Los Alamitos, CA, 1991, pp. 500–509.

[29] N. Roussopoulos and H. Kang, "A Pipeline n-Way Join Algorithm based on the 2-Way Semijoin Program," *IEEE Trans. Knowledge and Data Eng.*, Vol. 3, No. 4, Dec. 1991, pp. 486–495.

[30] D. Schneider and D. DeWitt, "A Performance Evaluation of Four Parallel Join Algorithms in a Shared-Nothing Multiprocessor Environment," *ACM SIGMOD Conf.*, ACM Press, New York, NY, 1989, pp. 110–121.

[31] *Teradata DBC/1012 Database Computer Concepts and Facilities, Release 3.1 Edition*, Teradata Document C02-0001-05, Teradata Corp., 1988.

[32] P. Valduriez, "Join Indices," *ACM Trans. Database Systems*, 1987, pp. 218–146.

[33] C.B. Walton, A.G. Dale, and R.M. Jenevein, "A Taxonomy and Performance Model for Data Skew Effects in Parallel Joins," *Proc. VLDB Conf.*, 1991, pp. 537–548.

[34] J.L. Wolf et al., "An Effective Algorithm for Parallelizing Hash Joins in the Presence of Data Skew," *Proc. Int'l Conf. Data Eng.*, IEEE CS Press, Los Alamitos, CA, 1991, pp. 200–209.

[35] G. Zipf, *Human Behavior and the Principle of Least Effort*, Addison-Wesley, 1949.

Chapter 4

A Performance Evaluation Tool for Parallel Database Systems

C.A. van den Berg, M.L. Kersten, and Fred Kwakkel

Abstract. *The three methods for performance evaluation, mathematical analysis, simulation, and measurement, when applied to parallel database systems, have in common that they quickly lead to a complex and time-consuming analysis. The system's performance is determined by a large number of factors. To increase the insight into the behavior of the system, a range of values needs to be examined for each factor. This makes performance tuning and evaluation a complex and time-consuming task. In this chapter a tool is presented which supports the database engineer in the performance tuning and evaluation process. The main objective of this tool is to offer a user friendly environment which allows the engineer to concentrate on the system and its performance metrics and relieve the engineer of the design and management involved in the experimentation process.*

4.1 Introduction

The demand for high volume databases and complex query processing has resulted in the development and design of parallel database systems. The conception and initial design of parallel database machines started in the early 1980s with the development of the early research prototype systems Bubba [2], Gamma [6], and Prisma [1]. Today, an increasing number of commercial parallel database systems are offered on the market [5, 13]. Although all these systems are relational database systems, their system architecture is totally different from one system to the next, taking advantage of specific hardware properties. As a result, their performance characteristics differ. A comparison of these systems requires a thorough analysis using a diverse set of workloads to uncover their strengths and weaknesses.

Performance evaluation is an invaluable tool in all stages of the development of parallel database systems. From the preliminary design to the construction of prototype systems and in the evaluation and tuning of operational systems, performance evaluation methods are used.

There are basically three methods for performance evaluation: analytical modeling, simulation, and measurement. The key consideration in deciding which technique is used is the stage the system is in. In the early system design, analytical models provide an insight into the major design tradeoffs. Once the design becomes more detailed, specific analytical modeling becomes mathematically intractable. Simulation allows analysis of more detailed designs. Alternative designs can still be compared relatively easily, but the number of parameters that influence the performance is increasing. Measurements performed on the actual (prototype) systems give the most accurate information on the system characteristics.

Parallelism has added to the complexity of performance analysis. It has resulted in new approaches to architecture and algorithmic design leading to a large number of factors that influence the performance. Furthermore, synchronization issues of parallel processes have become an important issue. The performance analysis should uncover bottlenecks in the system resulting from contention for shared resources or synchronization problems. Of particular interest in the analysis of parallel systems is also the speedup and scale up that can be reached with a system.

In the following section we will, in short, discuss the various approaches to performance evaluation and discuss their strong points and weak points with respect to the cost, accuracy, scalability, and possibility to tradeoff different designs. Then, we will introduce a tool for supporting the performance analysis process. Finally, we will discuss the application of this tool to a parallel database system.

4.2 Performance Evaluation Methods

4.2.1 Analytical Modeling

In the early stages of a design, when a product does not yet exist, analytical modeling and simulation are the only techniques available for performance analysis. The advantages of analytical modeling are that the time required is small compared to simulation and measurement and it is easy to determine the effects of various performance parameters and their interactions.

The main disadvantage of analytical modeling is that it requires so many simplifications and assumptions that the accuracy is low. In general, a performance prediction based on an analytical model should be questioned without a validation, either obtained through a simulation or through measurement.

Usually, analytical modeling is based on queueing theory or on time complexity. In a database system, transactions and queries require access to a number of resources before they are completed. In general, these resources are shared among concurrently running transactions, so that each transaction has to wait before it can be serviced. Queueing theory helps in determining how long a transaction has to wait for a certain resource. The sum of the time each transaction has to wait and the time it uses a resource determines the total runtime.

In a queueing model a system is described by *clients* and *services*. Given the arrival time of the clients, the number of services, the service time distribution, and the service discipline, the average waiting time of a client and the average queue length can be determined. More complex systems can be decomposed into a number of different services where the clients leaving a service enter the queue of another service. Unfortunately, only a limited number of queue network topologies can be analyzed analytically. An excellent overview on queueing theory can be found in [9].

Time complexity is used primarily to analyze and predict the performance of algorithms. In this approach an algorithm is decomposed into elementary operations such as the time to fetch a page from disk and the time to compare tuples. Once a cost estimate is available for the basic operations, it is possible to estimate the total execution time for a particular algorithm. Examples of this modeling technique applied to parallel database systems can be found in [3]. This approach disregards the timing of the individual operations and the effect of the distribution of the input data on the performance.

By combining probabilistic techniques with time complexity, more can be said on the effect of variations in the input on the performance. For instance, in [10, 12], the effect of nonuniform attribute value distributions is studied for join algorithm. In [14], a similar technique is used to study the performance of a dynamic query optimization method for a parallel system.

The main disadvantage of mathematical models is that many simplifications and assumptions need to be made to be able to do the analysis. Therefore, without a validation of the model through measurements or through simulation, the predictability is low.

Simulation models allow more detailed designs to be analyzed. This is particularly useful for the analysis and comparison of load balancing and scheduling algorithms. The effort required for building a simulation model, however, is considerable. Similar to analytical models, simulation model predictions should not be trusted without a proper validation.

4.2.2 Benchmarks

For existing DBMSs, benchmarks and test suites provide the common tools for performance analysis or performance tuning. Standard benchmarks provide a means to compare and evaluate systems. Well-designed benchmarks such as Wisconsin [7] or AS3AP [4] measure a particular function or operation in the system. By analyzing the outcome of the benchmark, the strengths and weaknesses of the system can be revealed. The TPC-A and TPC-B benchmarks [11] focus on bank-teller applications. Although they were originally intended to be representative for OLTP applications, they now only provide a simple comparative measure of a small part of the system. Currently, the TPC addresses this issue by defining benchmarks for more complex application domains such as decision support and order entry.

A potential danger of benchmarks is that the workload is no longer representative of today's requirements. Another problem is that the systems' capacities have grown to such an extent that the benchmark does not reveal the systems' full potential and bottlenecks. For example, the Wisconsin benchmark, designed in 1983, must be scaled up so that it becomes useful considering the amount of main-memory present in today's shared memory multiprocessor systems. Furthermore, benchmarks only measure a limited set of points in the workload space. Therefore, if a user offers the system a workload which is slightly different from the one measured, the user may face a bad system performance.

4.2.3 Observations

Three different approaches to performance analysis have been discussed so far: mathematical analysis, simulation, and benchmarks. The choice between them depends on the problem to be solved. Mathematical analysis, through the use of queueing models and time complexity, is more suitable for the analysis of initial designs and the comparative study of algorithms. Simulation, which allows the use of more detailed models and therefore can offer greater accuracy, is used in the design phase and for performance prediction. Benchmarks, finally, if well designed, provide a measure for comparing systems and can give insight into the performance characteristics of system prototypes.

All three approaches have in common that to increase insight into the behavior of a system and raise the confidence level of the results, a large number of parameter ranges need to be examined in an experiment. The organization and collection of the experimental results can grow prohibitively large. Assuming an experiment with a full factorial design where the k different factors range over n different values, a total of n^k possible factor combinations are examined.

Knowing that each experiment involves a certain amount of work, the experimenter's objective would be to organize the experiment in such a way that a maximum amount of information is obtained after a short number of experimental runs. For instance, in a transaction router simulation for an OLTP system, typical performance factors would be the distribution functions for the arrival of new transactions, the lock probability, and the CPU and I/O time each transaction requires. The scheduler itself is implemented using three different algorithms. Assuming that changing the distribution function parameters requires a rerun of the simulator and that changing the scheduling algorithm also requires a partial recompilation, it is wise to plan the experiments carefully.

In the case of benchmarks, it is necessary to run the benchmark for more parameter settings than prescribed. The extensive reliance on benchmarks like TPC-A and TPC-B for the comparison of (parallel) database systems has been known to lead to situations where the systems are tuned to perform well within the ranges of the benchmark. Once outside this range, for instance by doubling the record size, the system performance degrades rapidly.

For tuning a parallel database system, the system configuration parameters must also be taken into account in the experiment. Unfortunately, most database systems require a restart before the new configuration becomes effective.

All in all, the performance analysis is a formidable task requiring a clever design of the experiment, a good organization of the collection of the results, and knowledge of proper statistical techniques for the analysis of the results.

A software tool for systematic performance evaluation can facilitate the experimentation process. In the Esprit project, such a tool, "Pythagoras," has been developed. In the following section we discuss the Software Testpilot [8] and its application to an experiment on the Oracle/Ncube system.

4.3   The Software Testpilot

The Software Testpilot is a tool designed to aid the DBMS engineer and user in the performance analysis of software systems in general and database systems in particular. It has proven its usefulness in testing the performance of a range of systems like Ingress, Oracle on various platforms using various benchmarks like TPC -A/B, Wisconsin, and AS3AP.

Running an experiment with the Software Testpilot basically requires a specification of the experiment in terms of *factors*, *responses*, *actions*, and a hypothesis, which is a functional description of the expected performance. The Software Testpilot uses this specification to explore a large workload search space to find the slope, top, and knees of performance figures quickly.

The Software Testpilot iteratively selects DBMS workload parameter values, constructs an experimentation plan, and performs the experiment, such that the performance characteristics and quality weaknesses are determined at minimal cost (that is, time). The Software Testpilot performs the experiments against the target DBMS and uses the measurement results to update the model parameters and the confidence level attained for the hypotheses given. The confidence levels are fed back into the Software Testpilot, where they are used to decide if more experiments are required to prove or disprove the hypotheses. Furthermore, the results are visualized to monitor progress and the produced *diagrams*, the *test suite*, and a *history* of the testing process are included in a session report. A user can edit this report and enter observations and comments alongside the testing processing.

4.3.1   The Experiment Specification

The user describes the performance study of a target system with a *test suite*. This test suite is written in a language, called Test suite Specification Language (TSL). A TSL program contains all components required by the Software Testpilot to cover the workload search space and to interact with the target system. In the following, we illustrate the components of a TSL script using an aggregate query workload. The experiment involves computing an aggregate value min, max, count, sum, or avg on one of the attributes key, signed, or int grouped on one of the attributes key, signed, int, name, or code.

Each TSL script contains an *experiment* specification. It defines the name of the experiment and enumerates the factor and response variables used in the experiment.

```
experiment => [ name:    single_user,
                factor:  [ aggFunc, aggAtt, groupAtt,sel ],
                response: [ cpu, dio, bio ],
                design:  random ].
```

Factor and *response* variables span the workload space. Factors denote the target system input for an experiment and response variables denote the output measured on the target system. Factors and response variables have an underlying type (for example, integer, real, categorical) and range to describe permissible values. An experiment is an assignment of values to factors and obtained response values.

```
factor  => [ name:   aggFunc,
             type:   symbolic,
             range:  [ min,max,count,sum,avg ],
             state:  no ].
factor  => [ name:   aggAtt,
             type:   symbolic,
             range:  [ key,int,signed ],
             state:  no ].
factor  => [ name:   groupAtt,
             type:   symbolic,
             range:  [ key,int,signed,name,code ],
             state:  no ].
factor  => [ name:   sel,
             type:   float,
             range:  [ 0..1.0 ],
             state:  no ].
response => [name:    cpu,
             type:    integer,
             unit:    sec,
             range:   [ 0 ..  100000 ] ].
response => [name:    dio,
             type:    integer,
             unit:    page,
             range:   [ 0 ..  100000 ] ].
```

The interface with the target system is described with a collection of *actions*. In essence, each action object describes a small experiment to measure a given response given a fixation of the factors. Hypothesis objects describe relationships between factors and response variables. They describe expected response behavior of parts of the experimental space.

```
action => [ name:   measure,
            before: [ aggFunc:F,aggAtt:A,groupAtt:G,sel:S ],
            response: [ cpu:T, dio:D, bio:B ],
            body:  ( sql_query([
                                select,G,', ',F,'(',A,')',
                                'from hundred',
                                'where key<25000*',S,
                                'group by ',G],
                                (T,D,_ ))) ].
action => [name:   disconnect,
           body:   disconnect ].
```

In many cases a simple default test suite suffices. This applies to programs that can be interfaced using factor values as (positional) arguments and which return the response parameters on standard output like simulators.

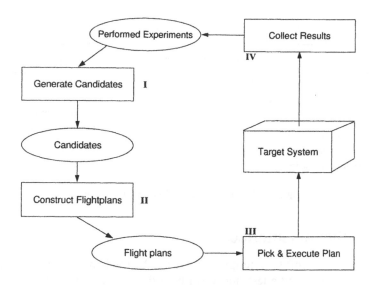

Figure 4.1: Performance assessment cycle.

4.3.2 The Performance Assessment Cycle

The Software Testpilot, after initialization of the target system, selects a point in the space spanned by the factors for experimentation. The point chosen depends on the hypothesis given and results of previous experiments. Given a point of interest, it performs an experiment by bringing the target system to the required initial state and by executing the action to obtain the response value. This process is repeated until the required confidence level has been attained or the system is stopped by the user.

The processing cycle (Figure 4.1) starts with the generation of candidate experiments (I) which are stored in a candidate pool. A user-defined threshold on the number of candidates in this pool limits the number of experiments taken into account for flight plan construction and execution. The Software Testpilot uses the performance hypothesis and performance data gathered in previous cycles to identify candidate workspace parameters with high probability to (dis)qualify user-defined and system-generated hypotheses. Thereafter, the best flight plan is constructed for each candidate experiment (II). A flight plan is a sequence of target operations that bring the target system to the correct state (as required by the candidate) and operations to measure the response variables. Each flight plan has an associated cost estimating the execution time of the flight plan. Among the candidate flight plans, process (III) selects one of high value and low cost and executes it on the target system. The processing cycle closes with collecting the results of the executed experiment (IV) which can be used to generate new candidates in the next round. As a side effect, the Software Testpilot adjusts the behavioral model when measurements disprove the models' assumptions. Thus, the outcome of a session is both improved statistical knowledge on the performance characteristics and a (possibly) modified behavioral model of the target system.

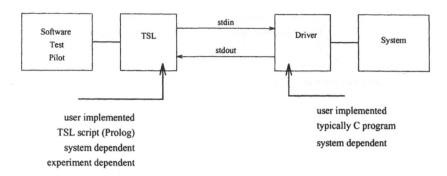

Figure 4.2: The general STP system interface.

4.3.3   The System Interface

In general, before the Software Testpilot (STP) can be used for system experiments, an interface to that system and a test suite describing the experiment must be defined. The interface consists of a system driver (typically a C program) that can initialize and control the system under test. It reads the parameter settings requested by the STP from standard input, performs the test, measures the response parameters, and returns the result as a list of key-value pairs (see Figure 4.2).

To build the driver software, a good understanding of both the Software Testpilot and the system is required. A system experimenter's prime concern is the system under test. He has knowledge about important system parameters and measures, but not necessarily knowledge of TSL. The effort required for the design and implementation of the STP system interface and the specification of the TSL script must therefore be as small as possible. Therefore, the STP must be customized for a particular system, which involves the design and implementation of the system driver and the development of a tool for generating TSL scripts.

In the following section we discuss how the Software Testpilot is customized for the Oracle/Ncube parallel database system.

4.4   The Software Testpilot and Oracle/Ncube

So far we have discussed the general ideas of the Software Testpilot. In this section we report on the use of the Software Testpilot in the performance assessment of Oracle V 7.x on the Ncube parallel database system.

The Ncube/Oracle installation is used by a large Dutch national bank for OLTP and complex queries for Decision Support Systems. In the current situation, performance measurements on the Oracle/Ncube system are done manually using a large collection of *real life* queries and OLTP suites in order to find the best configuration parameter settings. In the measurement process the queries and the configuration parameters are modified by hand to evaluate the effect of the variations in the parameter values on the overall performance. The result of these runs is basicallly a set of total runtime figures and is not broken down into, for instance, I/O and CPU cost.

The objective of this project is twofold. First, to deliver a user friendly performance evaluation environment for complex queries and OLTP on Oracle. Second, to test and explore the Oracle/Ncube installation at the ING bank for several generally known and ING-specific complex queries and OLTP benchmarks using the delivered testing environment.

The main objective of this environment is to facilitate the experimentation process on the Oracle/Ncube system by automating the generation and measurement of the workload and to allow interactive steering of the experimentation process. The ideal is that the collection of test queries and scripts can be reused with only a very small effort in the performance assessment environment. To this end, a graphical tool has been designed which allows an experimenter to define the experimentation factors, specify a parameterized query, and select a number of performance parameters maintained in Oracle's dynamic performance tables.

An essential component of the performance test environment is the Software Testpilot and its interface to the Oracle/Ncube system. To deliver a practical and useful performance testing environment, we investigated several options for this interface, ranging from using the Oracle-supplied tool tkprof, an embedded SQL application retrieving performance figures, to a platform-specific Oracle utility.

The remainder of this section is structured as follows. First, we describe the basic structure of the Oracle/Ncube installation. Second, we describe the particular requirements for performance measurement and testing of database systems for OLTP and complex queries. Third, we present the three different approaches we studied for interfacing the system under test (Oracle/Ncube) and the performance assessment tool (Software Testpilot). Finally, we show some results obtained with this system on the Oracle/Ncube system.

4.4.1 Database System Performance Assessment

In the general performance assessment of database management systems, three classes of factors determine the system performance: database characteristics, DBMS configuration, and query formulation. The performance measures for a given workload and system configuration include both the DBMS and OS resources used for processing the workload.

In the design of the performance assessment tool for the Oracle/Ncube system, we consider each of these classes and their manifestation in everyday practice.

Both synthetic and real databases are used for the performance analysis of the Ncube/Oracle installation. The synthetic databases used are defined by the OLTP benchmarks TPC-A and TPC-B and the AS3AP benchmark for complex query processing. The real database consists of a snapshot of the financial reports from all bank holdings. The synthetic databases are characterized by their size and attribute distribution functions, while the real databases are used as is.

The system configuration for the Oracle/Ncube installation is described by two configuration files. They describe the specific resources allocated to each database process. For instance, in the configuration file one can specify the number of processors used for the global file system, the dimension of the subcube for running the Oracle DBMS, or the size of the log buffer. Effecting a change in a configuration parameter involves, in the worst case, a shutdown and restart of the DBMS and hardware, which is a time consuming task. In fact, a cold restart is not always required as a configuration parameter may only involve a single Oracle instance. The Oracle/Ncube system distinguishes eight different restart levels for this purpose.

The workload consists of the OLTP transactions defined by TPC-A and TPC-B benchmarks and the AS3AP complex queries. For the performance experiment for decision support a real, very large aggregate query is used. For experimentation one would like, for instance, to change the interarrival time for the OLTP transactions, the selectivity of complex queries, and experiment with optimizer hints in the formulation of the aggregate query.

Based upon this everyday practice, we have formulated the following requirements for the performance assessment system:

- Database generation is supported by synthetic database generation tools for AS3AP and TPC-B. For "real-life" databases a sampling utility is required, which returns a proper subset of the existing data.

- A tool is required for changing DBMS configuration parameters and restarting the system at the appropriate restart level. This tool determines, given the set of changed parameters, at which level (inst, ora, arch, redo, lock, log, gfs, and cube) a system restart should take place.

- The workload can be specified using parameterized scripts or queries. The scripts are intended to accommodate the OLTP transaction generators and the differently formulated complex queries. The parameterized queries are intended to be used for complex SQL queries as found in the AS3AP benchmark. The user supplies a query in textual form and specifies parameters by prefixing them with a dollar sign (for example, $min_value or $selectivity).

To facilitate the specification of the performance factors, the database experimenter is provided with a form-based interface for specifying the experiment parameters, the response parameters of interest, and the query itself.

This interface allows the user not only to modify the settings of the configuration parameters, but also to introduce new parameters, which can then be used in the query specification. For each parameter the experimenter can set the type and range. For configuration parameters, the type is preset and cannot be changed, but the range can be adjusted.

The screen dump (Figure 4.3) shows in the left column the list of performance parameters consisting of the configuration parameters cube_dim (dimension of the Ncube subcube) and num_inst (number of oracle instances) and the user-defined variables aggregate_function, grouping_attribute, and min_value. At the top of the left column, the aggregate_function is defined as a *categorical* factor that ranges over the symbolic values min, max, count, avg, and sum.

The right column enumerates all the possible response factors that can be obtained by the Oracle/Ncube driver. The user has selected the CPU used measures, session connect time, and session memory as response factors.

The bottom area is used to specify the workload. In this case, it consists of a parameterized aggregate SQL query.

The tool generates a complete test suite including the proper interfaces with the driver software. This test suite can then be loaded and started by the user in the Software Testpilot.

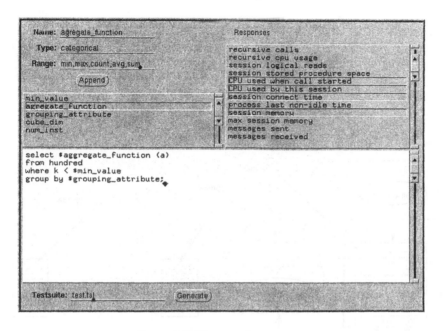

Figure 4.3: The test suite generator.

4.4.2   The Oracle/Ncube Interface

The Software Testpilot generates experiment specifications in a textual form which consist of the setting of the performance factors. It expects the results of an experiment, also in a textual form, consisting of a list of response variable-value pairs. The interface to the system under test is responsible for performing the experiment on the target system and retrieving the measurements.

In short, the system driver performs the following tasks:

- reads the performance factors from standard input

- builds the database if required

- reconfigures the system if required

- takes the measurements before execution

- executes the workload

- takes the measurements after execution

- outputs the performance measures

The basic problem to solve in the design of a system driver is the retrieval of the measurements, its cost, and the level of detail the measurements offer. Three different designs have been considered. The first design is based on the Oracle performance measurement utility, `tkproff`. This choice is motivated by the fact that it comes with the Oracle product. The second design exploits the dynamic performance tables maintained by the Oracle

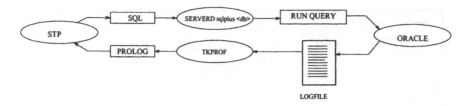

Figure 4.4: The tkprof-based driver.

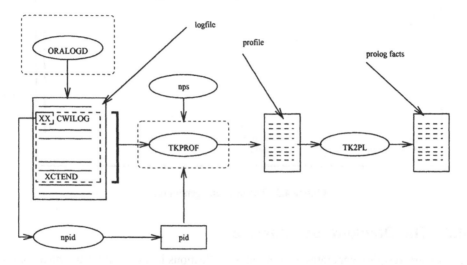

Figure 4.5: Dataflow for extracting tkprof profile data.

kernel. More than 100 different performance measures are maintained in these tables. In the last approach we considered the design of a monitoring process which runs concurrently with the Oracle instances and which inspects the dynamic performance tables without consuming database resources.

These options are discussed in the following paragraphs.

Solution I: TKPROF

In the first approach the functionality is split over two parts. One part connects to the database server to execute the test query using the SQL interface. The other part retrieves the performance figures of the query execution using the Oracle post session analysis utility, tkprof. The design of the system driver based on tkprof is shown in Figure 4.4.

The process for extracting the performance figures from the logfile generated by the Oracle logdaemon is automated. The dependencies and dataflow between the programs are illustrated in Figure 4.5.

Although the tkprof-based driver has the advantage that it is based on a standard Oracle performance measurement utility, it is rejected because tkprof offers only a limited set of performance figures, the performance is bad, and the process for obtaining the figures is too complex and unstable.

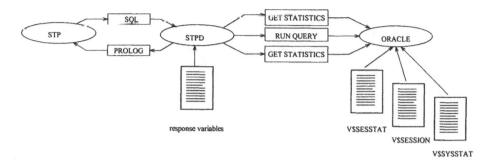

Figure 4.6: The embedded SQL driver.

Solution II: Embedded SQL

The second solution is based on the dynamic performance tables maintained by Oracle, the so-called V$ tables. Two tables, v$sesstat and v$statistics, provide enough information to monitor a single query.

In this case, the driver consists of a single embedded SQL program. Before it executes the query it receives from the Software Testpilot, the driver measures a user-indicated subset of the response factors by querying the dynamic performance tables. This measurement is performed again after the query has been run. These measurements are finally passed to the testpilot.

To perform its task, the driver program takes two parameters: the database name and a configuration file specifying the response parameters of interest. This configuration file is generated by the tslgen program and corresponds to the generated test suite.

4.5 Preliminary Results

We tried out the embedded SQL interface on the Oracle/nCube platform for a query studying the parallel behavior of the system.

Parallel Behavior

In this query we illustrate how we can vary the parallel servers and the number of instances used in the execution. We choose to use the parallel hint option for this purpose. In the parameterized query as specified below, the parameter I signifies the number of parallel instances, the parameter P is the number of parallel servers per instance, and the parameter S is used to vary the total workload. The query returns the cardinality of joining a portion of two relations, hundred.

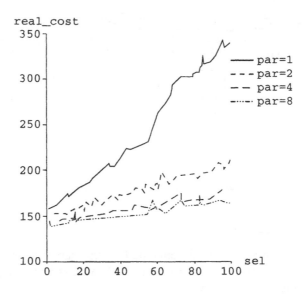

Figure 4.7: Parallel performance.

```
CREATE TABLE RESULT(a) AS
SELECT /*+ PARALLEL(h1,P,I) PARALLEL(h2,P,I) */' COUNT(*)
FROM hundred h1, hundred h2
WHERE  h1.k < size(h1) * S AND
h2.k < size(h1) * S AND
h1.k = h2.k
```

In Figure 4.7 we show the effect of varying the selectivity as a percentage and the degree of parallelism I on the real cost (wall clock time) measured in seconds by the Software Testpilot.

We see that increasing the degree of parallelism from four to eight instances has only a small effect on the processing time compared to increasing the degree of parallelism from one to two instances. This signifies that the sequential part forms a significant portion of the complete execution.

If we set out the execution time actually measured by the Oracle instance against the selectivity and the degree of parallelism, we can make two interesting observations (see Figure 4.8):

1. When the query is executed by a single instance, we see a sudden change in the slope of the performance curve when approximately more than 50 percent of the relation participates in the query. It appears as if a different algorithm is used to calculate the query. This discontinuous behavior is not yet explained.

2. The degree of parallellism does not affect the query execution time measured by a single instance. Apparently, the execution time spent by the participating instances for executing the subqueries issued by the coordinating instance is not added to the time measured by the coordinating instance.

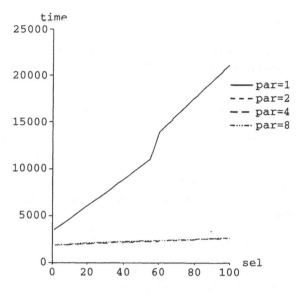

Figure 4.8: Ratio.

The latter effect has serious consequences for obtaining measurements from a parallel Oracle platform. It is impossible to retrieve information on the parallel execution time using the dynamic performance tables maintained by the Oracle instances. In other words, with the embedded SQL interface it is only possible to measure the performance of the coordinating instance and not of the complete query execution.

For this reason we have considered a third driver, which continuously monitors the dynamic performance tables stored in the SGA of the parallel running Oracle instances. Unfortunately, the design and implementation of this driver is impossible without knowledge of the SGA storage structures used for the dynamic performance tables. Fortunately, such a tool, known as statdaemon, is currently being developed by Oracle. The development of a driver based on this tool is therefore postponed until the tool is made available.

4.6 Conclusion

In this chapter we have reviewed three techniques for performance evaluation: analytical modeling, simulation, and measurement. We have argued that the performance analysis of a parallel database system in all the stages of its development is a complex task.

We have presented the Software Testpilot, a tool which reduces the time and effort for performing, managing, and visualizing the performance analysis of systems.

Finally, we have shown how the Software Testpilot can be customized for performance analysis of database systems. In particular, we have illustrated the use of the system in a practical situation on Oracle v7.x running on a 64 node Ncube.

Bibliography

[1] P.M.G. Apers et al., "PRISMA/DB: A Parallel Main Memory Relational DBMS," *IEEE Trans. Knowledge and Data Eng.*, Vol. 4, No. 6, Dec. 1992, p. 541.

[2] H. Boral et al., "Prototyping Bubba, A Highly Parallel Database System," *IEEE Trans. Knowledge and Data Eng.*, Vol. 2, No. 1, Mar. 1990, pp. 4–24.

[3] D. Bitton et al., "Parallel Algorithms for the Execution of Relational Database Operations," *ACM Trans. Database Systems*, Vol. 8, No. 3, Sep. 1983, pp. 324–353.

[4] D. Bitton, C. Orji, and C. Turbyfill, "The AS3AP Benchmark," *Database and Transaction Processing Sys. Performance Handbook*, J. Gray, ed., Morgan Kaufmann, San Mateo, CA, 1991.

[5] D.D. Davis, "Oracle's Parallel Punch for OLTP," *Datamation*, Aug. 1, 1992, p. 67.

[6] D.J. DeWitt et al., "The Gamma Database Machine Project," *IEEE Trans. Knowledge and Data Eng.*, Vol. 2, No. 1, Mar. 1990, p. 44.

[7] D. DeWitt, J. Naughton, and D. Schneider, "An Evaluation of Non-Equijoin Algorithms," *VLDB*, 1991, pp. 443–452.

[8] F. Kwakkel and M.L. Kersten. "Design and Implementation of a DBMS Performance Assessment Tool," *4th Int'l Conf. Database and Expert System Applications, Lecture Notes in Computer Science, No. 720*, Maryk, Lazansky, and Wagner, eds., Springer-Verlag, Sep. 1993, pp. 265–276.

[9] L. Kleinrock, *Queueing Systems*, John Wiley & Sons, New York, 1976.

[10] E. Omiecinski. "Performance Analysis of a Load Balancing Hash-Join Algorithm for a Shared Memory Multiprocessor," *VLDB*, G.M. Lohman, ed., Barcelona, Spain, Sep. 1991, pp. 3755–385.

[11] O. Serlin, "The TPC Benchmarks," *Database and Transaction Processing Sys. Performance Handbook*. J. Gray, ed., Morgan Kaufmann, San Mateo, CA, 1991.

[12] S. Salza and M. Terranova, "Evaluating the Size of Queries on Relational Databases with Non-Uniform Distribution and Stochastic Dependence," *Proc. ACM SIGMOD Conf.*, ACM Press, New York, NY, 1989, p. 8.

[13] E. Tseng and D. Reiner, "Parallel Database Processing on the KSR1 Computer," *Proc. ACM SIGMOD Conf.*, ACM Press, New York, NY, 1993, p. 453.

[14] C.A. van den Berg and M.L. Kersten, "An Analysis of a Dynamic Query Optimization Scheme for Different Data Distributions," *Query Processing for Advanced Database Applications*, J.C. Freytag, G. Vossen and D. Maier, eds., Morgan Kaufmann, San Francisco, CA, 1994, p. 449.

Chapter 5

Load Placement in Distributed High-Performance Database Systems

Björn Schiemann, Lothar Borrmann, and Eike Born

5.1 Introduction

Within the past five years, there has been a noticeable shift in the area of high-performance database servers, from expensive centralized mainframe systems to scalable, moderately priced distributed and parallel systems [5]. Powerful professional systems like Oracle with its Parallel Server configuration [10] are nowadays even available on clustered systems with PC-compatible architecture, thus delivering high performance at extremely low prices. In this situation, effective load management strategies become extremely important in order to use the existing resources with optimum efficiency. Figure 5.1 sketches the main load management approaches for the example of a distributed database management system (DBMS) where each node of the underlying system is associated with one DBMS instance.

Before the users' queries enter the DBMS instances for execution they will be preprocessed. Here they can be *partitioned* into subqueries or the corresponding subtransactions. *Transactions* (TA) are the internal representation of the users' queries. A good partitioning can support load balancing issues [6, 12] especially in shared nothing DBMS architectures, where each DBMS instance only has access to that part of the database which is stored on its node's disks. For database sharing architectures, where each of the DBMS instances can access the entire database, a dedicated load balancer will assign the partitioned transactions to the available instances or the corresponding nodes. This is called *load placement* or load assignment.

Internally, the DBMS instances use several server processes which are responsible for executing the incoming transactions. *Dispatching* and *scheduling* allow the load-dependent assignment of transactions to the available server processes. Furthermore, the number of these processes can be dynamically increased or reduced. An optimized disk architecture,

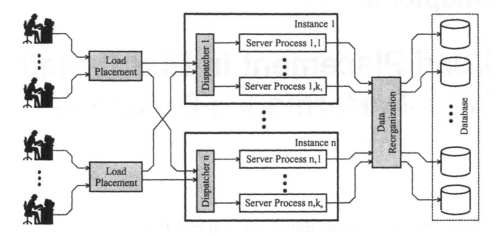

Figure 5.1: Load management for distributed database management systems.

which for instance may be a RAID architecture [11], benefits from the intelligent distribution of the database over the available disk drives. Then faster access times can be achieved. From time to time the database needs to be *reorganized* depending on the recent access history.

The investigations described in the following sections focus on the placement of newly arriving transactions onto the instances of a distributed DBMS with a database sharing architecture. Due to the particular architecture of parallel database systems, well-known load balancing schemes which work on the operating system level are not suitable here. Database specific schemes have to be found. The correlations between load balancing [3, 7, 20] and the system to be balanced, especially the DBMS application, are not well known. To overcome this, we investigated the impact of different basic load placement policies onto a distributed DBMS by means of event-driven simulation. To obtain realistic results, the load scenarios were derived from traces of a production system running customer applications. Buffering and locking mechanisms are crucial for the performance of a DBMS. Our simulation approach gives us insight into the behavior of these mechanisms under the influence of the respective load management strategy. This knowledge can be used for developing more intelligent strategies which react with respect to a system's applications' needs.

5.2   Investigated System

5.2.1   System Architecture

The DBMS we investigated has a heterogeneous *database sharing* architecture where the entire database is distributed over all of the system's disks. The basic architecture model (see also [10]) is depicted in Figure 5.2 below. A couple of variants, in particular, larger systems with different interconnect networks, have also been simulated, showing mostly similar results.

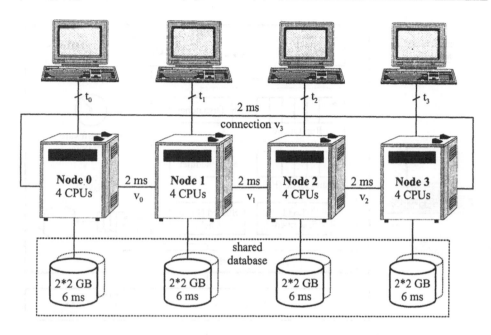

Figure 5.2: Simulated DBMS.

The architecture under test consists of four nodes each having four CPUs. The nodes' interconnection network is a peer-to-peer ring. Each node has two local disks with a total of 4 Gbytes for storing part of the 16-Gbyte shared database. Each node can access all disks. The high-performance disk architecture yields a mean disk response time of 6 ms. Disk and network contention are part of the simulation model.

In general, distributed DBMSs like the Oracle Parallel Server can support several instances per node. In our scenario, each node is associated with one DBMS instance which has a 64-Mbyte shared buffer cache (SBC). This is a software-controlled fully associative buffer with LRU replacement for the data most recently used by the processed transactions (cf. the basic architecture of an instance in Figure 5.3). Its blocksize is 4 Kbytes. A dedicated cache manager is responsible for maintaining the SBCs' coherency.

Corresponding to the architecture of the Oracle Parallel Server (OPS) [10], there are several server processes per instance which process the incoming stream of transactions. These processes run in a multitasking environment. Internally, they use multithreading for processing the assigned transactions. This enables a *hidden loading* mechanism: If the data requested by a transaction (TA) cannot be found in the SBC, a fast thread switch will be performed to activate another TA. Only if no TA can find its data in the SBC, the CPUs will perform an active wait until the data is available.

Each DBMS instance is equipped with a transaction monitor (TM). Thus queries can be represented by requests for specific transaction programs, which are identified by their transaction code (TAC). Without such a monitor, queries would be sequences of statements given in a database query language (such as SQL). Thus with a TM the network overhead caused by load placement can be limited to transmitting quite short requests and the TAs' results.

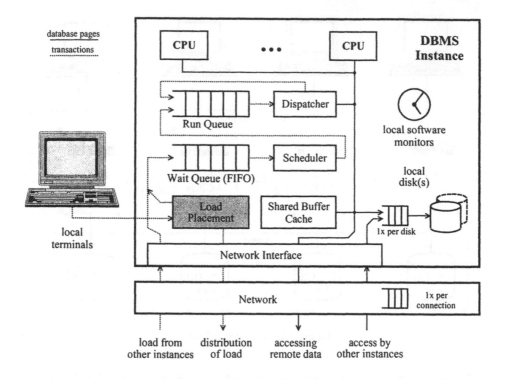

Figure 5.3: Architecture of a DBMS instance.

Node 0 and 2 of this ring have 250 connected terminals each, while the remaining two have only 125 terminals each. Each terminal is associated with one active user who sequentially generates queries. In between two queries he or she pauses, for example, for making inputs or for collecting new input data. Up to 12 queries are correlated. They form a sequence, called a *conversation*, where the corresponding TA references part of the data its predecessor (if there is one) has also used.

Load differences between the nodes of the simulated ring can be created by means of the number of terminals as well as by influencing the users' pauses between the generation of successive TAs. This enables the creation of hot or cool spots.

All DBMS instances are equipped with a couple of software monitors which extract performance data from the system by counting events as well as by periodically looking at internal status variables.

A distributed lock manager (DLM) enables the TAs to exclusively access the data stored in the database. Locking is performed with row level granularity which means that only specific parts of the data or tables will be locked. If some TAs compete for the same lock a deadlock could occur. One of the competitors would then be selected at random to be restarted. This causes all its locks to be freed and introduces additional system overhead.

5.2.2 Load Scenarios

For each of the DBMS instances the specification of the transactions can be set up individually (see also [22]). These TAs emerge from a synthetic load generator which is initialized from the analysis of real DBMS traces. This approach enables a close-to-reality load generation and allows for stressing the system under test even with extreme load situations in order to check its robustness and stability. The load generator associates each TA with a transaction code (TAC) which denotes the number of the transaction program (TAP) necessary to execute it. TAs are basically represented by a *reference string* which consists of a number of different page addresses within the address space of the entire database. This granularity corresponds to the page-oriented mechanisms used for the SBCs. Depending on the TAC, the following characteristics are set for each TA:

- The amount of pages in the reference string that will be modified during a TA's execution.

- An affinity factor expresses that fraction of a TA's pages which will also be used by the succeeding TA within the same conversation.

- In a distributed DBMS, each of the involved instances has local mass storage. Due to our database sharing approach, this storage is accessible by all other instances via the interconnection network. Another parameter describes a simple disk access distribution: it stands for the percentage of page addresses within a TA's reference string that use the local disks instead of the remote ones. As an alternative, a common disk pool could be modeled.

- Each of the pages in the reference string is used only once. But the evaluation of our traces shows that there will usually be multiple references to each page. Thus, a factor specifies how often the pages have to be used before the TA terminates.

- A TA acquires all required locks when a page address to be written will be executed for its first time. The TA keeps these locks until termination. Then they will be freed, and all modified pages will be committed and written back to the disks *(deferred write)*.

Besides the characteristics outlined above, further aspects of the simulation model can be configured. This includes the CPU performance as well as the overhead for lock management, multitasking, transmitting the requests' results via the network, and load management. The latter comprises additional CPU load and network load. Furthermore, the scheduler which transfers TAs from the wait queue into the run queue can be configured (see Section 5.4).

5.2.3 Trace Analysis

In order to make our simulations as close to reality as possible, several DBMS access traces have been used as a basis for our load patterns. These traces contain load characteristics which are independent from the underlying system architecture. The systems monitored were symmetric multiprocessors (SIEMENS 7.500) running the CODASYL database handler UDS [1, 18, 19] and the transaction monitor UTM [13]. Within every application program of the transaction monitor (TM), several transaction programs (TAP) are linked together with runtime libraries and interface adapters enabling communication with the transaction monitor and the database handler (DB-H). This system is fairly typical for commercially used mainframe environments.

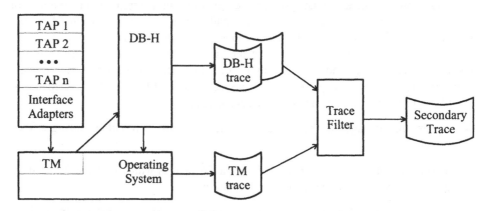

Figure 5.4: Collecting and preprocessing DBMS traces.

The customer loads under observation are the order and delivery processing at a large manufacturing company and a large customer help desk system for information technology support. All transactions within about an hour were recorded, totalling between 1,500 and 20,000 transactions. To hide the particular features of different software monitors, and to obtain a common basis for further evaluation, recording and evaluation of the customers' load environments are performed in three steps (see Figure 5.4):

First of all, primary traces are recorded online by both the DB-H and the TM. These traces have different formats. Then, a specific filter merges the primary traces into secondary traces and performs some further processing. Finally, the secondary traces can be evaluated by means of statistical schemes.

For the primary trace, the monitored events cover every TM application request directed to either the transaction monitor or to a database handler and also some DB-H internal calls. TM-specific events are recorded in a system global trace file, but each DB-H process writes a private trace file. Thus, atomic actions of the transaction monitor and the database handler are recorded in separate files.

For the secondary traces, the different primary traces are merged in such a way that load data, such as accessed DB pages or access modes, are collected per transaction. This is done by a dedicated filter program [9]. Correlation of information from different primary traces is based on time stamps and process identifications. Table 5.1 summarizes the main contents of the resulting secondary trace. BOT and EOT mark begin and end of a transaction, LOGREF describes an access to a database page.

Based on the secondary traces, our statistical evaluations cover various load characteristics, for example, the mean and standard deviations of the number of accessed or modified database pages per TA. Each item was evaluated for a given clustering of the transaction load, thus giving a picture of the different resource requirements of different load classes. In the following, the workload classes are defined by the identification of the transaction

record type	header	body
BOT	timestamp transaction-ID	application-ID, session-ID conversation-ID, TAC, terminal-ID, user-ID
EOT	timestamp transaction-ID	termination type
LOGREF	timestamp transaction-ID	database-ID database page number modification intention

Table 5.1: Contents of secondary traces.

monitor programs (TAC). For the observed workload such a clustering gives a more homogeneous class-specific behavior than a clustering which is based on the terminal-ID or the user-ID.

5.2.4 Load Setup

From the traces described in the previous section the following load characterizations were derived. They give a good picture of real-life workloads and were used for setting up the introduced load generator.

Load Profile 1

The first trace represents a heterogeneous load with 12 different types of transactions which are characterized by their transaction codes ranging from 0 to 11. Figure 5.5 shows the TAs' length given as the mean number of different database pages accessed (the reference string). Furthermore, the related percentage of the modified pages which had to be written back to the database is shown. Finally, the TAs' nearly exponentially distributed execution count is given.

Load Profile 2

The load profile represented by our second trace is more homogeneous than the previous one (Figure 5.6). It comprises 82 different transaction codes. For convenience, only the first 32 TACs are mentioned in the following statistics. Compared to profile 1 there are clear differences concerning the percentage of modified pages as well as the length of the respective TAs' reference strings. As can be further seen, there are no TAs which access a much larger amount of database pages than others. Thus, the access variance is quite low (for profile 1 it is high).

The introduced load profiles are the base for setting up the simulator. All simulations are initialized by randomly filling all the instances' shared buffer caches and by executing 100,000 TAs. This covers the caches' warm-up phase and leads into a stable state. Then the actual simulation of typically 500,000 TAs begins. Simulations were performed for a number of various system architectures and load scenarios. For instance, the variations covered the number of disks, their latencies, the network architecture, and the CPU processing

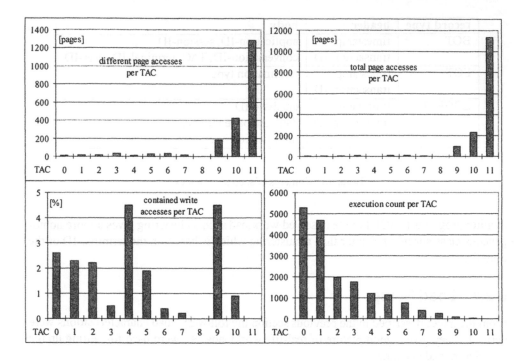

Figure 5.5: Load profile 1.

power, as well as the data affinity between a conversation's TAs or the distribution of the database over the available disks. Even heterogeneous systems were investigated where the nodes had different processing performance or different cache sizes. The variations mentioned are a great challenge for a system's load management.

5.3   Load Placement Strategies Investigated

Our simulations focus on load placement for database sharing architectures. It is assumed that every DBMS instance possesses the program code (that is, the transaction programs) necessary to process the incoming TAs, thus their code does not have to be migrated, and load placement can focus on the transactions' requests for transaction programs. Furthermore, in larger systems there is usually a permanent stream of new load which can be used for alleviating load imbalances by means of placement.

In our simulations each DBMS instance is equipped with its own load balancer which is responsible for load placements. This is a *distributed load management* scheme. The basic placement strategies covered by our simulations are outlined below. All dynamic strategies (3 to 5) use an activiation threshold. Thus, load arriving at one instance can only be directed to another instance if the load difference between this instance and the potential destination exceeds this threshold.

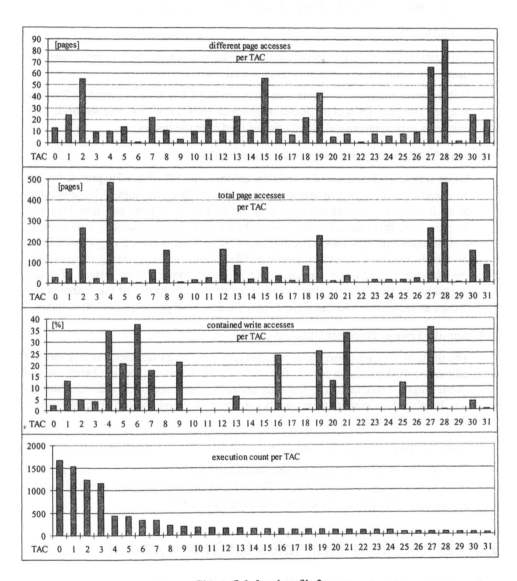

Figure 5.6: Load profile 2.

1. No Load Placement   *(No)*

   This is the reference situation which is the current standard for many commercial systems. All TAs will be executed on that DBMS instance and its corresponding node on whose terminals the respective queries were generated.

2. Round Robin   *(RR)*

   This static strategy works similarly to the well-known scheduling scheme of the same name. No information about the system's load status is evaluated.

   If there are n instances available then an incoming TA will be executed on instance $k < n$. The next TA will be placed on instance $(k + 1) \bmod n$, and so forth. This ensures a very symmetrical distribution of load over the instances.

3. Join-the-Shortest-Queue with Conversations   *(Co)*

   Using simple load measures for decision making is a well-adopted approach for low overhead algorithms in load management strategies. Here, the sum of TAs contained in an instance's wait and run queues is the decision criterion, and new load will be placed on that instance which currently has the shortest queues. This strategy is well known as *Join-the-Shortest-Queue* (JSQ). Since a certain degree of affinity or correlation can be assumed between TAs belonging to the same conversation, the placement granularity was chosen to be entire conversations instead of single transactions. This strategy is expected to improve the behavior of the shared buffer caches as successive TAs can benefit from the data their predecessors left in there.

4. Join-the-Fastest: Processor Utilization   *(Pr)*

   The utilization of processors is a different indicator for an instance's utilization and efficiency. It depends on several factors like SBC behavior, locking behavior, and queue length. Thus, incoming TAs will, under consideration of the activation threshold, be placed on that instance and its corresponding node whose processors show the lowest utilization.

5. Join-the-Fastest: Response Time   *(Rt)*

   This algorithm places incoming conversations on that DBMS instance which recently showed the fastest response times. These times are distinguished per TAC which allows for better adaptation to heterogeneous load profiles.

5.4   Scheduling Strategies for Transactions

Scheduling has a high impact on the overall system performance which became evident in our simulations. The scheduler is responsible for moving jobs, that is, TAs, from an instance's wait queue into its run queue (cf. Figure 5.3). The set of TAs contained in the run queue denotes an instance's working set. The size of this working set, and thereby indirectly the instance's SBC behavior, can be influenced by the scheduler. If the working set becomes excessive, there will be many TAs competing for an SBC's contents, and this might decrease its hit rate.

In our model, TAs will never be thrown back from the run queue into the wait queue. This assumption is legal because TAs do not produce any intermediate results—they are atomic. Thus, from the user's point of view, it cannot be observed whether a TA started execution. The only event becoming visible is a TA's termination, corresponding to the delivery of its results. Up to now, two basic scheduling strategies have been investigated:

1. Limiting the size of the run queue to a certain TA count.

   The scheduler limits the length of the run queue depending on the number of contained TAs, irrespective of their characteristics.

2. Limiting the run queue size depending on load characteristics.

   Using well-informed scheduling algorithms which evaluate information about the underlying system's state is a well-adopted strategy for high-performance scheduling. Furthermore, load characteristics like the typical length of a TA's reference string should be taken into consideration. This should be supported by a load classification which can be based on the respective TAs' transaction codes or application-IDs.

   The scheduler will limit the number of TAs in the run queue by means of the sum of the lengths of their reference strings. If this sum adequately relates to the size of an instance's shared buffer cache, a *cache-oriented scheduling* algorithm will be in charge of the system. An improved behavior of the SBC can then be expected (cf. [14] and [17]). This is due to the fact that the queue will contain only the amount of TAs such that most of the pages these will reference will fit into the SBC. This in turn reduces SBC conflicts.

Furthermore, it is possible to combine both the basic scheduling strategies. For instance, one strategy could be applied for TAs with a short reference string, while the other one will be used for those with a long reference string.

5.5 Simulation Results

5.5.1 Influence of Scheduling

Our simulations indicate that the performance of a system heavily depends on the chosen scheduling strategy. This has a large impact, especially on the behavior of the shared buffer caches, which is quite independent of their respective sizes. Thus, an appropriate scheduling helps reduce the load of network connections and hard disks.

The efficiency of the introduced scheduling strategies was investigated for SBC sizes from 16 to 192 Mbytes. It became evident that the limitation of the run queue by means of the number of contained TAs can best be used with homogeneous load profiles. Much better results were achieved by means of cache-oriented scheduling strategies which limit the length of the run queue via the lengths of the contained TAs' reference strings. This leads to a dynamic adaption of the DBMS instances' working sets to the size of their SBCs, and the tuning of the allowed maximum queue lengths becomes much easier.

Without cache-oriented scheduling, the DBMS instances' run queues might get overloaded with long running TAs or those with a long reference string. This might lead to a bad SBC behavior and high network or disk load. Thus, especially for heterogeneous load profiles, a cache-oriented scheduling is a must if good response times and a high through-put have to be achieved. This is mainly due to an improved SBC behavior which alleviates or even eliminates bottlenecks at network connections or hard disks. If the scheduling fur-ther supports an out-of-order execution which gives selected TAs (for example, those with a short reference string) a higher priority, then the mean response times of these preferred TAs will be improved while the response times of the remaining TAs will get worse.

However, the investigated form of cache-oriented scheduling does not consider data access affinities between arbitrary TAs. If these could be easily detected, then the schedul-ing efficiency could be further improved. Yet no low-overhead scheme could be identified which can be used at system runtime. If the typical lengths of the TAs' reference strings are not known, then the mean response time could also be exploited for scheduling pur-poses. This can be recommended for those load profiles where a long reference string is not necessarily an indicator for an expected long response time.

5.5.2   Evaluation of the Load Placement Strategies

In general, the surveyed load placement strategies need a minimum load difference between the system's nodes or DBMS instances to be efficient. Thus, a careful tuning of the algo-rithms' thresholds is required to avoid unnecessary activations. The thresholds of 10–20 percent used for the simulations mostly led to reasonable results.

The figures on the following pages give a graphical comparison of some results for the described system (Figure 5.2) running the load profile 2 (Figure 5.6) and using a cache-oriented scheduling scheme. Figure 5.7 shows the following characteristics achieved with selected load placement schemes:

For each algorithm one row with three diagrams is shown. The first diagram depicts the *placement behavior*. It shows how many of the TAs generated on an instance's termi-nals were executed on which of the available instances. Corresponding to Figure 5.2 the instances are numbered from 0 to 3. The next diagram shows the number of *net accesses* used. The figures have been distinguished for each of the system's network connections. Finally, the *utilization* of the simulated system's DBMS instances is given as a percentage which represents the mean of their nodes' CPUs' utilization. It separates into:

- Processing TAs: This item (iExec) covers all DBMS-specific CPU load that relates to executing submitted TAs.

- Active waiting time (iWait): If none of the TAs being held in an instance's wait queue can find its data in the SBC, the CPU has to wait until the data of at least one TA is available. Then execution can be resumed.

- Overhead for acquiring and releasing locks (iLock): Even the unsuccessful attempt at acquiring a lock increases CPU load.

- Further overhead (iAddCode): This covers tasks like process switching and TA mi-gration. The migration overhead is quite low here because only requests for transac-tion programs had to be placed.

The diagrams in Figure 5.7 show the results for homogeneous systems (indicator 'hom') as well as those for a heterogeneous system where the processing performance of node 1 was reduced by 50 percent (indicator 'het'). Next, Figure 5.8 gives an overview of the response time distributions which the load placement schemes achieved. Scheme *No* is the reference system without placement.

a) Scheme *RR*

The static Round Robin scheme leads to acceptable results in many application cases. One of its major advantages is that it can be easily implemented. In the long term, a symmetrical throughput of all instances is achieved.

Compared to other algorithms *RR* shows the highest number of remote placements where TAs will be executed on another instance than the one on whose terminals they were generated. This loss of locality does not necessarily introduce a high network load. Due to high SBC hit rates, in some cases only a small number of network and disk accesses was used. The reasons behind this are asymmetric behavior and instabilities: *RR* tends to temporarily overload some DBMS instances while the others will have a low load leading to good SBC hit rates and very short response times. For heterogeneous load profiles, the overload is due to assigning a lot of TAs with a long reference string (or high expected response time) to the same instance because the static *RR* is not able to dynamically adapt to overload situations. Thus, even overloaded instances will be assigned further load: in a scenario with 1,400 active terminals, the overloaded instance reached a queue length of more than 700 TAs. However, from time to time the overloaded instances may recover and others will take over their role. The outlined effects are less severe on homogeneous systems with a homogeneous workload. But even a small architectural heterogeneity like a node with a little less computing power can be expected to cause huge load differences when the system has to cope with a large transaction stream. Furthermore, *RR* often leads to an increase in lock conflicts.

Summarized, scheme *RR* should only be used on homogeneous systems whose nodes should be exclusively available for the DBMS application (no background load). Even the placement of conversations instead of TAs could not avoid the observed effects. Without an out-of-order scheduling, *RR* often cannot achieve similar response times on the DBMS instances. In some scenarios the outlined unstable behavior could lead to a high increase in the transaction throughput.

b) Scheme *Co*

Scheme *Co* is a join-the-shortest-queue scheme which places entire conversations. This is superior to placing single transactions when there is data access affinity between a conversation's TAs. In this case, a transaction uses data of its predecessor, thus leading to a better utilization of the shared buffer cache (SBC). This means an increase in SBC hit rate and a decrease in disk and network accesses compared to other placement schemes (Figure 5.7). As a consequence, the mean response times will improve (Figure 5.8). The higher the affinity between a conversation's TAs, the better results will be achieved. With affinity factors below 20 percent, no significant advantages over an algorithm which places single transactions could be observed. However, due to the larger placement granularity, the tuning of the

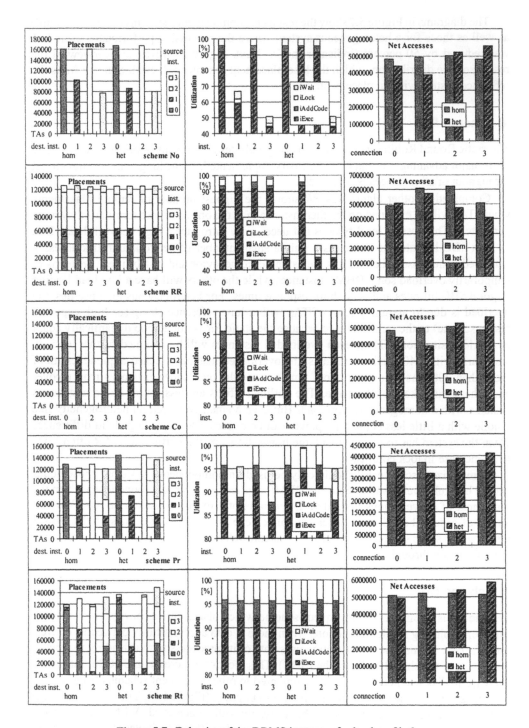

Figure 5.7: Behavior of the DBMS instances for load profile 2.

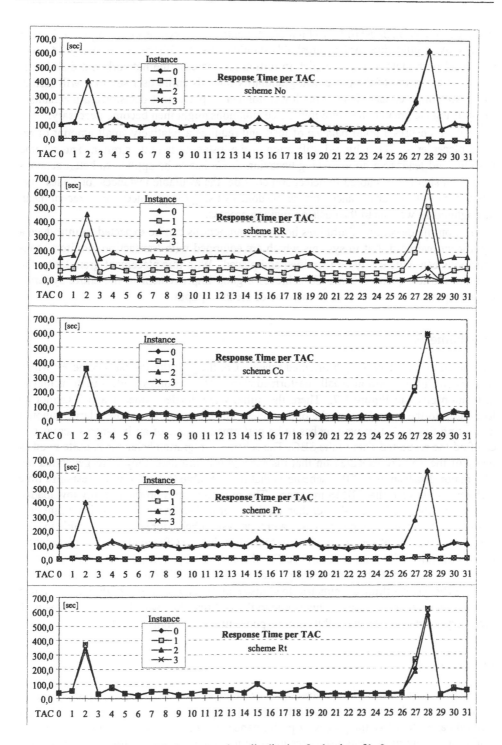

Figure 5.8: Response time distribution for load profile 2.

scheme's activation thresholds is a bit more difficult if conversations will be placed instead of TAs. As a guideline, higher thresholds should be used. Otherwise too many TAs will be placed on remote instances which in turn might increase the network and disk loads. A further extension of the placement granularity towards entire user sessions will further emphasize these effects. Due to the lower number of placement decisions, a mechanism for splitting the granule in severe imbalance situations might then become necessary.

But *Co* ensures a good balance of load and requires a relatively small amount of remote placements. The achieved utilization of the instances is quite similar. The scheme is stable and leads to a good locking behavior. If *Co* has to be applied to heterogeneous systems it should be enabled to detect and consider the available instances' or nodes' different capabilities. For instance, this can be done by using the instances' most recent mean throughputs as weights in the decision-making process.

The online detection of affinities between transactions can be expected to introduce a significant overhead, but in systems which are equipped with transaction monitors, conversations can quite easily be identified and placed. With this placement granularity, the join-the-shortest queue scheme *Co* achieves a good improvement in the entire system's mean response times as well as an increase of the throughput.

c) Scheme *Pr*

Compared to the queue-length-oriented scheme *Co*, the join-the-fastest scheme *Pr* which focuses on CPU utilization usually performed worse. This becomes evident in the achieved utilization given in Figure 5.7. There the initially low loaded nodes 1 and 3 cannot be loaded up to the same level as the other nodes. Furthermore, they show a larger amount of waiting times. Active waiting has to be performed if none of an instance's active TAs can find the requested data in the SBC. The scheme's migration behavior is quite good as many of the TAs are executed on that instance whose terminals they were generated on. The major disadvantage of this scheme is that it is not able to level out the response time differences between the DBMS instances. The response times on the initially low loaded nodes are still significantly shorter than on the other nodes. In some cases this might be a desired characteristic but in most cases a unique system behavior should be visible to all a system's users. The observed effect is due to the fact that the CPU load can be high for short queues as well as for long queues. The *Pr* scheme will stop assigning an instance further load as soon as a minimum queue length leads to a high CPU utilization. As observed for scheme *RR*, the resulting asymmetric load distribution may lead to a high overall system throughput in some scenarios. This is due to the fact that the lower loaded instances with their very short queues can exhibit short response times and high throughput.

d) Scheme *Rt*

This scheme is a join-the-fastest strategy. Due to the evaluation of mean response times it is suited even for heterogeneous systems since the response times directly depend on architectural parameters like the processor performance. If *Rt* has to be used for heterogeneous load profiles, the mean response times must be measured separately for some transaction classes. Here the TAs were distinguished by means of their transaction code (TAC).

The investigated form of Rt places entire conversations. If single TAs were placed it sometimes happened that the instances specialized on TAs with certain TACs: some instances preferred TAs with a long reference string while others preferred those with shorter strings. This is contradictory to the idea of avoiding the remote placement of short running TAs since the expected performance gain usually does not outperform the placement-related overhead. If single TAs have to be placed, additional mechanisms which avoid this specialization should be applied (for example, 'aging' of response time measurements).

If entire conversations are placed, the placement decision will be based on the observed mean response time for a conversation's first TA. Compared to other placement schemes Rt now achieves quite similar response times on all a system's DBMS instances. This even holds for heterogeneous systems and load profiles. The instances' utilization measures are quite similar. However, if compared to successful scheme Co, sometimes a higher number of network and disk accesses could be observed. This was due to the fact that even low loaded instances will have some of their conversations placed remotely. To avoid this, further activation thresholds should be introduced. For instance, only those instances with a high TA arrival rate could be enabled to place some of their load on remote instances.

Summarized, scheme Rt achieves a good improvement of the system throughput. Its main advantages are quite similar mean response times on all instances as well as its suitability for heterogeneous architectures and load profiles.

5.5.3 Lessons Learned

This section summarizes the lessons learned out of the assessment of load placement strategies. Several conclusions are in line with previous work. If not all a system's nodes are initially overloaded, then the load placement strategies assessed generally improve the transaction throughput of our distributed DBMS. This is, in most cases, accompanied by an improvement in the overall mean response time for transactions. This improvement is asymmetric in the sense that the relative improvement is smaller for complex transactions when the load profile is heterogeneous. Furthermore, load placement typically leads to reduced response times on heavily loaded instances but slower responses of lightly loaded instances. Dynamic strategies in many cases introduce a nearly uniform distribution of response times. If the goal of load placement is to present a unique system behavior to all its users, then strategies which mostly rely on CPU utilization are not suited. Our Pr scheme was not able to achieve similar TA response times on all the entire system's nodes.

The locking behavior is considerably improved, particularly for schemes Co and Rt. This is related to the throughput improvement. Under high throughput conditions, TAs complete faster and thus keep their locks for shorter time intervals thereby allowing following TAs to proceed. The number of transactions restarted due to locking conflicts is significantly reduced. In our scenarios lock handling did not introduce a significant CPU load but a considerable part of the network load.

The benefit of load balancing depends on the scheduling policy used. A load-adaptive scheduling is beneficial, particularly with heterogeneous load where the transactions' response times vary. With homogeneous load the scheduling policy is less relevant, but still allows for better utilization of resources, especially buffers. Scheduling policies which adapt to the shared buffer caches of our DBMS showed the importance of considering the cache behavior within scheduling decisions. They limit the number of running TAs depending on the utilization of the instances' shared buffer caches.

The load balancing mechanism should only be activated on demand when the imbalance reaches a certain level. This can be implemented using an imbalance threshold which is determined during system tuning. It was further shown that single decision criteria like queue lengths are usually not sufficient for implementing efficient load balancing schemes which can cope with varying load situations and which can be applied to heterogeneous systems.

Static load assignment schemes appear to be inappropriate for heterogeneous architectures. In this situation these schemes show a tendency to become unstable, as was shown for the popular *Round Robin* scheme. However, static schemes may behave quite well in homogeneous systems with homogeneous and static load conditions (for example, none of the nodes further executes a varying amount of nondatabase load) if the network provides a high performance and if the load placement overhead is low.

Load profiles with strong heterogeneity put a heavy burden on buffering mechanisms and may cause overloading of the shared buffer cache. This only occurred when the response time distribution of our transactions exceeded a certain level of imbalance. An example is our load profile 1: If transaction type 11 is removed from the profile, throughput and lock conflict rate are substantially improved. This result underlines the requirement for well-selected benchmark loads which are used for estimating a system's performance: Only if the benchmark load models the real application appropriately can reliable results be obtained.

If load profiles show a certain locality of reference, this locality may be partially lost when the load is balanced. This leads to increased communication load and may evidently have a negative effect. The improvement in throughput gained by load balancing alleviates bottlenecks on DBMS instances, but on the other hand, it can lead to new bottlenecks, especially in the area of network resources and mass memory. To cope with this, the hit rate of the SBCs (shared buffer caches) should be maximized. This can be achieved by evaluating related performance measures in the load balancer and the scheduler. In general, well-behaved SBC access is crucial for the success of a particular load balancing scheme. SBC hit rates on lightly loaded instances are sometimes decreased by load balancing. On the other hand, this figure is usually improved on instances with heavy load. In cases of severe disk hot spots, none of the investigated load balancing schemes was able to help. The SBCs were not able to cache a sufficient number of accesses. A reorganization of the database is required to cope with such issues.

Summarized, relatively simple load placement schemes based on the introduced join-the-shortest queue scheme *Co* or the join-the-fastest scheme *Rt* are well suited for database management systems with a database sharing architecture. The best performance gains in terms of mean response time and throughput improvement were achieved if entire conversations instead of single TAs were placed. This especially holds if there is a high data access affinity between a conversation's TAs. Due to the larger placement granularity, higher activation thresholds should be used for the placement schemes. In particular, the join-the-shortest queue schemes should be extended so that they can recognize the current performance of DBMS instances, making them applicable even to heterogeneous system architectures. The join-the-fastest scheme *Rt* does not require such an enhancement since the mean response times which are used as the decision criterion depend directly on architectural parameters.

Compared to DBMSs which do not use load placement, all of the investigated schemes were able to improve the overall throughput and, in most cases, even the system's overall mean response times. If a hidden loading of the shared buffer caches is used, the differences between the respective schemes' throughput gains diminish if a high-performance network and disk are available! All schemes have different requirements concerning the number of performed network and disk accesses. This might have an impact on the maximum achievable throughput. If some instances have a low load or if the network or disks become overloaded, the hidden loading might not be able to compensate for the bad SBC behavior of some placement schemes. Then the observed waiting times will occur. Now, not the maximum throughput of the processors, but the maximum throughput of the network or the disks will determine the transaction throughput. Irrespective of the fact of whether a hidden loading is used or not, those placement strategies which show the better SBC behavior will be superior. Furthermore, the SBC behavior has a huge impact on response times since SBC misses will cause an increase. With hidden loading in place this is due to thread and process switches, while in the other case the system must wait until the requested data is available. As a consequence, we identified two major criteria for choosing a placement scheme:

- Good *SBC behavior*: The better the achieved SBC behavior, the less network and disk accesses can be expected. If the SBC's hidden loading cannot compensate for bottlenecks at these components, then the SBC behavior will mainly determine the achievable system throughput.

- Good *response time behavior*: If all the available placement schemes lead to good SBC behavior, which includes efficient and effective hidden loading, then the response time will be the primary criterion for choosing a scheme. The response time behavior should be characterized by similar short response times on all a DBMS's instances.

5.5.4 Decision Parameters Used

Load balancing schemes use different load parameters for their decision making. The parameters we used for our investigations are summarized in Figure 5.9. They are characterized as follows:

- The *CPU Utilization* covers all a processor's tasks. It is well suited for general purpose systems but proved to be less efficient for load placement decisions in a distributed DBMS. However, when used together with the part of the overall utilization which belongs to the DBMS's processes, then a distinction of DBMS-specific and non-DBMS load can be performed. This in turn can be a valuable input for load balancing decision making.

- The *queue lengths* of the run or wait queues of the DBMS instances can be used effectively for load balancing decisions. However, the evidence is limited in systems with heterogeneous load, or in systems which do not dedicate all their nodes' performance to the database application.

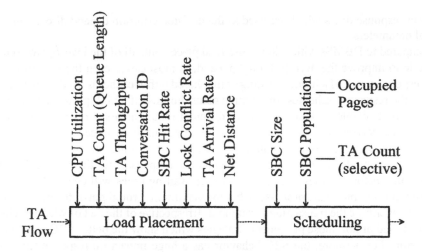

Figure 5.9: Load metrics used during simulation.

- SBC (shared buffer cache) *hit rates* can easily be obtained through software monitoring. These rates are a first measure of conflicts between a DBMS instance's active transactions. Experiments with a load balancing scheme which was based solely on this measure did not show uniformly acceptable results since high hit rates can occur either for high or low access rates.

- The *lock conflict rate*, the ratio of locks requested versus locks granted, did not seem to be a suitable criterion in our experiments. It may be useful as a secondary measure in certain situations where lock conflicts determine the system performance.

- The *transaction throughput* of the individual instances proved to be an appropriate measure to account for imbalances which are due to different performance capabilities of the respective underlying system components.

- *Transaction arrival rates* at the DBMS instances can be used to detect lightly loaded nodes. Furthermore, this figure provides valuable input for calculating activation thresholds for the load balancer. These help to avoid load migration from instances with a "naturally" light load to instances with a higher load arrival rate. It may thus help to avoid instability.

- The *net distance* between DBMS instances (hop count) is useful as an additional criterion to restrict the load placement distance and to define *migration domains* in a system. The distance must be defined in such a way that it is a meaningful scale factor for the cost of a specific migration.

In addition to these parameters which have been used in our experiments and in our previous work, there are a few further measures which seem especially relevant for load balancing in systems which apply a transaction monitor.

- The *transaction code* denotes DBMS queries which belong to a given transaction. It can be used to classify load items. For further classification purposes it might be helpful to also consider the respective application-ID of a database application as well as the issuing user's user-ID and terminal-ID.

- The *mean number of different database pages* referenced by transactions of a given class should be derived offline, for example, by analyzing traces. Measuring the length of this reference string online can be expected to introduce significant overhead. This length criterion enables a high performance scheduling (see Section 5.4) as well as a more sophisticated load management which may then focus on long running or data intensive jobs. Alternatively, the TAs' mean response time could be used which can be obtained online quite easily.

5.6 Conclusion and Open Issues

Our analysis has shown that even simple load placement schemes lead to a considerable performance improvement in distributed database management systems (DBMS). In most cases this is related to an improvement in the overall throughput.

Heterogeneous systems or systems with mixed applications, that is, systems which are not exclusively dedicated to the database server function, raise additional problems. Among the schemes assessed, only the join-the-fastest scheme, Rt, which evaluates the TAs' mean response times seems to be suited for this class of systems. Other schemes like the introduced join-the-shortest queue scheme, Co, have to be enhanced, based on the parameters discussed above (for example, by also considering the instances' throughputs). On the other hand, Co was very successful for homogeneous systems.

A load classification which is, for example, based on transaction codes, the mean length of the TAs' reference strings, and their mean response times will help in characterizing load items in advance. This enables load management to focus on selected classes of transactions, for example, on computationally or data intensive ones. Furthermore, the placement of conversations instead of single transactions leads to performance gains which are due to data access affinity between a conversation's TAs.

Based upon the introduced placement schemes, we further tried to develop more intelligent placement schemes which evaluate more decision parameters [17]. These should have been able to evaluate dependencies between decision parameters. Such decision making is capable of considering tradeoffs like the following one: If a decision improves the behavior of component 1 then the behavior of component 2 will get worse. But the resulting overall system behavior should still improve. For instance, the SBC hit rates and the lock rates were considered. It became evident that highly sophisticated schemes were more specialized and thus required much more tuning effort to avoid instabilities. This limits their suitability for a wider range of DBMS applications and load profiles. Furthermore, they were not able to achieve a significantly higher throughput but often showed a worse SBC behavior than schemes Co and Rt (see Section 5.5.3). This in turn leads to asymmetric mean response time distributions of the underlying DBMS instances.

Summarized, enhanced join-the-shortest queue strategies based on our scheme Co as well as response-time-oriented join-the-fastest strategies like our scheme Rt can be regarded as best suited for a broad range of database sharing architectures and load profiles.

Another important result is the requirement for cooperation of the load placement strategy with the scheduler of the database server instances. It was shown that cache-oriented scheduling schemes which consider the characteristics of the shared buffer caches used by a distributed DBMS can significantly improve the overall performance.

The comparision of load placement schemes provides a valuable input for our current research activities: We implement a front end for a heterogeneous distributed DBMS by means of the technology of Interface Definition Languages (IDL). In particular, the CORBA standard is used [2]. The IDL technology will be enhanced by transparently integrating load balancing mechanisms [15, 16, 17] based on the investigated schemes.

Bibliography

[1] *Technical Report 1971*, CODASYL Database Task Group.

[2] *CORBA 2.0 / Interoperability, Specification of CORBA 2.0*, OMG TC Document 95.3.xx, Mar. 20, 1995.

[3] P. Dickman, "Effective Load Balancing in a Distributed Object-Support Operating System," *Proc. Int'l Workshop on Object Orientation in Operating Systems*, Palo Alto, CA, Oct. 17–18,1991, pp. 147–153.

[4] D.L. Eager, E.D. Lazowska, and J. Zahorjan, "The Limited Performance Benefits of Migrating Active Processes for Load Sharing," *Proc. ACM Sigmetrics Conf. on Measurement and Modeling of Computer Systems*, Santa Fe, NM, May 1988, pp. 63–72.

[5] T. Haerder, "On Selected Performance Issues of Database Systems," *Informatik-Fachberichte 154*, Springer-Verlag, 1987, pp. 294–312.

[6] K.A. Hua, W. Tavanapong, and H.C. Young, "A Performance Evaluation of Load Balancing Techniques for Join Operations on Multicomputer Database Systems," *Proc. 11th Int'l Conf. on Data Eng.*, Taipei, Taiwan, Mar. 6–10, 1995, pp. 44–51.

[7] C. Jacqmot and E. Milgrom, "A Systematic Approach to Load Distribution Strategies for Distributed Systems," *Proc. Decentralized and Distributed Systems*, IFIP, Elsevier Science, 1993.

[8] E. Born, T. Delica, and W. Ehrl, "Characterization of Commercial DB/DC Workloads," Internal report from LYDIA (ESPRIT project 8144) basic research activity. Siemens Nixdorf Informationssysteme AG, 1996.

[9] T. Manzke, *Erstellung und Filterung von Referenzstrings für UDS/UTM-Anwendungen*, diploma thesis, Univ. of Kaiserslautern, Germany, 1986.

[10] *Oracle Parallel Server for Pyramid Systems*, Oracle White Paper, 1993.

[11] D.A. Patterson, J.L. Hennessy, and R.H. Katz, "A Case for Redundant Arrays of Inexpensive Disks (RAID)," Rep. No. UCB/CSD 87/391, Univ. of California, Berkeley, 1987.

[12] E. Rahm, "Dynamic Load Balancing in Parallel Database Systems," *Proc. EURO-PAR 96*, Lyon, France, Aug. 1996.

[13] H. Sattler, *Transaktionssystem BS2000*, Reihe BS2000 Technische Beschreibung, Siemens AG, 1989.

[14] B. Schiemann and J. Plankl, "Leistungsoptimierung durch Cache-orientierte Seitenvergabe / Performance Optimization through Cache-Oriented Paging," *Proc. 3. Fachtagung Arbeitsplatz-Rechensysteme*, Hannover, Germany, May 17, 1995.

[15] B. Schiemann and L. Borrmann, "A New Approach for Load Balancing in High Performance Decision Support Systems," *Proc. Int'l Conf. on High-Performance Computing and Networking, HPCN '96*, Brussels, Belgium, Apr. 16–18, 1996, pp. 571–579.

[16] B. Schiemann, "A New Approach for Load Balancing in Heterogeneous Distributed Systems," *Proc. Int'l Workshop on Trends in Distributed Systems TreDS'96*, Aachen, Oct. 1–2, 1996.

[17] B. Schiemann, *Intelligente Lastverteilung für Datenbank-Management-Systeme*, Ph.D. thesis, Tech. Univ. of Munich, 1997.

[18] *Performance Evaluation Report UDS-D*, Internal Report, Siemens AG, Munich, Germany, 1989.

[19] *UDS-Application Programming*, Manual U930-J-Z55-7600, Siemens AG, Munich, Germany, 1989.

[20] M.C. Wikstrom et al., "Myths of Load Balancing," *Proc. Int'l Conf. on Parallel Computing 91*, London, UK, Sep. 3–6, 1991, pp. 531–549.

[21] M.H. Willebeek-LeMair and A.P. Reeves, "Strategies for Dynamic Load Balancing on Highly Parallel Computers," *IEEE Trans. on Par. and Distrib. Systems*, Vol. 4, No. 9, Sep. 1993, pp. 979–993.

[22] P.S. Yu et al., "On Workload Characterization of Relational Database Environments," *IEEE Trans. on Software Eng.*, Vol. 18, No. 4, Apr. 1992, pp. 347–355.

Part II

Parallel Machine Architecture

Chapter 6

Modeling Recovery in Client-Server Database Systems

Lory D. Molesky and Krithi Ramamritham

Abstract.   *In the study of database recovery, one is often presented with a myriad of seemingly disconnected assumptions and implementation techniques. Some reasons for these phenomena include (a) the recovery subsystem must be able to handle a node crash at any point in the history of operations on the database, (b) the volatile and stable state of the database at the time of a node crash must be considered, and (c) the related recovery mechanisms must be designed to exhibit low runtime overheads and to allow for efficient recovery. These difficulties are further compounded when we consider more elaborate architectural platforms, such as client-server systems, where the state of the database is defined by a collection of nodes.*

To address these issues, we introduce a framework for recovery analysis, based on the ACTA formalism. We use this framework to specify the various requirements, policies, and mechanisms associated with crash recovery. We first apply this formalism to characterize uniprocessor recovery, then we address the more difficult recovery problems associated with client-server database systems. This approach offers a logical framework which facilitates a concise description of recovery, and enables a comparative analysis of recovery approaches of client-server database architectures.

6.1   Introduction

One of the major trends in high performance database design involves the use of multiple processor/node systems [1, 18]. This trend is fueled by the price/performance advantages of such systems. The three main types of multiple node architectures are *shared nothing* (SN), *shared disk* (SD), and *shared memory* (SM). In SN systems, processing nodes do not share disks nor do they share memory. Communication between nodes occurs by sending messages across a communications network. In addition to providing a communications network, SD systems also provide a single disk or set of disks shared among all nodes in the system. SM database systems are generally a superset of SD systems; SM systems additionally provide shared memory.

One increasingly popular variant of SN database systems is the client-server (CS) database system. In the CS model, access to the database is provided by one or more server nodes, allowing client nodes to access the database by communicating with the server. This model of data sharing exploits the economies associated with using commodity components, allows for flexible connection establishment (even to geographically remote hosts), and enables the construction of highly scalable systems.

In this chapter, we consider crash recovery in CS architectures. Even in uniprocessor database systems, the recovery subsystem can be very complex. When a node crashes, the contents of volatile memory are lost, potentially resulting in an inconsistent database state. Correctness of database crash recovery requires that *failure atomicity* be restored—after a node failure, all effects of committed transactions should persist, and no effects of aborted transactions should persist. Furthermore, in designing the mechanisms which ensure failure atomicity, performance considerations are a critical concern. Recovery in CS architectures is further complicated by the existence of multiple independent volatile memories [5, 10, 11, 13, 14, 15, 16].

Given the large volume of work done in this area, it is appropriate to ask *what are the relative merits of each of these CS recovery architectures?* What features of the architectural model facilitate transaction recovery? Our approach to this comparison is based on first establishing clear recovery *requirements*, then showing how associated *policies* and *mechanisms* meet these requirements. In order to concisely express these differences, we employ the ACTA formalism [3, 4], tailored to address crash recovery. Requirements describe the essential conditions which the recovery system must meet. Policies describe a specific course of action among many alternatives. Mechanisms achieve the requirements or policies potentially in cooperation with other mechanisms.

In Section 6.2 we review the objectives of recovery and to establish a baseline for this comparison, we introduce our formalism in the context of uniprocessor database recovery. Section 6.3 describes some general problems common to all multiple node architectures. Section 6.4 uses the formalism introduced in Section 6.2 to model and analyze the recovery architectures of three different client-server database systems—ESM-CS (the Client-Server version of the *Exodus Storage Manager*) [5], ARIES/CSA (the Client-Server version of *Algorithms for Isolation Exploiting Semantics*) [14], and CD (*Client Disks*) [16]. Our conclusions are presented in Section 6.5.

6.2 Uniprocessor Recovery and Formal Approach to Modeling Recovery

The basic objective of database crash recovery is to ensure the *failure atomicity* of transactions—all the effects of committed transactions should persist, and no effects of uncommitted transactions should persist. The main challenge in ensuring this objective is that in the event of a node crash, the contents of volatile memory are lost. By writing data to disk, it is possible to avoid the loss of data (and logged information) due to node crashes. However, performing a disk write takes about five orders of magnitude more time than performing a write to (volatile) memory [17]. This ratio underscores another crucial issue in recovery—ensuring failure atomicity while minimizing the performance degradation due to disk writes.

In this section, we consider the assumptions and issues in uniprocessor database crash recovery. This recovery material will serve as a baseline for the more elaborate TP architectures.

In conjunction with performing a database update, a *log record* is written to (volatile) memory. The systems we examine in this chapter employ both basic logging methods—*physical logging*, where log records describe blind writes to variables, and *logical logging*, where log records describe parameterized operations on variables [7]. We assume that *in-place* updating is used in conjunction with the *write-ahead log* (WAL) protocol. WAL requires that prior to writing a dirty page to stable database, any associated log records are first written to stable storage. The most flexible buffer management policy, No-Force/Steal, is used [8]. No-force allows transactions to commit without forcing updated pages to stable database. Instead, prior to the commit of a transaction, all the transaction's log records are propagated to stable storage. We also assume that locking-based concurrency control is used.

Recovery in a TP system can be viewed as two related components, a *runtime* component and a *restart recovery* component. The runtime component enforces certain policies during the normal runtime operation of the TP system, such as performing logging, ensuring the WAL protocol, and implementing commit processing. In the event of a crash, the task of restart recovery is to return the database to a consistent state—this generally requires ensuring that all the effects of committed transactions persist, and none of the effects of active transactions persist.

Section 6.2.1 introduces the basic formal concepts, and defines primitive events associated with database operations, logging, checkpointing, and recovery. Section 6.2.2 defines the basic mechanisms associated with logging. In Section 6.2.3, we specify the policies which are enforced during the normal runtime operation. In Section 6.2.4, we define numerous other data structures which are maintained during runtime for the purpose of efficiently performing restart recovery. In Section 6.2.5, we describe the process of restart recovery, based on the algorithms of ARIES [12, 9].

6.2.1 Basic Formal Concepts

During the course of their execution, transactions invoke operations on pages as well as transaction management primitives including Commit (C) and Abort (A). $op_x[p]$ denotes the event corresponding to the invocation of the operation op on page p by transaction x. We refer to the invocation of a transaction management primitive as a significant event. ϵ_t denotes the invocation of event ϵ by transaction t. We assume that the operations invoked by transactions operations consist of *read* (r) and *write* (w).

The concurrent execution of a set of transactions is represented by H, the *history* [2, 4] of the significant events, and events on data items invoked by these transactions. H also indicates the (partial) order in which these events occur. This partial order is consistent with the order of the events of each individual transaction, and with the order of the events executed at each individual node. H_{ct} (the current history) is used to denote the history of events that occur until a point in time. The predicate $\epsilon \to \epsilon'$ is true if event ϵ *precedes* event ϵ' in history H. It is false, otherwise. (Thus, $\epsilon \to \epsilon'$ implies that $\epsilon \in H$ and $\epsilon' \in H$.) Also, the notation $\epsilon \to \epsilon' \to \epsilon''$ is shorthand for $\epsilon \to \epsilon' \land \epsilon' \to \epsilon''$. We will use $pre(\epsilon)$ and $post(\epsilon)$ to denote the preconditions and postconditions, respectively, of an operation or a transaction management primitive ϵ. $op \in p$ denotes that the effects of op are in p, analogously, $op \notin p$ denotes that the effects of op are not in p. These *relations*, *events*, and *predicates* are summarized in Tables 6.1, 6.2, and 6.3, respectively.

Relation	Example Usage	Description
$\to$	$(\epsilon_1 \to \epsilon_2)$	Event ϵ_1 *happens before* ϵ_2
$\Rightarrow$	$(\epsilon_1 \Rightarrow \epsilon_2)$	Event ϵ_1 *implies* ϵ_2

Table 6.1: Summary of relations.

Event	Description
	Transaction-oriented events
$op[p]$	Operation op on page p Operations are either write w or read r
C_x	Transaction x Commits
A_x	Transaction x Aborts
$Crash$	A node crash occurs
	Events associated with logging and access to stable storage
$VLog[w[p]]$	$w[p]$ is appended to the volatile log
$Force[VLog]$	The volatile log is forced to stable storage
$Force[p]$	p is forced to the Stable DB
CP	A checkpoint is taken
	Events associated with restart recovery
$Redo(w[p])$	The effects of the write to page p are redone
$Undo(w[p])$	The effects of the write to page p are undone

Table 6.2: Summary of events.

For notational convenience, we also use *conditions*, which are based on the occurrence and relative ordering of other events. We use $SLog[w[p]]$ to indicate that $w[p]$ is appended to the stable log, defined as:

$$(SLog[w[p]] \in H_{ct}) \Leftrightarrow (VLog[w[p]] \to Force[Vlog]).$$

That is, stable logging ($SLog$) of a write operation ($w[p]$) is implemented by first volatile logging $w[p]$, then forcing the volatile log. We also use $lastCP$ to denote the last checkpoint appearing in the stable log.

Note that the evaluation of these predicates is relative to the current history, H_{ct}. We use this notation throughout this chapter to specify recovery-related properties. To aid the

$C(x)$	t_x has committed
	$C_x \in H_{ct}$
$U(x)$	t_x is uncommitted
	$C_x \notin H_{ct}$
$C(op_x[p])$	$op_x[p]$ was performed by a transaction t_x which has committed
	$op_x[p] \rightarrow C_x$
$A(op_x[p])$	$op_x[p]$ was performed by a transaction t_x which has aborted
	$op_x[p] \rightarrow A_x$
$Dirty(p)$	p is dirty
	$(w[p] \in H_{ct}) \wedge \not\exists Force[p] \| (w[p] \rightarrow Force[p])$

Table 6.3: Summary of predicates.

reader in the interpretation of this notation, we provide English descriptions of the resulting property. As a first example, using our notation, we next specify our recovery objective, achieving *failure atomicity:*.

REQUIREMENT: **Failure Atomicity**
In the event of a failure, ensuring *failure atomicity* requires that the following two properties are restored:

- All effects of committed transactions persist.
  $\forall x, C(x), w_x[p], (w_x \in p)$
  The notation $(w_x \in p)$ means that page p reflects the effects of w_x. Thus, the above reads as follows: all write operations to page p $(w_x[p])$ performed by committed transactions $(C(x))$ must be reflected in page p.

- No effects of active transactions persist.
  $\forall x, U(x), w_x[p], (w_x \notin p)$
  $(w_x \notin p)$ means that page p *does not* reflect the effects of w_x. Thus, the above reads as follows: all write operations to page p $(w_x[p])$ performed by uncommitted transactions $(C(x))$ must not be reflected in page p.

Note that the above conditions are *postconditions* of recovery. We will revisit these conditions at the end of this section when we show how uniprocessor recovery policies and mechanisms enable the recovery process to ensure these postconditions.

Next, we specify the fundamental mechanisms associated with logging.

6.2.2 Logging Mechanisms

In order to achieve durability of operations, transaction processing systems employ logging. In this section, we employ our formalism to express some of these mechanisms which are associated with WAL-based TP systems, such as volatile and stable logging.

In conjunction with performing an update to a database page, a record is appended to the *volatile* log.

MECHANISM: **Volatile Logging**

$(w[p] \in H_{ct}) \Rightarrow (VLog[w[p]] \to w[p]).$

That is, if a write to p appears in the history, then before the write affects p, the write operation must be volatile logged.

The volatile log ($VLog$) can be made stable ($SLog$) by forcing the in memory portion of the volatile log to stable storage. The stable log is guaranteed to survive node crashes.

MECHANISM: **Stable Logging**

$(Force(VLog) \in H_{ct}) \Rightarrow \forall op[p]|(op[p] \to Force(VLog), SLog[op[p]] \in H_{ct}).$

That is, after the $VLog$ is forced, all operations that preceded the force are now stable.

Each log record has a unique LSN (*Log Sequence Number*), which is assigned at the time a record is appended to the log. LSNs are sequenced in ascending order. Only transaction-oriented events, such as $op[p]$, A_x, C_x, are logged.

In addition, the $SLOG$ data structure is used in the specification of recovery algorithms. For restart recovery, we use $(w[p] \in SLOG)$ to indicate that $w[p]$ was stable logged prior to a node crash: $(w[p] \in SLOG) \Leftrightarrow (w[p] \to SLog[w[p]] \to Crash).$

6.2.3   Runtime Policies for Ensuring Correctness

In this section, we consider some of the runtime policies which allow for correct recovery in the event of a node crash. For example, WAL requires that prior to writing a dirty page to the stable database, any associated log records are first written to stable storage. If this were not enforced, an inadvertent node crash would result in uncommitted data being written to the stable database, without sufficient information (log records) to undo the changes required to restore failure atomicity. Consider a specification of the WAL requirement.

POLICY: **WAL**

$(w[p] \to Force[p]) \Rightarrow (SLog[w[p]] \to Force[p]).$

This specification is interpreted as follows: if a write to p ($w[p]$) precedes the force to disk of p ($Force[p]$), then the log record corresponding to $w[p]$ must be written to the stable log ($SLog[w[p]]$) prior to the force of p.

Unlike force, no-force commit does not require the operation to be committed to the database. Instead, no-force commit allows a transaction to commit after all its log records have been written to the stable log. Consider a specification of *no-force commit*:

POLICY: **No-Force Commit**

$(w_x[p] \to C_x) \Rightarrow (SLog[w[p]] \to C_x).$

This specification is interpreted as follows: If t_x performs a write to some page p and eventually commits, a log record corresponding to that write must be written to the stable log prior to commit. In practice, an actual implementation of no-force involves first appending a commit record to the end of the volatile log, then forcing the log up to this commit record.

IMPLEMENTATION: **No-Force Commit**

$(w_*[p] \to C_x) \Rightarrow (SLog[w_*[p]] \to C_x).$

Thus, *any* write (w_*) operation which happens before the commit of t_x will be stable logged prior to the commit of t_x.

Finally, for completeness, we specify another related policy, *No-Steal*. No-steal does not allow a page containing uncommitted data to be written to the stable database.

> POLICY: **No-Steal**
> $(w_x[p] \to C_x) \Rightarrow \not\exists Force[p], (w_x[p] \to Force[p] \to C_x).$

A *Steal* policy does not incur this restriction.

These last two sections, 6.2.2 and 6.2.3, have shown how our formalism can be applied to concisely express some of the standard mechanisms and policies associated with the normal runtime recovery provisions associated with a uniprocessor TP system. Moreover, understanding these mechanisms and policies is essential to understanding the more elaborate recovery mechanisms of multinode database systems. Next, in Section 6.2.4, we consider some additional data structures maintained during normal runtime, which allow for *efficient* restart recovery.

6.2.4   Data Structures Maintained for Efficient Recovery

Restart recovery relies on a number of data structures which are maintained at runtime [6, 7, 12]. These data structures enable efficient restart recovery by (a) establishing a bound on the earliest point where the log must be processed, and (b) for a given page, determine whether a particular update needs to be redone. Note that many of these data structures are page oriented, because the page is the unit of I/O (to disk). These data structures include the following:

PageLSN Each database page has a PageLSN field which contains the LSN of the log record that describes the latest update to that page. The PageLSN is used during restart (and media-recovery) to determine which logged updates have been applied to the page. Specifically, redo is performed if (PageLSN < LSN). In our specification, the notation $(w \in p)$ corresponds to this implementation of determining if a page contains a particular write operation.

DPT (Dirty Page Table) An entry is included in the DPT for each dirty page, that is, those pages which contain updates that are not reflected on stable store. Each entry of the DPT contains two fields, the *PageID*, a unique page identifier, and the *RecLSN*, which indicates the earliest update made to a page.

When a database update is initiated which results in a nondirty page being fixed into the buffer pool, the dirty page table is updated. This involves assigning the current LSN (the LSN of the log record which will contain the current update) to RecLSN. Thus, a page's RecLSN is the LSN of the update that caused a page to become dirty. RecLSN is used during restart recovery to determine the earliest point in the log which needs processing. The *firstLSN* is derived from the RecLSNs—it is the minimum of all RecLSNs, and determines the (earliest) point in the log for redo processing.

Transaction Table Contains an entry for each active transaction.

The DPT is used to aid in implementing checkpointing, and for enforcing the WAL protocol. Periodically, ARIES writes a fuzzy checkpoint [2] to disk. This involves writing the contents of the transaction table and the DPT. We use $lastCP$.DPT to indicate the DPT written during the last checkpoint.

6.2.5   Restart Recovery—The ARIES Approach

The ARIES [12] recovery method follows the repeating history paradigm and supports no-force/steal, and fine granularity locking. We study the ARIES approach to recovery because of these features, and because many subsequent proposals for high performance architectures supporting transactional semantics have been based on ARIES.

Recovery under the repeating history paradigm follows a redo/undo strategy, and consists of three phases, *analysis*, *redo*, and *undo*. For a crashed node, prior to performing redo and undo, starting from the last checkpoint, an analysis phase examines the log to reconstruct the dirty page table and the transaction table, and links undo log records belonging to the same transaction. The transaction table indicates which transactions are active, and the dirty page table indicates which pages possibly need redo. The dirty page table is used to determine where the redo pass must start. The redo phase scans the log in chronological order, performing redo for all updates (except those that had already been propagated to the stable database). The undo phase scans the log in reverse chronological order, performing undo for all loser transactions.

In order to bound the amount of logging during recovery (in the case of repeated crashes during recovery), CLRs (compensation log records) are written in conjunction with performing undo operations. CLRs point to the previous logged update performed by the same transaction. Note that this can be performed efficiently since, during normal operations, log records generated by the same transaction are chained together. However, in the interest of space, we do not include the mechanisms related to CLRs in our recovery specification.

Analysis Pass:

The function of the analysis pass is to transform information that is available in the stable log to a more efficient, tabular representation of the two data structures. For example, based on the log, the transaction table is reconstructed in order to efficiently evaluate the predicate $U(x)$. A more complex task is to determine which pages are dirty, in order to efficiently evaluate $Isdirty(p)$:

> REQUIREMENT: **Analysis of Dirty Pages**
> $post(AnalysisPass) \Rightarrow \forall U(x)|(w_x[p] \in SLOG),\ Isdirty(p)$. That is, for all uncommitted transactions that wrote to p, p is marked as dirty.

In a uniprocessor database system, this can effectively be determined as follows:

> IMPLEMENTATION: **Analysis of Dirty Pages**
> In ARIES, a page p is considered dirty if either p appears in the DPT logged in the most recent complete checkpoint prior to the crash, or an update log record for p appears in the stable log *after* that checkpoint. This is specified as

follows: $Isdirty(p) \Leftrightarrow (p \in lastCP.DPT) \vee ((lastCP \rightarrow w[p]) \wedge (w[p] \in SLOG))$.

After a node crash, redo is performed only for dirty pages, and undo is performed for all operations performed by active transactions.

Redo Pass:

REQUIREMENT: **Redo**
After the completion of the redo pass, all stable logged operations are reflected in the associated database page. $post(RedoPass) \Rightarrow \forall (w[p] \in SLOG), (w \in p)$.

In order to process the log efficiently, *firstLSN* is used to bound the log scan—this avoids having to scan the entire log.

IMPLEMENTATION: **Redo**
All stable logged operations which are not already reflected in the associated database page. This is accomplished via a forward pass of the log, from $firstLSN$ to $lastLSN$. $\forall (w[p] \in SLOG_{(firstLSN,lastLSN)}), Isdirty(p) \wedge (w \notin p) \Rightarrow (Redo(w[p]) \in H_{ct})$.

Note that notation $SLOG_{(firstLSN,lastLSN)}$ indicates that the Stable Log is scanned from $firstLSN$ to $lastLSN$.

Undo Pass:

REQUIREMENT: **Undo**
After the completion of the undo pass, no updates made by uncommitted transactions are reflected in any database page. $post(UndoPass) \Rightarrow \forall U(w_x[p]) \in SLOG, (w_x \notin p)$.

IMPLEMENTATION: **Undo**
For all stable logged uncommitted operations, undos are performed in reverse chronological order. This is accomplished via a backward pass of the log, from $lastLSN$ to $firstLSN$. $\forall U(w_x[p]) \in SLOG_{(lastLSN,firstLSN)}), Undo(w_x[p]) \in H_{ct}$.

Note that notation $SLOG_{(lastLSN,firstLSN)}$ indicates that the Stable Log is scanned from $lastLSN$ to $firstLSN$.

If the above recovery requirements are satisfied, we can prove that our objective of *failure atomicity* is met. First, consider proving that *all effects of committed transactions persist*. This follows from (A1), which is implied by No-Force Commit, and from (A2), which follows from the requirements of the postcondition of the Redo Pass.

A1: $(C_x \in H_{ct}) \Rightarrow \forall w_x[p], (SLog[w_x[p]] \rightarrow C_x)$
A2: $post(RedoPass) \Rightarrow \forall (w[p] \in SLOG), (w \in p)$
(A1 $\wedge$ A2) $\Rightarrow \forall C(x), w_x[p], (w \in p) \square$

Likewise, the proof that *no effects of uncommitted transactions persist* follows directly from WAL (A1) and from the postcondition of the Undo Pass.

A1: $(w[p] \rightarrow Force[p]) \Rightarrow (SLog[w[p]] \rightarrow Force[p])$

A2: $post(UndoPass) \Rightarrow \forall U(w_x[p]) \in SLOG, (w_x \notin p)$

(A1 $\wedge$ A2) $\Rightarrow \forall U(x), w_x[p], (w \notin p)\square$

Thus, we have shown that our recovery objectives have been met. Next we consider some common recovery problems in multinode architectures, then we apply our formalism to recovery in client-server systems.

On a single node or centralized database system, a single log stores all log records. This is not true in a multinode system, where multiple logs are used. One major obstacle to recovery is establishing a global ordering between these log records, and this is discussed next.

6.3 LSN Sequencing Techniques for Multinode Systems

In this section, we consider some of the issues which are common to virtually all multinode database systems (SN, SD, and SM). One design strategy which has emerged in multinode database architectures is the use of multiple logs, one for each processing node. This approach is attractive from a performance perspective because it allows each system a high degree of autonomy when processing log records, thus allowing for a high degree of concurrency between nodes. However, with respect to a particular page, the order of operations performed at recovery must adhere to the order that writes were performed during normal runtime operation. To meet this requirement, two LSN sequencing techniques have been developed.

- Globally Sequenced LSNs—Globally sequenced LSNs establish a total order between *all* update operations. During recovery, it is possible to determine the runtime generation order of all (of the many nodes) log records.

- Page Sequenced LSNs—For any page, page sequenced LSNs establish a total order between *all* update operations. During recovery, it is possible to determine (a) the runtime generation order of all *local* log records, and (b) the runtime generation order of all log records corresponding to a given page.

In the context of multiple-log SD systems, [13] proposes a method for globally sequenced LSNs. This method requires that the clocks of all nodes are synchronized, enabling log records are globally sequenced by generating LSNs as timestamps. Another possibility, feasible if low-latency remote memory access is provided (as in SM systems), is to access a global counter for the generation of globally sequenced log records. However, this approach may lead to high contention if many nodes are supported.

The sufficiency of page sequenced LSNs follows from the fact that the repeating history recovery paradigm only requires that for a given page, redo recovery operations must be performed in the same order as they had during normal runtime operations. One advantage of this method is that synchronized clocks are not needed.

An LSN generation technique which avoids the need for synchronized clocks was first proposed in [10], also in the context of multiple-log SD systems. This method ensures page sequenced LSNs as follows: Each time a page is updated, a sequence number within the page (PSN)[1] is incremented, then the LSN and the PSN are written to the update log record. The PSN is used at recovery time to determine the next log record that should be applied to the page. The PSN technique has also been adopted in other multinode database designs, notably the client-server designs of [5] and [16], which are discussed in Section 6.4.

Another method for ensuring paged sequenced log records is discussed in [14]. When a log record is generated, the next LSN is assigned to one greater than the maximum of the associated pages' PageLSN and the current local log's LSN $(max(PageLSN, LSN) + 1)$ This new value is used as the LSN on the local system and as the PageLSN in the updated page.

Because of the high communication costs associated with SN architectures, client-server database designs [5, 14, 16] have not opted to implement globally sequenced LSNs. As we will see in the next section, the absence of globally sequenced LSNs requires additional mechanisms to ensure efficient recovery in these client-server database systems.

6.4 Recovery in Client-Server Database Systems

In this section, we consider approaches to implementing client-server database systems which employ *data-shipping*.[2] With data-shipping, data is shipped from servers to clients, where clients perform transactional operations on the locally buffered data. By allowing clients to operate on the locally buffered data, this approach has the potential to reduce the computational load at the server. However, artifacts of the above design decisions pose additional recovery problems (beyond those encountered in uniprocessor database systems) for data-shipping client-server database systems. The specific artifacts stemming from the CS architecture include the following:

CS1: Clients lack efficient assignment of LSNs, thus globally sequenced LSNs are not implemented [5].

CS2: The server can have log records for updates for which it does not have the corresponding affected database pages [5].

$$(VLog^s[w^c[p]] \in H_{ct}) \land w^c \notin p^s).$$

p^s denotes the *server's* copy of page p, while p^c will be used to denote the *client's* copy of page p. Also, w^c denotes a write performed by a *client*, and $Vlog^s$ indicates that $Vlog$ was performed on the *server*. Thus, the server has volatile logged a write to p performed by the client $(VLog^s[w^c[p]])$, but the server does not have the copy of p that contains the write performed by the client $(w^c \notin p^s)$.

---

[1]Originally denoted *BSI* in [10].

[2]In the alternative approach, *query-shipping*, clients ship queries to the server for execution; once executed, the server sends the results back to the client. In query-shipping systems, all logging and recovery functions are implemented at the server, and thus the recovery issues are basically the same as in a uniprocessor database system.

CS3: There may be pages that are dirty at a client but not at the server [5].

$$\exists p|\ Dirty(p^c)\ \wedge\ \neg Dirty(p^s).$$

In the following subsections we discuss recovery mechanisms which have been proposed to handle these artifacts. In Section 6.4.1, we consider solutions presented in the context of client-server EXODUS, and in Section 6.4.2, we consider solutions presented in the context of ARIES/CSA [14]. In Section 6.4.3, we consider the recovery issues of the proposals of [16], which we call *CD* (client-disks).

The features provided by these systems and their architectural assumptions have a significant impact on the design of the recovery algorithms. Table 6.4 summarizes some of these differences.

	ESM-CS	ARIES/CSA	CD
Unit of Sharing	Page	Page	Page
Granularity of Locking	Page	Record	Page
Client Storage	Diskless	Diskless	Clients have Disks

Table 6.4: Architectural and functional summary of client-server systems.

As Table 6.4 indicates, in all systems, the unit of sharing (data transfer) between the client and server is the page. However, only ARIES/CSA allows locking to be performed at the granularity of a database record. Both ESM-CS and ARIES/CSA assume that clients are diskless, while CD addresses recovery in the context of clients which have disks.

6.4.1   Client-Server EXODUS (ESM-CS)

Client-server Exodus (ESM-CS) [5] is a client-server database system based on the ARIES approach to recovery. During a transaction, clients cache data and index pages in their local buffer pool. The server is responsible for lock management and major recovery functions, while both server and client participate in log management. Note that since clients are diskless, the stable log is maintained only at the server. The server is ultimately responsible for performing the actual commit or abort of the transaction via access to stable store.

Prior to caching a copy of a page, clients must first request locks from the server. Once a page is locked and cached, clients may perform read and update operations to cached pages. The granularity of sharing between the client and the server is the page, and data is locked at a page or coarser granularity.

When clients perform updates, log records are written locally, but in order to commit, clients must send log records and the associated pages to the server. In order to support WAL, clients must send log records to the server *prior* to sending the pages on which the updates were performed. This is denoted *Force-to-Server-at-Commit*, and is specified as follows:

POLICY: **Force-to-Server-at-Commit**
Before committing a transaction, the client sends all the pages modified by the transaction to the server. $(op_x^c[p] \to C_x) \Rightarrow (op_x^c[p] \to Send^{(c,s)}[p] \to C_x)$.

The Force-to-Server-at-Commit policy distinguishes ESM-CS from other client-server database systems, and this policy influences the design of other recovery support mechanisms.

Next, consider how the absence of global LSNs affects the assignment of RecLSNs. Recall that RecLSNs track updates to dirty pages, enabling restart recovery to determine the earliest point in the log to start the redo pass. In a centralized system, a page's RecLSN is the LSN of the update that caused a page to become dirty. In ESM-CS, when a client first dirties a page, the client does not know the current LSN at the server. To handle these conditions, RecLSN assignment is done with an *Approximate RecLSN*.

REQUIREMENT: **RecLSN Assignment**
When a page p is first dirtied, clients must assign a RecLSN to p.

MECHANISM: **Approximate RecLSN**
An approximation of the RecLSN is attached to each newly dirtied page. Every server reply sent to a client is augmented with the current LSN (the last LSN used at the server). When a client first dirties a page, the latest LSN supplied by the server is assigned to RecLSN, called *approximate RecLSN*. The approximate RecLSN is guaranteed to be less than or equal to the LSN which is eventually assigned to the log record (during commit processing at the server).

This mechanism bounds the amount of log records which must be processed during crash recovery.

Next, we consider how CS2 can cause difficulties in implementing rollbacks during normal operation. Recall that, due to CS2, there may be log records on the server for which it does not have the corresponding affected database pages. During restart recovery, due to CS2, using unconditional undo could result in incorrect recovery if the corresponding page did not reflect the update to be undone. This could incorrectly lead to spurious undos.

REQUIREMENT: **No Spurious Undos**
Undos should only be performed on log records that have actually been applied.

$$(w \notin p^s) \Rightarrow (Undo(w, p^s) \notin H_{ct}).$$

MECHANISM: **Conditional Undo**
Undos are performed in reverse chronological order, for all stable logged uncommitted operations, *which do not have their effects present in the corresponding page*. Undo will only be performed if the stable log record's PSN is *greater than or equal to the page's PSN* ($w \in p$). As in uniprocessor recovery, this is accomplished via a backward pass of the log, from $lastLSN$ to $firstLSN$.

$$\forall (U(w_x[p]) \in SLOG_{(lastLSN, firstLSN)}), (w \in p) \Rightarrow (Undo(w_x[p]) \in H_{ct}).$$

With conditional undo, in order to properly handle CLRs, additional considerations must be addressed. In order to ensure forward progress of undo in the event of node crashes, *fake CLRs* are written for undo log records for which undo is not performed. However, the page's PSN remains unchanged as a result of the fake undo. This enables the detection of undo log records which should be skipped that appear earlier in the log.

Next, we consider the artifacts of client-server which require extensions of the basic ARIES recovery algorithms in order to (a) detect all dirty pages which need recovery, and (b) determine a redo recovery log position which is sufficiently early to enable the redo of all unapplied write operations. Thus, we are concerned with the general requirement of ensuring *correct analysis*.

In ARIES, if a page is not dirty at the time of a checkpoint, then all updates logged prior to the checkpoint are guaranteed to be reflected in the copy of the page on stable storage. The above is not true in a CS database environment, due to CS2. That is, when the server takes a checkpoint, pages which are only dirty at the client will not be included in the server's checkpoint record, and may cause problems if the server were to subsequently crash. This problem requires extensions to the original ARIES recovery algorithms.

PROBLEM: **Missing Redos**

$(p \notin lastCP.DPT) \wedge (SLog^s[w^c[p]] \rightarrow lastCP)$.

We consider two variations on the problem of missing redos, one related to uncommitted transactions, and the other related to committed transactions. First, consider a variation of the Missing Redo problem which affects uncommitted transactions:

PROBLEM: **Missing Redos V1**

$(p \notin lastCP.DPT) \wedge (Slog(w_x^c[p]) \rightarrow lastCP) \wedge$
$(lastCP \rightarrow Slog(w_x'^c[p])) \wedge \not\exists C_x \mid (C_x \rightarrow Crash^s)$.

Version 1 of the Missing Redo problem arises when, at the time of the last checkpoint, page p is not dirty at the server, but redo log records corresponding to uncommitted updates for p are stable logged before and after the last checkpoint. If the server crashes under these circumstances, under the original ARIES approach to recovery, the log records before the checkpoint will be (incorrectly) skipped, but the log records appearing after the checkpoint will be redone, potentially corrupting the page. To avoid this, ESM-CS ensures the *Redo-Consecutive Pages* property:

REQUIREMENT: **Redo-Consecutive Pages**

If any redos were made to page p by t, then all preceding redos made by t to p have been applied. $\forall U(t), Redo(op_x[p]) \Rightarrow ((op_x'[p] \rightarrow op_x[p]) \Rightarrow (Redo(op_x'[p]) \rightarrow Redo(op_x[p])))$.

To accomplish this, the starting point of the redo pass is conservatively set to the earliest update of any uncommitted transaction.

MECHANISM: **startLSN**

To ensure *Redo-Consecutive Pages*, for any uncommitted transaction t, the redo recovery point begins no later than the LSN corresponding to the first update made by t. This is accomplished by augmenting the transaction table with a field called $startLSN$. At the end of analysis, any entries to the DPT added on behalf of an uncommitted transaction have their RecLSN replaced by startLSN.

Next, consider missing redos in the context of committed transactions.

> PROBLEM: **Missing Redos V2**
> $(p \notin lastCP.DPT) \wedge (SLog^s[w_x^c[p]] \rightarrow lastCP)$
> $\wedge (lastCP \rightarrow Send^{(c,s)}[p] \rightarrow Crash^s) \wedge (C_x \rightarrow Crash^s).$

Version 2 of the Missing Redo problem arises when, at the time of the last checkpoint, page p is not dirty at the server, and (a) redo log records corresponding to committed updates for p are stable logged before the last checkpoint, and (b) p was sent back to the server after lastCP but prior to the crash of the server. Clearly, these pages must be recovered, but with the original ARIES analysis method, they would not be considered dirty. To handle missing redo records for committed transactions, ESM-CS proposes an additional mechanism:

> MECHANISM: **CommitDPL**
> When a client sends a dirtied page p to a server, p and its associated RecLSN are added to the *CommitDPL* (Commit Dirty Page List). The contents of this list are stable logged prior to logging the commit record for the transaction. When a page is forced, it is removed from the list. During analysis, if a logged CommitDPL is encountered, those pages (which are not already in the DPT) are added to the DPT. $(op_x[p^c] \rightarrow C_x) \Rightarrow (Send^{(c,s)}[p] \rightarrow SLog[CommitDPL[p]] \rightarrow C_x).$

Thus, CommitDPL enables the analysis pass to detect pages which may have been missed, thus ensuring durability of committed transactions.

Table 6.5 summarizes the ESM-CS approach to recovery, based on the requirements, the mechanisms that satisfy the requirements, and the artifacts that lead to the requirements. It is important to keep in mind that the mechanisms used to satisfy the requirements in ESM-CS are predicated on the use of the Force-to-Server-at-Commit policy.

Requirement	Mechanism	Artifact		
		CS1	CS2	CS3
RecLSN Assignment	*approximate RecLSN*	√		
No Spurious Undos	*Conditional Undo*		√	
Redo-Consecutive Pages	*startLSN*		√	
Redo All Unforced Committed Updates	*CommitDPL*		√	√

Table 6.5: Summary of recovery mechanisms in ESM-CS.

6.4.2 Client-Server ARIES (ARIES/CSA)

Another example of a data-shipping client-server architecture is client-server ARIES (ARIES/CSA) [14]. There are many similarities between ARIES/CSA and ESM-CS, including (a) clients perform their updates on cached pages and produce log records, (b) the server is responsible for lock management, (c) recovery is performed by the server on behalf of the clients, and (d) LSNs are not globally sequenced. But these two client-server architectures are significantly different in two respects:

- Unlike ESM-CS, in ARIES/CSA, pages are *not* required to be forced to the server when a client transaction commits (force-to-server-at-commit).

- ARIES/CSA supports fine-granularity locking (record level).

In order to overcome many of the problems associated with client-server database architectures (such as those stemming from CS1, CS2, and CS3), one policy recommended by ARIES/CSA is to require clients to take checkpoints, and these checkpoints are *coordinated* with the server's checkpoint. Client checkpoints consist of a *Dirty Page List* (DPL), and the associated RecLSNs for each page.

MECHANISM: **Coordinated Checkpointing**
Coordinated checkpointing requires servers to synchronize their checkpointing with client checkpointing. Specifically, the server initiates a coordinated checkpoint by requesting the DPL (and associated RecLSNs) from all clients. After receiving all the client DPLs, the server merges these lists with its own DPL, and eliminates duplicate entries by selecting the smallest RecLSN from the multiple entries.

With coordinated checkpointing, server checkpoints contain a list of pages which are dirty at either the server or any client. This effectively solves the problem of *missing redos* discussed in Section 6.4.1. Thus, the coordinated checkpointing mechanism of ARIES/CSA achieves the objectives of the CommitDPL and startLSN mechanisms of ESM-CS.

RecLSN Assignment

MECHANISM: **Mapping RecLSNs to Server Log Addresses**
In ARIES/CSA, the RecLSNs delivered by the clients do not correspond to physical server log addresses. This problem is resolved by mapping from logical RecLSNs to physical server log addresses (*RecAddrs*). This mapping is done as the client's log records are added to the server's log. If the server already had a dirty version of the page, the current RecAddr is retained. This allows the analysis pass to determine a lower bound for the redo pass.

Mapping RecLSNs to server log addresses satisfies the RecLSN assignment requirement in ARIES/CSA, while in ESM-CS, the RecLSN assignment requirement is satisfied with the *ApproximateRecLSN* mechanism.

By implementing client checkpoints, ARIES/CSA can avoid the need for the conditional undo mechanism of ESM-CS. This allows ARIES/CSA clients to initiate rollbacks during normal operation, and thus avoids the complications which may arise during the server-initiated rollback of client operations in ESM-CS.

In order to support fine-granularity locking, short term locks on pages are provided in addition to the longer term locks (typically of transaction duration) on records [13, 14]. In order to effectively handle recovery in [14], a client is not allowed to relinquish a page p's update privilege until the latest version of p has been received by the server. This ensures that, in the case of a client crash, only updates made by the client will be lost. In the case of a server crash, for a given page, it may be necessary to redo updates from multiple clients.

6.4.3   Shared Nothing Clients with Disks (CD)

In [16], recovery algorithms are presented for a shared nothing system where each client node may have a local disk. These local disks are used for permanent storage of (local) databases and logs. This recovery architecture has many similarities with the two client-server systems discussed previously [5, 14]. The basic data-shipping paradigm is followed—data items referenced by a transaction are fetched from the server[3] by the client node before they are accessed. For performance reasons, pages are cached locally. Each node has a local log, the unit of locking and intersystem transfer is the page, and no-force/steal is supported. Page Sequenced LSNs are used, as defined in [10].

Each node has a DPT, all nodes periodically take checkpoints. This allows transaction rollback to be handled by each node, as in [14]. However, unlike the coordinated checkpointing of [14], checkpoints in [16] are asynchronous.

The assumption that each node has stable storage for the local log simplifies the solutions to many of the problems addressed in [5, 14]. Since each client has access to stable storage, the commit process does not need to ship log records (or the associated pages) to the server. Instead, clients force their local log to commit their local transactions.

Even with client disks, the tricky problem of *missing redos* may arise. For example, consider page p at server s. Suppose p was updated by a client transaction, and then was transferred back to the server's cache, after the server's last logged checkpoint, then the server crashes. This results in a dirty page which (a) was present only in the cache of the server, (b) is not in the crashed server's lastCP.DPT, and (c) was not updated by the crashed node after lastCP.DPT. These are essentially the same conditions for which *missing redos* may result in ESM-CS and ARIES/CSA.

To properly recover these pages in the event of a server crash, CD uses a mechanism called *coordinated recovery*, which merges information from the DPTs of all clients at recovery time, in order to determine which pages need redo.

MECHANISM: **Coordinated Recovery**
The protocol discussed in [16] involves each remote node sending its (a) list of cached pages owned by the crashed node, and (b) and all entries in the DPT owned by the crashed node. After this is complete, the crashed node merges these and its own DPT to determine which pages are dirty. Once this is determined, both servers and clients participate in the redo and undo phase of recovery. This is done without requiring a merged log [13], by transferring pages which need recovery between nodes.

Note that this mechanism is possible because each client has a local stable log. This combination facilitates the analysis of all dirty pages, and the determination of the redo scan point (based on the RecLSN stored in merged DPT).

---

[3] In [16], each node can function as a server and a client, depending on which of the many node's databases is accessed.

6.4.4   Summary of Recovery Approaches in Client-Server Architectures

For the three client-server systems analyzed in this chapter, Table 6.6 summarizes the recovery requirements and the mechanisms which ensure these requirements. In scanning this table, it is important to keep in mind that the assumptions on which these systems are based differ, as was detailed in Table 6.4.

	ESM-CS	ARIES/CSA	CD
RecLSN Assignment	Approximate RecLSN	Map RecLSNs to Server Log Addrs.	Coordinated Recovery[4]
Correct Analysis	startLSN, CommitDPL, Force-to-Server-at-Commit	Coordinated Checkpointing	Coordinated Recovery
No Spurious Undos	Conditional Undo	Client Checkpointing, Client-Initiated Rollback	Client Checkpointing, Client-Initiated Rollback

Table 6.6: Summary of recovery requirements and mechanisms in three client-server systems.

Proper RecLSN assignment is achieved with two basically interchangeable techniques in ESM-CS and ARIES/CSA. In ESM-CS, server log addresses are assigned at the client end—via a server-supplied lower-bound of the LSN. This lower-bound is guaranteed to be smaller than or equal to the LSN eventually assigned at the server end for this log record. In ARIES/CSA, the mapping of RecLSNs to server log addresses is done at the server end, when the client log records are actually written to the server's log. Thus the ARIES/CSA method is more accurate. In CD, the provision of client disks allows for client checkpointing and coordinated recovery, obviating the need for a RecLSN assignment mechanism.

As we saw in Section 6.4.1, the possibility of a page being dirty on the client but not dirty on the server requires extensions to the original ARIES analysis algorithm. In ESM-CS, correct analysis is achieved with three mechanisms, startLSN, CommitDPL, and Force-to-Server-at-Commit. In ARIES/CSA, these problems are solved with coordinated checkpointing, while in CD, these problems are solved with coordinated recovery.

In ESM-CS, although clients generate log records locally, they do not take checkpoints. Furthermore, rollback under normal database operation is performed by the server, leading to the need for conditional undo. In contrast, in ARIES/CSA and CD, clients perform checkpointing and are responsible for performing rollback under normal database operation.

6.5   Conclusion

In this chapter, we have introduced a new approach to modeling recovery, based on the ACTA formalism. We first applied this formalism to express some of the requirements,

---

[4]In CD, *Coordinated Recovery* is made possible via the provision of stable storage on each client. Neither ESM-CS nor ARIES/CSA assumes that clients have local access to stable storage.

policies, and mechanisms associated with uniprocessor recovery, we then applied this formalism as a basis for the comparison of recovery in three client-server database systems, ESM-CS [5], ARIES/CSA [14], and CD [16]. This approach facilitated a concise specification of the problems and solutions associated with each recovery system, and leads to a better understanding of the various approaches to recovery.

Although in this chapter we have focused on the traditional atomic transaction model, the ACTA framework facilitates the formal description of properties of extended transaction models. Future work in this area will involve synthesizing new database recovery systems based on the requirements of extended transaction models. The approach specifying requirements, policies, and mechanisms presented in this chapter will be used as a basis for this synthesis.

Bibliography

[1] "Panel Discussion on Shared Nothing, Shared Disk, and Shared Memory Database Systems," *Proc. 1994 ACM SIGMOD Int'l Conf. on Management of Data*, Vol. 23, May 1994.

[2] P.A. Bernstein, V. Hadzilacos, and N. Goodman, *Concurrency Control and Recovery in Database Systems*, Addison-Wesley, Reading, MA, 1987.

[3] P.K. Chrysanthis and K. Ramamritham, "ACTA: A Framework for Specifying and Reasoning about Transaction Structure and Behavior," *Proc. 1990 ACM SIGMOD Int'l Conf. on Management of Data*, May 1990, pp. 194–203.

[4] P.K. Chrysanthis and K. Ramamritham, "Synthesis of Extended Transaction Models using ACTA," *ACM Trans. Database Systems*, Vol. 19, No. 3, Sep. 1994, pp. 450–491.

[5] M. Franklin et al., "Crash Recovery in Client-Server EXODUS," *Proc. 1992 ACM SIGMOD Int'l Conf. on Management of Data*, Vol. 21, June 1992, pp. 165–174.

[6] J. Gray, *Notes on Data Base Operating Systems*, IBM Research Report: RJ2188, IBM Research, CA, Feb. 1978.

[7] J. Gray and A. Reuter, *Transaction Processing: Concepts and Techniques*, Morgan Kaufmann, 1993.

[8] T. Haerder and A. Reuter, "Principles of Transaction-Oriented Database Recovery," *ACM Computing Surveys*, Vol. 15, No. 4, Dec. 1983, pp. 287–317.

[9] D. Kuo, "Model and Verification of a Data Manager Based on ARIES," *ACM Trans. Database Systems*, Vol. 21, No. 4, Dec. 1997, pp. 427–479.

[10] D. Lomet, *Recovery for Shared Disk Systems Using Multiple Redo Logs*, Digital Equipment Cambridge Research Laboratory Technical Report (4), Oct. 1990.

[11] D. Lomet and M.R. Tuttle, "Redo Recovery after System Crashes," *Proc. 21st Int'l Conf. on Very Large Data Bases*, Zürich, Sep. 1995.

[12] C. Mohan et al., "ARIES: A Transaction Recovery Method Supporting Fine-Granularity Locking and Partial Rollbacks Using Write-Ahead Logging," *ACM Trans. Database Systems*, Vol. 17, Mar. 1992, pp. 94–162.

[13] C. Mohan and I. Narang, "Recovery and Coherency-Control Protocols for Fast Intersystem Page Transfer and Fine-Granularity Locking in a Shared-Disk Transaction Environment," *Proc. 17th Int'l Conf. on Very Large Data Bases*, Vol. 17, 1991, pp. 193–207.

[14] C. Mohan and I. Narang, "ARIES/CSA: A Method for Database Recovery in Client-Server Architectures," *Proc. 1994 ACM SIGMOD Int'l Conf. on Management of Data*, Vol. 23, 1994, pp. 55–66.

[15] L. Molesky and K. Ramamritham, "Recovery Protocols for Shared Memory Database Systems," *Proc. 1995 ACM SIGMOD Int'l Conf. on Management of Data*, May 1995, pp. 11–22.

[16] E. Panagos et al., "Client-Based Logging for High Performance Distributed Architectures," *Proc. 13th IEEE Conf. on Data Engineering*, 1996.

[17] C. Ruemmler and J. Wilkes, "An Introduction to Disk Drive Modeling," *IEEE Computer*, Mar. 1994, pp. 17–28.

[18] A. Silberschatz, M. Stonebraker, and J. Ullman, "Database Research: Achievements and Opportunities into the 21st Century," *Report of an NSF Workshop on the Future of Database Systems Research*, May 1995.

Chapter 7

Parallel Strategies and New Concepts for a Petabyte Multimedia Database Computer

Felipe Cariño Jr. and Warren Sterling

Abstract. *This chapter provides a comprehensive analysis of the new concepts and technical solutions that multimedia and objects introduce into the traditional alphanumeric database paradigm. We provide a technology roadmap of how we believe multimedia objects will be deployed in three waves. To illustrate how the emerging "multimedia object/relational" paradigm requires changes to databases, networking, and applications, we describe our notion of a Multimedia Data Warehouse. We also describe a five-year National Institute of Standards and Technology (NIST) medical knowledge bank program that uses the framework, concepts, and multimedia object/relational database systems described in this chapter. We analyze the Teradata Multimedia Database System (Teradata-MM) and the Teradata Multimedia Object Server architectures and parallel technical issues that petabyte (10^{15} bytes) and larger systems must handle. We describe our parallelism strategy which uses parallel infrastructure, computer platforms (like the DBC/1012 and WorldMark 5100M), and the Teradata Relational Database System. This chapter addresses our key contributions and strategies pertaining to: (1) new concepts, new components, and new functionality; (2) system integration of diverse technology, like networking, workflow, client GUIs, and other nondatabase components, into the database paradigm; and (3) user-defined function (UDF) exegesis concerning parallel execution and tuning of UDFs within a massively parallel, shared nothing system. The UDF analysis addresses parallel execution flow, spatial indexing, a new virtual column facility, and a "pragma" tuning facility to provide hints to the optimizer.*

139

7.1   Introduction

Teradata-MM (formerly MoonBase [7]) is a multimedia object/relational [21] database system being developed for emerging multimedia applications. Teradata-MM defines a framework to integrate multimedia islands of information and related technologies. This chapter uses the term 'Teradata-MM' to refer to both the product and new concepts that integrate these diverse technologies. Our first implementation employs an extensible federated relational database coordinator that nonintrusively adds selected SQL3 [23] and multimedia capabilities to existing relational [9] database management systems such as the Teradata Database [6, 29]. SQL3 is an emerging (that is, still evolving) standard allowing users to define abstract data types (ADTs) and user-defined functions (UDFs) that operate on the ADTs, thereby extending the types known to the underlying relational database system. In this chapter, we refer to the SQL3 subset we are implementing to support ADTs and UDFs as M-SQL. Teradata-MM uses the parallel Teradata Multimedia Object Server [11] (formerly Prospector [10]) to store, manipulate, and analyze multimedia objects based on their content. The Teradata-MM federated coordinator generates parallel execution plans for three logical 'database' components: a relational database, a Teradata Multimedia Object Server, and other special object servers (such as video servers).

Database support for multimedia required that we integrate and develop new concepts to define and manage: (1) multiple networks, (2) data security, (3) system administration, (4) user-interfaces, (5) information workflow, (6) retrieval and updating of multimedia tuples, (7) multimedia object feature extraction and indexing for content-based retrieval, (8) query optimization, and (9) performance enhancement. These topics are discussed below with respect to scalable, very large parallel systems. We describe the massively parallel architecture, infrastructure, hardware, and software strategies used by the Teradata Database system. This provides readers a foundation to understand the rationale behind the architecture and design choices made.

Data warehousing is a business concept for storing and manipulating data. We describe and analyze how multimedia information, especially continuous ADTs, like video, requires an evolution of the well-known alphanumeric-based Data Warehouse concept.

This chapter is organized as follows: Section 7.2 provides the vision of how multimedia objects will change applications. It describes: Multimedia Data Warehouse, three waves of multimedia database commercialization, and the medical Knowledge Bank NIST program that uses Teradata-MM to store and analyze healthcare information. Section 7.3 describes the computer platform, infrastructure, and software used to exploit parallelism. Section 7.4 analyzes our integrated framework, the Teradata-MM architecture, new concepts needed to run multimedia queries, and the Teradata Multimedia Object Server used to store objects and execute UDFs for content-analysis and object transformations. Section 7.5 concludes with an analysis of: UDF optimizer issues, a new UDF value persistence facility, a pragma facility to tune query plans, and spatial indexes that operate on features extracted from the objects.

7.2   Multimedia Data Warehouse, Databases, and Applications

Data Warehouse [15, 16] is a business concept to convert raw enterprisewide (company-wide) data into strategic and timely information available to the entire enterprise. Wal*Mart "process re-engineered" the retail business [6] with their innovative data warehouse model and use of parallel-processing computers and software from Teradata. Figure 7.1 shows our multimedia data warehouse and the information flow through the warehouse.

Data warehousing applications use tools to collect information and store them in relational databases. The database system query facility is then used to convert the raw data into information. Data warehousing [4] uses include: (1) cross-functional views of data across an enterprise; (2) data precision to identify specific information; and (3) discovery of trends or information that challenge conventional enterprise assumptions.

As shown in Figure 7.1, the data warehouse [2] information concept is defined as: (1) assemble operational data; (2) transform raw data in warehouse form; (3) distribute the information into the warehouse; and (4) access the data or mine for information from the warehouse. Reference [14] emphasizes the dynamics of data and metadata flow. Multimedia objects provide richer and more visual raw data for information repositories, object data mining for information, and information workflow. The Teradata-MM multimedia information workflow concept and capability is an efficient way to distribute complex and more visual information.

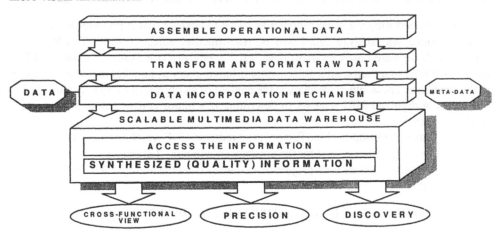

Figure 7.1: Multimedia data warehouse.

7.2.1   Three Waves of Multimedia Database Development

Multimedia technology and multimedia database systems [13] and applications can be categorized into three waves: (1) multimedia communications; (2) content storage and retrieval; and (3) content-based analysis.

Wave (1) uses multimedia as a communication mechanism. Video conferencing, say for telemedicine, is an example of multimedia communications. The problem with Wave (1) multimedia communications is that once a multimedia communication occurs its content is lost (that is, lacks multimedia data persistence).

Wave (2) provides persistence to the multimedia communication (for example, digitally storing a telemedicine video conference). AT&T systems that provide multimedia persistence include: Rapport [1], a multimedia collaboration system that provides persistence for collaboration, and Nemesis [18], a database containing talks given at AT&T along with the related viewgraphs and documents. Wave (2) multimedia information, like video, requires a technology, infrastructure, and use that we believe will result in a database paradigm shift. Wave (2) stores multimedia data, such as a video of a surgery, so that it can be retrieved or broadcast to others at another time. In the Wave (2a) example below, the query retrieves an object based on an alphanumeric-coded data predicate.

Wave (2a): SELECT name, age, MRI FROM PatientTable WHERE name = 'Elisa Doe';

In the Wave (2b) example, the information is also retrieved based on an alphanumeric-coded data predicate. A "projection" or "transformation" UDF ZoomIn() is applied to the retrieved MRI columns containing MRI scan sets (multiple MRI images). MRI stands for magnetic resonance imaging, a technique for creating images of cross sections, or "slices," of parts of the body, such as the brain.

Wave (2b): SELECT name, age, ZoomIn (MRI) FROM PatientTable WHERE name = 'Gaby Doe';

Wave (3) performs the same function as Wave (2) except that it provides a facility to locate, retrieve, and analyze data based on (multimedia) object content. The Wave (2) examples above were based on traditional SQL2 predicates (for example, name = "Elisa Doe"). We refer to a multimedia object content-based query as one that includes functions in the predicate. These functions analyze the content of an object, like find a face in a video or analyze a digitized MRI scan set to determine if a tumor is detected within a certain confidence level.

In the Wave (3) example, "FindTumor" is a predicate UDF which analyzes an MRI scan set and returns a confidence level for the presence of a tumor. "LateralView" is a projection UDF which returns a lateral view projection extracted from the multiple MRI images in the MRI scan set.

Wave (3): SELECT name, age, LateralView(MRI) FROM Patient WHERE FindTumor(MRI) > 0.8;

7.2.2 National Medical Practice Knowledge Bank Application

The following is a description of a real-world healthcare application that requires a multimedia database. The Teradata Multimedia Database System will serve as the multimedia registry for a National Medical Practice Knowledge Bank. This knowledge bank is being developed as part of a five-year NIST program whose goal is to revolutionize healthcare management, patient care, remote consultation and diagnosis, computer-assisted diagnosis and treatment decision making, specialist training, and procedural rehearsal.

Figure 7.2 shows the knowledge bank global view of the architecture, applications, components, and information flow that currently are not integrated or managed by a single system. The knowledge bank requires that multimedia data warehouse tools and special programs be developed to import and format hospital legacy and equipment data so that it can be stored in Teradata-MM.

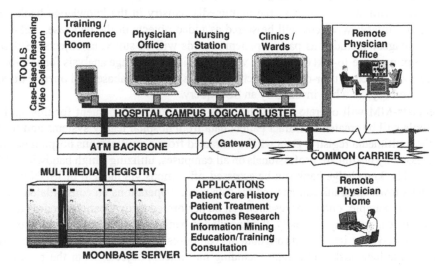

Figure 7.2: Knowledge bank.

The National Institute of Standards and Technology Advanced Technology Program (NIST-ATP) sponsors high-risk technology programs in conjunction with private industry, with the goal that successful programs are commercialized, resulting in broad national benefit. In the area of healthcare, NIST awarded a five-year contract to a joint venture led by Allegheny Health, Education, and Research Foundation to develop a National Medical Practice Knowledge Bank.

Initially, the knowledge bank will be limited to the medical domain of neurosurgery, expanding to cardiology and oncology in later stages of the program. NCR Parallel Systems is a member of this joint venture and will supply the Multimedia Registry, a multimedia database which is the main repository of medical data for the knowledge bank. It will hold the following types of data: (1) patient records, including digitized medical imagery and other complex objects representing medical data; (2) videos of surgical techniques; (3) video interviews with specialists covering diagnosis, treatment, surgical technique, and other medical subjects; and (4) critical pathways for patient treatment and recovery (decision trees for patient care based on patient observations, accepted treatments, and expected outcomes).

The key technological innovations which will drive this project are: (1) a massively parallel object/relational database system with petabyte storage capability; (2) the ability to manipulate and analyze objects within the context of a database query; (3) voice-to-text translations; (4) automated video indexing and segmentation; (5) case-based reasoning (CBR) tools for computer-assisted patient diagnosis; and (6) user interfaces which require minimal physician training.

There are two primary modes of access to the multimedia registry. In the first, users located at interactive endpoints can perform updates and queries against the registry. These endpoints are clients in a client-server environment. In the second, two or more video endpoints can participate in a video collaboration session. All participating endpoints can simultaneously access and view data from the registry.

Teradata-MM will function as the multimedia registry in the knowledge bank. The training and interview videos will be stored as video objects in the database. Likewise, medical imagery included as part of patient records will be stored as objects. Software for performing voice-to-text conversion, video indexing, and image analysis for case-based reasoning are stored as user-defined functions (UDFs) in the database, and operate directly on the stored objects when invoked by an SQL query.

Teradata-MM will operate in a typical data warehouse environment for this application. Tools will be created to extract patient data from hospital legacy systems and format it for the multimedia registry. Data will be extracted from a multicampus hospital network and accessed by healthcare professionals on all campuses, utilizing a high bandwidth ATM network. The knowledge bank can be accessed off campus via modem or ISDN connection. The knowledge bank can be used for data mining operations on consolidated patient records. For example, outcomes research can be performed against patient records to evaluate the critical pathways. Finally, the knowledge bank must be accessible by the video collaboration system installed throughout the campuses to allow video-conference participants to simultaneously view data, including multimedia objects, from the multimedia registry.

7.3 Massively Parallel Architecture, Infrastructure, and Technology

Teradata Corporation developed the DBC/1012 [6] parallel computer hardware and Teradata Relational Database management system based on a loosely-coupled shared nothing architecture [27]. The DBC/1012 and Teradata Relational Database system were able to scale to the terabyte level by employing a parallel infrastructure consisting of: (1) the Ynet interconnection network (an active synchronous interconnection bus) used to communicate and share data between the processors, (2) a proprietary operating system designed for parallelism, and (3) system partitioning for fault-tolerance.

The Teradata database on the DBC/1012 generates query plans [29] to exploit the massively parallel architecture. On the DBC/1012, interface processors (IFPs) handle mainframe connections and communication processors (COPs) handle workstation and PC connections. The access module processors (AMPs) have disks where the actual data is stored. The key to exploiting parallelism is to generate a parallel query plan. On the DBC/1012, the Teradata database query plan module generates Steps that are broadcast to the AMPs via the Ynet interconnection network. Steps are parallel pseudo-database operations used to exploit shared nothing parallel processing with support from the interconnection network.

The next-generation computer platform, WorldMark 5100M, evolved the DBC/1012 (IFP, COP, AMP) uniprocessor design to a symmetric multiprocessor (SMP) architecture [8]. The WorldMark 5100M (Figure 7.3) SMP nodes are called Processor Module

Assemblies (PMAs). Each PMA manages a disk array. The maximum theoretical configuration consists of 4,096 PMAs and based on the size of the disk array, the WorldMark 5100M could support petabyte-size database applications. Other WorldMark 5100M design evolutions are to host AMP, IFP, and COP functionality on virtual processors, and to logically group SMP processors into "cliques" for fault tolerance reasons. The WorldMark 5100M also has a parallel infrastructure that uses a next-generation interconnection network, the BYNET. A comprehensive exegesis of the Teradata database, Ynet, and BYNET interconnection networks can be found in [8, 29].

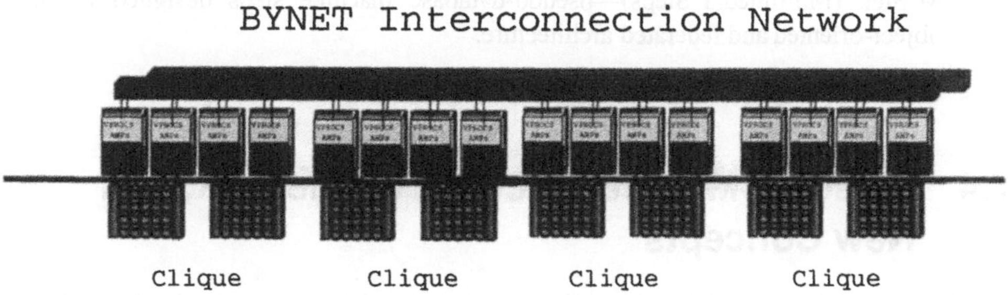

BYNET Interconnection Network

Clique   Clique   Clique   Clique

Figure 7.3: WorldMark 5100M architecture (in cliques).

7.3.1 Parallelism

There are a number of components comprising a parallel architecture: multiple processors, an interconnection network, an operating system that supports parallelism, and a database system that supports parallelism. An analysis of how the Teradata Relational Database achieves scalable parallelism [8] on the WorldMark 5100M yields the following:

- UNIX/Parallel Database Extensions (UNIX/PDE) operating system—which provides virtual processor (Vproc) and globally distributed object (GDO) facilities. Vprocs are a way of encapsulating the database functionality in an SMP environment. This encapsulation is done to provide availability and independence of the physical node where the Vproc runs. The PDE facilities automatically restart all Vprocs from a failing node on other nodes that share the I/O connectivity.

- BYNET interconnection network—provides the necessary bandwidth to distribute/redistribute the data and synchronize the parallel processes.

- Step instruction set—provides a parallel pseudo-database intermediate language. The query plan generator and optimizer can generate Steps that utilize the Vproc facility and interconnection network services to exploit system parallelism.

Teradata-MM uses the existing and developed new parallel infrastructure for large multimedia objects. We reused the Vproc facility since it is scalable and has been proven reliable in very large applications. We specifically developed the following new parallel infrastructure:

- Multimedia Infrastructure (MI)—provides a scalable infrastructure to get, put, send, or receive data or messages. MI provides a mechanism to execute functions on Vprocs where worker processes work on their share of the data. MI provides transparent execute migration to other Vprocs and hides the details of the underlying operating system from the developers and system code.

- Agent/Event—an internal communication system to send and receive data. It is designed based on the software agent paradigm [12].

- M-Step (Multimedia Steps)—pseudo-database machine steps designed for our object-oriented and federated architecture.

- Object Server Connectivity—high speed secondary network manager.

7.4 Teradata-MM Architecture, Framework, and New Concepts

Teradata-MM [7] is an SQL3 multimedia object/relational database extension to the Teradata Relational Database. A federated coordinator lets us nonintrusively add ADT objects and UDF capabilities to one or more heterogeneous relational databases. Multiple heterogeneous database issues and solutions are described in [5]. This section discusses our first implementation that adds multimedia object data to the Teradata Relational Database system.

7.4.1 Teradata-MM Architecture

Figure 7.4 shows the Teradata-MM architecture which logically integrates: (1) the Teradata database system, (2) the Teradata Multimedia Object Server, and (3) other object servers via a special application interface. Figure 7.5 shows a video server application programmable interface (API).

7.4.2 Key New Concepts

Multimedia and object data required new functionality and concepts [26]. The key new concepts not found on or traditionally part of object or relational database systems include:

- Two-Pass Paradigm for multimedia object retrieval

- Object Server Connectivity (OSC) network management

- Multimedia Object Locators (MOLs)

- Multiple Data Receivers for information workflow

- Kerberos security tickets used with MOLs

- Object extensions to the Call Level Interface

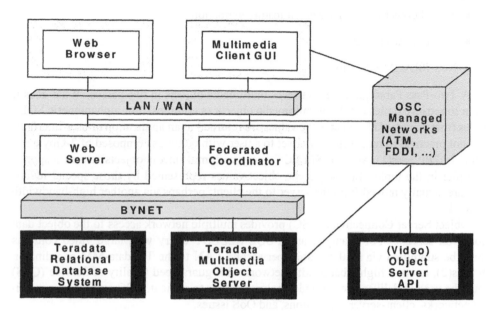

Figure 7.4: Architecture and data flow.

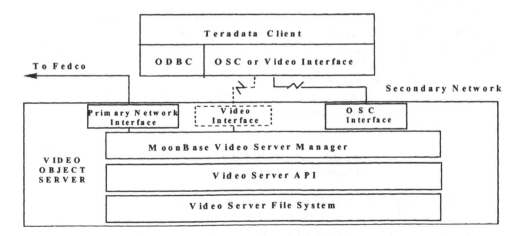

Figure 7.5: Video server API.

- UDF value persistence facility to compute UDF values only once

- Spatial object indexing based on feature extractions

- New optimizer strategies

- New PRAGMA facility

A Two-Pass Paradigm (2PP) retrieves multimedia objects in two passes. What does it mean to retrieve tuples that have multimedia objects as columns? For alphanumeric SQL2 tuples (that is, not ADT objects), the values are returned to an application or user-interface. It is not practical to return an answer set to a user with columns composed of 2-Gbyte objects. In 2PP pass(1), an SQL SELECT query with multimedia objects returns a special identifier in the tuple. In pass(2), the object values represented by those special identifiers are actually moved from the server to the client; perhaps via another high-bandwidth network.

Object Server Connectivity (OSC) provides multiple network access to the object data stored on servers. For example, an M-SQL SELECT query with large video columns could be submitted via a 10 megabits per second LAN to the Teradata-MM coordinator. In pass(2), another higher bandwidth network with guaranteed Quality of Service (QoS) could be used to deliver selected video column values to a client. OSC manages the multiple networks, client-server connections, and QoS issues.

Multimedia Object Locators (MOLs) are internal special identifiers generated to point to a multimedia object location. A MOL is like an Internet Universal Resource Locator (URL). MOLs provide a mechanism to create a specific link to an internal database file where the object is stored. This is important in shared nothing, multinode, and/or distributed systems to minimize messages and data being routed to client(s).

A MOL is created by a *transform* operation that logically concatenates a MOID (Multimedia Object Identifier), a network address, and Kerberos ticket into a unique locator. The Teradata-MM Object Identifier (MOID) contains the directory and file information needed to locate an object. The network address is of the node where the object is stored. The optional Kerberos security ticket is used for user identification. Kerberos is part of a Distributed Computing Environment (DCE) [25] and provides a secure mechanism to authenticate users who want to retrieve ADT objects.

The user interface (UI) has to evolve to incorporate our 2PP and MOL data retrieval process for ADT objects. We illustrate the new UI concepts with an example. The interactive UI lets the user specify a query like:

SELECT name, age, ShowTumor (MRI) FROM patient WHERE age > 40
AND FindTumor (MRI) > 0.1 ORDER BY age;

The above query shows the ADT and UDF capabilities of M-SQL. In this example, the user defined an MRI ADT and used it as a column of a table. The Teradata-MM Answer Set Manager returns <name, age, MRI.MOL> and the UI displays an ICON or ADT object thumbnail as shown in the left-hand side of Figure 7.6.

Then, when a user selects a specific MRI by clicking on the ICON or thumbnail, the MOL is used to create a connection to where the data object is stored. In this case, a ShowTumor() UDF is executed only on the selected MRI object and displayed (see the right-hand side of Figure 7.6) in the second pass. A user may choose to retrieve all the objects in the first pass, but frequently this is not practical.

NAME	AGE	ShowTumor()
Carino	40	MRI
Sterling	50	MRI
Simon	39	MRI

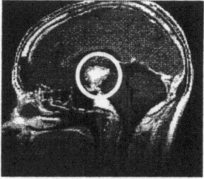

Figure 7.6: *(left)* First pass display, *(right)* Second pass display.

Multiple Information Workflow Receivers (Figure 7.7) are a concept where the results of an M-SQL query are sent/broadcast to multiple receiving clients. The implementation is like an electronic-mail system that notifies users that they have a message and the message is retrieved and displayed when selected by a user. Teradata-MM Answer Set Manager (ASM) transforms each MOID into a MOL and when the multiple receiver option is used, a message is sent to the receivers. A receiver can retrieve the answer set, and then retrieve specific ADT objects contained within the tuples.

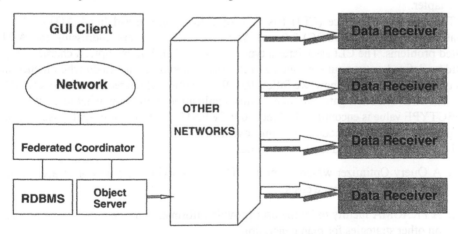

Figure 7.7: Multiple data receivers (for workflow).

Keeping answer sets for long periods can require large amounts of disk space. A system option determines how long to keep an answer set. Teradata-MM releases the locks at the end of a transaction and the actual objects can change before a receiver fetches the object. In this case, we inform the user of the change. The user can then issue a query to retrieve the 'new' modified object values.

Database security is handled via SQL GRANT/REVOKE for security. Two new security problems and our solutions are:

- Kerberos security tickets [25] are an optional part of a MOL sent back to clients or receivers in pass(1). Kerberos tickets provide a user identification mechanism. The client/user interface presents the MOL and the Teradata-MM coordinator validates user identification and access rights to the object. If both are valid, then object retrieval can proceed.

- UDFs can be implemented in a programming language like C/C++. UDFs may read or write data which is stored in the Bell Labs Storage System (BeSS). BeSS handles unauthorized access and, for trusted code like Teradata-MM, protects control structures and blocks invalid data access. Also, a 'thin fire wall layer' prevents UDFs from using I/O to read/write objects. UDFs operate on one tuple at a time and only this data is accessible to the UDF.

System administration includes initial loading of multimedia objects into the system, backup, and restore utilities. For example, the bulk load utility provides a way to load videos into the Teradata Multimedia Object Server. It may not be feasible to back up a very large (for example, petabyte) multimedia database. In certain cases, it may be practical to only back up the relational data and have a disaster recovery system that loads the multimedia data and perhaps executes transforming UDFs to recover a database or database subset. A diagnostic utility navigates the tables to verify the integrity of MOID references in a database. There are many system administration and other issues, like evolving legacy SQL2 applications to include multimedia objects, that are beyond the scope and purpose of this chapter.

The call-level interface (CLI) has to evolve to handle user-defined ADTs. Open Database Connectivity (ODBC) 3.0 and ANSI SQL/CLI [28] are addressing the ADT-related problems. The CLI associates a type with a number. For example, a character type could be defined as type number, such as 128. The CLI knows what to do when it encounters type number 128. For now, we follow the ODBC notion which requires that every ADT have an ODBCTYPE negative number. Thus, applications will know what to do when an ODBCTYPE value is encountered. Hence, our CREATE TYPE requires that a user specify a negative number. This model needs improvement.

UDF new concepts and facilities include:

1. A Query Optimizer which supports UDFs, networking, remote object access, and temporary value storage costs.

2. A PRAGMA facility to let the user provide information to the query plan generator on other strategies for plan generation.

3. A precomputed UDF value persistence facility (designed for performance and conservation of system resources). We extended M-SQL to provide a mechanism whereby a UDF is executed only when a value is inserted, updated, and/or modified. UDF invocations can be expensive in terms of time, data movement, and internal resource consumption. Computing the UDF values and storing these internally lets the optimizer convert potentially expensive UDF invocations to hidden column references.

4. Object Feature Extraction and Indexing. This is a facility whereby content-based queries retrieve tuples based on object features. The pattern matching is done in feature space (features extracted from the object). Hence applying a potentially expensive UDF to every native ADT object is avoided.

7.4.3 SQL3

SQL3 is a nickname for a series of evolving standards (composed of: Framework, Foundation, Call Level Interface (CLI), Persistent Storage Model, Transactions, and Temporal). The term "object/relational" was coined for adding object support into the relational model. SQL3 is the leading standard object/relational effort. We call our SQL3 subset and extensions M-SQL.

7.4.4 Federated Coordinator

A Teradata-MM table is fragmented both horizontally and vertically. As shown in Figure 7.8, the Federated Coordinator facilitates vertical table partitioning among our three logical components: (1) Teradata Relational Database where alphanumeric data is stored, (2) Teradata Multimedia Object Server, and (3) third party object servers. The vertical fragmentation is done on the basis of column data type. Whereas the Teradata database distributes rows based on a hashing function, the object server supports multiple object distribution strategies, that is, hashing, range, round-robin, and so on.

Recall from the user interface and 2PP concept analysis how UDFs are executed and answer sets sent back to clients or receivers. The predicate (that is, where-clause) is evaluated and Teradata-MM returns the MOL values for ADT columns. The UDFs that appear in the predicate are evaluated in the first pass. The user can select one or more columns to view. In this case, a projection transforming UDF is applied to MRI column before sending the MRI to the client for viewing. For continuous data, such as audio or video, displaying or playing more than one at a time is not feasible.

SELECT name, age, ShowTumor(MRI) FROM patient WHERE age > 40
AND FindTumor (MRI) > 0.1;

The Teradata-MM first implementation requires that UDFs be written in C++. A UDF install utility validates data types, compiles, and installs a UDF on the object server. Also, a library of predefined ADTs and UDFs [4] will be supplied.

The Federated Coordinator receives user queries and generates a query plan composed of parallel steps, called M-Steps, that execute on both the Teradata Relational Database and the parallel Teradata Multimedia Object Server. The Teradata-MM components mirror those of the Teradata Relational Database.

These components are:

- Session Manager—manages sessions and interfacing with clients.

- Parser—converts SQL query into a parse tree.

- GDD Manager—maintains a GDD cache.

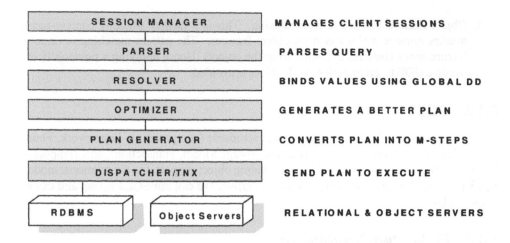

Figure 7.8: Federated Coordinator components.

- Security—enforces security based on GRANT/REVOKE privileges stored in GDD security table.

- Optimizer—optimizes for parallelism (see Section 7.5.1).

- Plan Generator—converts the query plan into M-Steps.

- Dispatcher—coordinates and sends the M-Step execution plan to the (Teradata) relational database, Teradata Multimedia Object Server, and other special servers.

- Answer Set Manager (ASM)—collects the intermediate results stored in temporary files. The ASM is responsible for merging the spool files from the relational database and object server(s).

- Transaction (TNX) Manager—determines whether to commit or rollback transactions.

7.4.5 Teradata Multimedia Object Server

Teradata-MM uses the Teradata Multimedia Object Server (Figure 7.9) to store ADT objects and execute UDFs that perform content-analysis (in predicates) and content-transformations (in projection list) in parallel. It is a general-purpose content-analysis server designed for symmetric multiprocessor and massively parallel processor environments. It provides the ability to define and manipulate user-defined functions (UDFs) which are invoked in parallel to analyze and manipulate the contents of objects.

The Teradata Multimedia Object Server incorporates:

- A generic platform that is application independent and extensible

- Programmable agents

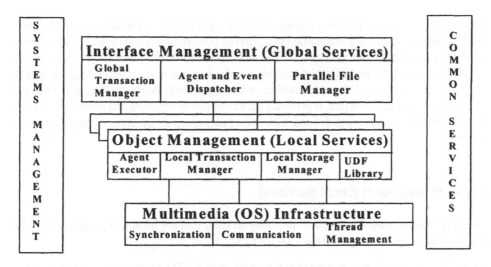

Figure 7.9: Teradata Multimedia Object Server.

- Content-based object analysis capabilities through UDFs

- Extensive support for large object data placement

- A UNIX-like file system API for accessing large objects

As shown in Figure 7.9, the software architecture consists of five major components:

1. An interface management component for global services

2. An object management component for local services

3. Multimedia (operating system) infrastructure

4. Common services component

5. Systems management component

Interface Management (Global Services)

The interface management component consists of the global transaction manager, agent and event dispatcher, and the Parallel File Manager.

Global Transaction Manager: provides interfaces to begin, prepare, commit, and abort transactions that conform to the XA standards.

Agent and Event Dispatcher: parallelizes a user request using agents and events over the appropriate Vprocs for processing. It transforms the user request into one or more agents and prior to dispatching, programs the agents with the sequence of the Vprocs to be visited and the operations (for example, a UDF) to be performed at the various Vprocs. Computation in the system is based on the execution of work by agents which is triggered by the receipt of events (messages).

Parallel File Manager: provides storage/retrieval capabilities with transactional semantics on all Vprocs. Objects are maintained in a parallel persistent storage system. The location of objects is hidden from the external user. The Teradata Multimedia Object Server provides an object identifier (OID) for each object. As the system is reconfigured, the objects are transferred from one Vproc to another in a transparent fashion and the same OID can be used to reference the object. It provides the capability to organize and group objects into directories. Each directory is defined with one of numerous distribution strategies over the Vprocs.

Object Management (Local Services)

The object management component provides services that are local to Vprocs and provide access to persistent storage and the UDF library.

Local Transaction Manager: provides the traditional ACID (Atomicity, Concurrency, Isolation, and Durability) transaction properties.

Agent Executor: provides computation capabilities by supporting programmable agents. During an agent's execution, it may trigger other events, create new agents, access the persistent storage, execute UDFs, and migrate to other Vprocs.

Local Storage Manager: utilizes BeSS (Bell Labs Storage System) storage manager as the core storage system to provide persistent storage and allocation, concurrency control, and recovery of objects. BeSS is a persistent file system that provides Two-Phase Commit (2PC) transaction and Two-Phase Locking (2PL) facilities. It does not impose any limits on the size of the objects. A single object may span multiple disks on a Vproc.

UDF Library: provides an extensible set of abstract data type (ADT) algorithms to do content-based analysis on objects. It provides the ability to load, store, and execute application-specific UDFs (for example, extract fingerprint features, compare fingerprint features, and so on).

Multimedia (OS) Infrastructure

The multimedia infrastructure provides synchronization, communication, and system resource management services across the Vprocs.

Synchronization: provides services to synchronize among the various object servers and application processes via monitors.

Communication: provides services to facilitate the communication among between the various object servers and application processes by transporting messages containing control and data information between the processes.

Thread management: provides a mechanism for executing and managing processes in the Teradata Multimedia Object Server environment.

Common Services

The common services component provides services that are utilized by all other components such as the tracing and the error handling facilities.

Systems Management

The systems management component provides system start-up, system shutdown, configuration, and postmortem analysis services.

7.5 Parallel UDF Execution Analysis

SQL3's new ADT and UDF capabilities create new challenges beyond optimizing SQL2 queries. Our parallel query plan generation, optimization, tuning, value caching, and indexing analysis is for shared nothing, MPP architectures (such as WorldMark 5100M). The Teradata-MM plan generator and optimizer main parallel execution issues are analyzed below via examples.

7.5.1 UDF Optimizations

SQL optimizers use cost estimation, tuple statistics, indexes, and/or sampling to optimize queries. Large multimedia databases that use UDFs introduce new complexity into each of these optimizer tools. Cost estimation of UDFs works when the average execution time has low variance. Consider a UDF that does content analysis of video columns where some videos are a few minutes and some 15 hours in length.

Sampling implies running a random instance of every UDF in the query and using this information to generate an efficient query plan. Sampling is the easiest to implement, but assumes that a UDF execution time is uniform across all objects. If sampling is used on a UDF with large execution cost variance, then nonoptimal plans may be generated. Of course, if the cost variance varies widely, an efficient plan may not be possible. The optimizer contains formulas evaluating the criteria used by the optimizer. The optimization criteria include: response time, throughput, disk space utilization, and networking costs.

First, we list the key UDF optimization issues:

1. Delay execution of projection UDFs to pass(2) of our two-pass paradigm retrieval scheme.

2. For predicates with multiple UDFs determine the order of execution and balance response versus throughput issues.

3. For UDFs with multiple ADT parameters determine which Vproc to execute the UDF. Also, what strategy should be used for the other ADT parameters in the UDF. Copy the ADT(s) to this Vproc or access via a remote procedure call (RPC) the other ADT(s) in the UDF parameter list.

4. For nested UDF invocations determine which UDFs can be executed in parallel and the mechanism to "pipe" results to the UDFs at the next level of nesting. The trade-offs are temporary files versus a real "UNIX-like pipe" which has partial result and tuple pairing complexity.

5. Update-in-place UDF is a special UDF that can "safely" write over an existing ADT object without creating integrity problems; this avoids making a copy of the ADT object being modified. An example would be a Time-Series UDF that appends stock tick values to the end of a {stock price, time} sequence.

6. UDF execution or resource usage variance based on ADT object values.

Case (1): Delay projection UDF execution to pass(2). Recall that a user can retrieve tuples in two passes with our two-pass paradigm. In pass(1), predicate UDFs are always evaluated. Also, projection or transformation UDFs evaluation can be delayed to pass(2).

SELECT LateralView (MRI) FROM PatientTable WHERE FindTumor (MRI) > 0.8;

The key performance optimization here is to delay the execution of LateralView() until pass(2). If a query returns 'n rows' and a user views k rows, then delaying the projection UDF saves (n-k) invocations of the projection UDF. This execution and resource usage is significant if $n \gg k$.

Case (2): For predicates with multiple UDFs the order to execute the UDFs could affect performance. The primary factor in determining UDF execution order is UDF selectivity (that is, percent row kept or rejected by the UDF). UDFs with 'high' variance for execution time and temporary resources are difficult to optimize since their execution time and resource usage are based on each individual object value. For example, assume that a video analysis UDF execution time and resource usage is based on the length of the video column, and that table contains video columns of diverse length. If the video column contains videos that greatly vary in length then the optimizer must use average statistics or default to an execution strategy.

SELECT * FROM PatientTable
WHERE UDF1(a1) AND UDF2 (a2) AND UDF3(a3) AND UDF4(a4);

UDF Name	SELECTIVITY (% Rows Accepted)	EXECUTION TIME (Scale: 1 to 100) (1→Low; 100→High)	RESOURCE USAGE (Scale: 1 to 100) (1→Low; 100→High)
UDF1	50%	50	30
UDF2	10%	90	10
UDF3	40%	60	70
UDF4	90%	10	50

Assume that for the preceding query the GDD has the following statistical information. UDF4() has high 90 percent selectivity (which means on average 90 percent of tuples are

accepted) and low execution time (mainly CPU) cost. Hence, for fast response time UDF4()
should be executed first. UDF2() has low selectivity and high CPU cost and should be
executed last. Using this criteria, UDF1() should be executed before UDF3(). Therefore,
the order of UDF execution should be: UDF4(), UDF1(), UDF3(), and UDF2().

Case (3): Another optimization issue concerns multiple ADT parameters in a UDF invocation. This optimization should minimize or eliminate large ADT data movement or remote
object access.

SELECT * FROM surgery WHERE UDF5 (ADT1, ADT2);

Assume that ADT1 and ADT2 objects needed for UDF5() are stored on different nodes.
Then the optimizer can generate two different plans:

1. Generate a query plan where the UDF execution node location is determined at
   compile-time, such that execution always occurs on a particular node (uses static
   average ADT size information). If the average size of ADT1 is greater than ADT2
   then "always" execute UDF5 at ADT1's location.

2. Generate a query plan where the UDF execution node location is determined at runtime. To determine node location at runtime requires obtaining object sizes and
   migrating processing to the pertinent node.

Case (4): Nested UDF invocations have parallel pipelining process and intermediate result
issues. Either approach requires the ability to migrate a process to the node where one of
the objects is stored.

SELECT * FROM PatientTable
WHERE UDF6 (UDF7(ADT1, UDF10(ADT2)), UDF8(ADT3), UDF9(ADT1));

Figure 7.10 shows the execution graph for UDF6. A strict serial execution of the graph
plan yields:

Time T1: Execute Tmp1 = UDF10 (ADT2); Tmp2 = UDF8 (ADT3);
    Tmp3 = UDF9 (ADT1)

Time T2: Execute Tmp4 = UDF7 (ADT1, Tmp1)

Time T3: Execute Answer = UDF6 (Tmp4, Tmp2, Tmp3)

This execution strategy generates a temporary (spool) file for each nested UDF invocation. With the temporary result set file approach it is easy to correctly align parameter
values. For example, for UDF6, generating the appropriate parameters is simply done by
reading temporary files <Tmp4, Tmp2, Tmp3> in sequential order.

Another execution model is to pipeline results as they are generated. In this model,
all UDFs execute in parallel and wait for their input. The executor must insure that the
pipelined results align properly. With the UDF6 example above the pipeline executor must
align parameters <Tmp4, Tmp2, Tmp3>—which are now pipes—in correct row sequence.

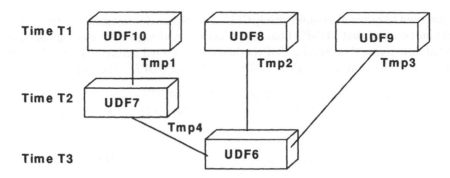

Figure 7.10: Nested UDF execution and dependency graph.

There are numerous flow control problems associated with the pipelining approach, hence we use the temporary result and serial approach.

Case (5): UDF updates ADT object value in place (without making a copy). A UDF with potentially a special behavior can appear in an SQL3 UPDATE command. This special case is where a UDF can update an ADT object without having to make a copy of the object. This "update-in-place" requires user designation at definition time or in the pragma since this requires UDF internal semantic knowledge. Otherwise, a copy of the object must be made during the update. An example of an update-in-place UDF is an append UDF where values are always written to the end of the object.

> UPDATE TimeSeries SET StockHistory = AppendValuesUDF (StockHistory, Price, Time);

Case (6): Collecting statistical information for UDFs that operate on objects that have large variance with respect to execution time and/or storage resources. As mentioned in Case (2), a key plan generation issue pertains to average statistics for time or space. If UDF(a1) takes time t1 with resources r1 to execute and the same UDF(a2) takes time t2 with resources r2, then if the differences between the two time and resources values are great, an optimal plan could be difficult to determine.

7.5.2   PRAGMA Facility

To address difficult plan generation and optimization issues a "pragma facility" was developed. Performance experts and database tuners have developed a portfolio of tricks to help the query plan and optimizer generate a specific execution plan. Some optimization requires semantic knowledge of UDF execution and optimal execution plans may depend on intermediate result set characteristics (for example, Case (6) above). Also, there are nonstandard queries that deviate from the normal database usage patterns.

Teradata-MM provides a pragma facility that lets a user tell the optimizer the user-desired order of execution. The complete pragma language extension is beyond the scope of this chapter, but we show how to tune queries using the examples from Section 7.5.1.

On the CREATE TABLE a user can specify "retrieve immediate" or "two-pass." For retrieve immediate ADT columns, users can override this default with a pragma directive, as follows:

SELECT LateralView (MRI) FROM PatientTable WHERE FindTumor (MRI) > 0.8
[PRAGMA: LateralView (MRI) = Pass(2)]; // Override one pass default for MRI

Recall, from Section 7.5.1, that the optimal UDF order execution plan based on internal statistics was: UDF4, UDF1, UDF3, and UDF2. If a "knowledgeable" user knows a better execution order it could be specified in the command as follows:

SELECT * FROM PatientTable
WHERE UDF1(a1) AND UDF2(a2) AND UDF3(a3) AND UDF4(a4)
[PRAGMA: UDF EXECUTION ORDER = UDF1, UDF3, UDF4, UDF2];

For UDFs with multiple ADT parameters, the default is to execute the UDF at the node with the largest ADT object and to access the other objects remotely. If ADT1 objects on average are larger than ADT2 objects, then UDF5 will normally execute at the node where the ADT1 object resides. This can be overridden as shown below:

SELECT * FROM surgery WHERE UDF5 (ADT1, ADT2)
[PRAGMA: Execute UDF5, @ADT2];

The following pragma for TS_UDF tells the optimizer that it is safe to update in place.

UPDATE TimeSeries SET StockHistory = TS_UDF (StockHistory, Price, Time)
[PRAGMA: UPDATE UDF IN PLACE = TS_UDF];

7.5.3 UDF Value Persistence Facility

In general, evaluating UDF expressions is (significantly) more expensive that retrieving a column (object) value. For UDFs that are expensive to evaluate and frequently invoked we designed a "UDF Value Persistence Facility." With this persistence facility UDFs are evaluated once and the value returned by the UDF is saved, hence our UDF value persistence nomenclature. After a UDF value is computed and saved (in a hidden column), the optimizer will convert UDF function invocations to column references.

Assume, for example, the FindTumor (MRI) UDF returns a floating point number. This could be a very expensive UDF because the UDF must analyze 40 to 64 slices—where each slice is at least 1 Mbyte—that compose an MRI scan. If the FindTumor (MRI) were a frequently invoked query, repeated evaluating of the UDF wastes resources and time. Therefore, for FindTumor and other UDFs of similar expense to evaluate, use of the persistence facility saves time. The extra space needed to store this value is negligible when compared to the resource and time cost required to evaluate the predicate at run time. Storing UDF values consumes disk storage, but for UDF queries that are expensive to evaluate this storage cost is affordable. This is especially true for an expensive UDF that returns an alphanumeric value.

UDF value persistence requires that the value returned by the UDF be stored. In our federated architecture, this means that scalar values are stored in the relational database, and object values are stored in the object server. Also, persistence implies postprocessing on SQL INSERT or SQL UPDATE that affect columns specified in a UDF. For FindTumor (MRI), every update or insert to the MRI column implies computing a new value for each modified or new MRI column.

The UDF mechanism for precomputing and storing of UDF values was added to SQL and is specified via a virtual column facility. It is completely hidden from the user. The optimizer detects the virtual column and converts UDF invocation to a column reference. In Teradata-MM, queries with alphanumeric-valued UDFs become simple Teradata SQL2 queries. Our SQL3 extension, is shown via an example:

> CREATE VIRTUAL COLUMN mri_value (float mri_scan) on PatientTable.MRI
> USING (float FindTumor(MRI)) ON (name, MRI);

The original query and the optimizer query rewrite are shown below.

Original: SELECT name, MRI FROM PatientTable WHERE TumorSize(MRI) > 0.8;
Optimized: SELECT name, MRI FROM PatientTable WHERE mri_value > 0.8;

7.5.4 Spatial Indices for Content-Based Querying

Content-analysis of very large ADT objects can be expensive and difficult. A UDF that analyzes an ADT object and looks for a match (for example, a face in an image) is both expensive and time consuming. To address content-based queries, Teradata-MM provides an indexing facility. An exegesis of feature extraction, indexing, and implementation issues can be found in [11].

The MRI ADT example used throughout this chapter is simple when compared to more complex types of content-matching. ADT object content-matching on the base ADT object itself is not always practical. Consider an airport customs security example where arriving passengers who are known security risks must be identified. Assume there is a table, SecurityRisk <name, country, face>, against which matching is done. A MatchFace(face, target_face) UDF can be written to perform the pattern matching. A better alternative, from a performance standpoint, is to extract features from the images in the "face" column, store them in the database, and perform the face matching operation against the extract features.

The indexing facility works as follows:

Step (1) a feature vector(s) of numeric values is created by executing UDF feature extract functions;

Step (2) UDFs perform content-analysis of the feature vector(s) and match objects with confidence levels between 0 and 1.

The attribute "characteristics" on the ADT "face" is a derived attribute. The point is that "characteristics" is a virtual (derived) attribute that is set with a UDF that is not in the actual query. More importantly, this attribute (in this case) is stored in the Teradata Multimedia Object Server. In this example, the feature extract may be a vector or vectors. Thus, to do the comparison, the Cartesian product is taken. Then, with each pair, it is evaluated with the Euclidean distance equation. The results of each pair are then summarized to determine the distance between the two faces. In general, the feature extraction should never by done at query time—but, done at insertion time. Mostly likely this will be done using a "lazy" feature extraction protocol. The reason being that response time will be several orders of magnitude worse on large data sets.

The following are MRI feature extract and indexing usage examples. Figure 7.11 shows two features extracted from the MRI scans. Figure 7.12 shows partitioning object clusters based on features. Then an R-Tree-like search can be (efficiently) done. R-Trees on shared nothing MPP systems are an active area of research and no "efficient" algorithm and evaluate strategy has been developed.

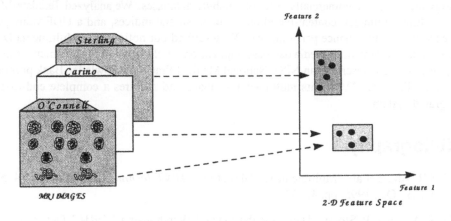

Figure 7.11: Feature extraction.

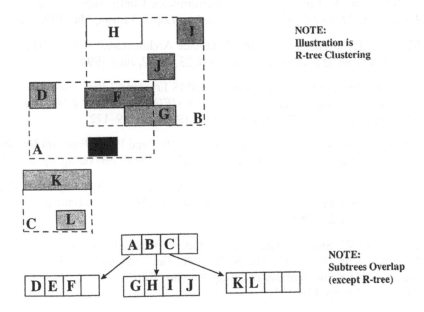

NOTE:
Illustration is
R-tree Clustering

NOTE:
Subtrees Overlap
(except R-tree)

Figure 7.12: Partitioning object clusters in feature.

7.6   Conclusion

In this chapter we analyzed several new concepts and parallel implementations we designed and developed for Teradata-MM. Teradata-MM integrates and manages the multimedia islands of information for database applications. We described the parallel processing technology that will be commercially sold for petabyte databases. We analyzed Teradata-MM architecture, optimizer, content-based querying on spatial indices, and a UDF value persistence facility to enhance performance. We described our notions of a Multimedia Data Warehouse and how multimedia database applications will evolve in the commercial marketplace. We also described an NIST National Medical Practice Knowledge Bank program that uses Teradata-MM for its multimedia database and requires a complete end-to-end integrated system.

Bibliography

[1]   S.R. Ahuja et al., "Multimedia Collaboration," *AT&T Technical Journal*, Vol. 74, No. 5, Sep./Oct. 1995, pp. 46–53.

[2]   S. Atre and P. Storer, "Data Distribution and Warehousing," *DBMS*, Oct. 1995, pp. 54–62.

[3]   A. Biliris and E. Panagos, "A High Performance Configurable Storage Manager," *Proc. IEEE 9th Int'l Conf. Data Engineering*, Taipei, Taiwan, Mar. 1995, pp. 35–43.

[4]   M. Bell, "The Montage Extensible Datablade Architecture," *Proc. ACM Special Interest Group on Management of Data*, Vol. 23, No. 2, June 1994.

[5]   F. Cariño, "HETERO—Heterogeneous DBMS Frontend," *Proc. Int'l Federation Information Processing Technical Committee (IFIPTC) 8/WG 8.4 Working Conf. on Methods and Tools for Office Systems*, Oct. 1986, pp. 159–172.

[6]   F. Cariño and P. Kostamaa, "Exegesis of DBC/1012 and P-90," *Proc. 4th Int'l Parallel Architectures and Languages Europe (PARLE '92)*, Springer-Verlag, pp. 877–892

[7]   F. Cariño, W. Sterling, and I.T. Ieong, "Teradata-MM—A Complete Multimedia Database Solution," *ACM Multimedia Workshop on Multimedia Databases*, San Francisco, CA, Oct. 21, 1994.

[8]   F. Cariño, W. Sterling, and P. Kostamaa, "Industrial Database Supercomputer Exegesis—The DBC/1012, The NCR 3700, The Ynet and The BYNET," *Emerging Trends in Knowledge and Database Systems*, IEEE Computer Society Press, Los Alamitos, CA, pp. 139–157.

[9]   E. Codd, "A Relational Model for Large Shared Data Banks," *Comm. ACM*, Vol. 13, No. 6, June 1970, pp. 377–387.

[10] W. O'Connell et al., "Prospector: A Content-Based Multimedia Object Server for Massively Parallel Architectures," *Proc. of ACM-SIGMOD*, Montreal, Canada, June 1996.

[11] W. O'Connell, D. Schrader, and H. Chen, "The Teradata SQL Multimedia Database Server," B. Shen, ed., *Technology For Multimedia*, IEEE Press, Dec. 1996.

[12] M. Geneserethm and K. Ketchpel, "Software Agents," *Communications of ACM, Special Issue on Intelligent Agents*, Vol. 37, No. 7, July 1994, pp. 48–53.

[13] A. Ghafoor, ed., "Special Issue on Multimedia Database Systems," *ACM Multimedia Systems*, Vol. 3, No. 5/6, 1995.

[14] R. Hackathorn, "Data Warehousing Energizes Your Enterprise," *Datamation*, Feb. 1995, pp. 38–45.

[15] W. Inmon, *Building the Data Warehouse*, QED Technical Publishing Group, Wellesley, MA, 1992.

[16] W.H. Inmon and R.D. Hackathorn, *Using the Data Warehouse*, Wiley-QED Publication, New York, 1994.

[17] N. Jayant, ed., "Multimedia Technology Special Issue," *AT&T Technical Journal*, Vol. 74, No. 5, Sep./Oct. 1995, pp. 46–53.

[18] H. Katseff and T. Robinson, "Predictive Prefetch in the Nemesis Multimedia Information Service," *Proc. ACM Multimedia*, San Francisco, CA, Oct. 1994, pp. 201–206.

[19] S. Khoshafian and A.B. Baker, *MultiMedia and Imaging Databases*, Morgan Kaufmann, San Francisco, CA, 1995.

[20] N. Koudas, C. Faloutsos, and I. Kamel, "Declustering Spatial Databases on a Multi-Computer Architecture," *Proc. Extending Database Technology*, France, Mar. 1996.

[21] M. Loomis, "Moving Objects into Relational Systems," *Proc. Database World and Client/Server World*, Vol. 1, June 14, 1993.

[22] J. Melton et al., "Database Language (SQL3)," *ISO/ANSI Working Draft, ANSI X3H2-92-93-091 and ISO/IEC JTC1/SC21/WG3/DBL YOK-003*, Feb. 1993.

[23] J. Melton and A.R. Simon, *Understanding the New SQL: A Complete Guide*, Morgan Kaufmann, San Francisco, CA, 1995.

[24] A.P. Sheth and J.A. Larson, "Federated Database Systems for Managing Distributed, Heterogeneous and Autonomous Databases," *ACM Computing Surveys*, Vol. 22, No. 3, Sep. 1990, pp. 183–236.

[25] J. Shirley, W. Hu, and D. Magid, *Guide to Writing DCE Applications*, O'Reilly and Associates, Sebastopol, CA, May 1994.

[26] W. Sterling and F. Cariño, "Multimedia Databases and Servers," *AT&T Technical Journal*, Vol. 74, No. 5, Sep./Oct. 1995, pp. 54–67.

[27] M. Stonebraker, "The Case for Shared-Nothing," *IEEE Data Engineering Bulletin*, Vol. 9, No. 2, 1986, pp. 4–9.

[28] M. Venkatrao and M. Pizzo, "SQL/CLI—A New Binding Style for SQL," *ACM SIG-MOD Record*, Vol. 24, No. 4, Dec. 1995, pp. 72–77.

[29] A. Witkowski, F. Cariño, and P. Kostamaa, "NCR 3700—The Next-Generation Industrial Database Computer," *Proc. 19th Int'l Conf. on Very Large Databases (VLDB '93)*, pp. 230–243.

Chapter 8

The MEDUSA Project

George M. Bryan and Wayne E. Moore

Abstract. *This chapter describes work on a prototype self-organizing multiprocessor database machine, MEDUSA. MEDUSA is based on a shared nothing architecture, each transaction node comprised of an INMOS T805 transputer and a T222 SCSI interface to a 180-Mbyte disk drive. MEDUSA employs two key technical ideas which give it an autonomous data management capability. The first key technical idea is the use of a dedicated processor for load balancing and data management as part of the overall transaction processing system. Second, the data storage structures used are designed as self-contained packets which may be moved between disk units with minimal overhead. By using these techniques MEDUSA is able to manage its own data declustering strategy to approach optimal performance, with minimal impact on transaction processing. The authors believe that the properties of autonomous data management and self-organization displayed by this prototype will be necessary in the next generation of database systems to make them commercially viable.*

8.1 Introduction

A decrease in the time taken to execute a given task can usually be accomplished by a division of labor among smaller subtasks. The application of this principle to the processing and retrieval of data has been recognized by industry and the research community for a number of years. As noted by DeWitt and Gray in [7], a number of database vendors such as Teradata and Tandem have produced purpose-built parallel database machines based on the above principle. A number of projects have been undertaken to explore the applications of parallel processing to database systems. Some examples of these projects are GRACE [9], Gamma [6], Bubba [2], COMFORT [11], and Dragon Net [13]. A second and equally important concept is that the time taken to accomplish a task that has been divided into a number of subtasks will be equal to the time taken to complete the slowest subtask.

A primary objective of a parallel database system is to partition data across the available processors in such a manner that the system's workload will be equally shared among its processors. Hau and Lee [8] have suggested that a balanced work load can be achieved by ensuring an even data distribution across the system's processors. Moenkeberg et al. [11] opted to achieve a balanced workload in the COMFORT project by balancing processor access rates. This was based on an idea first suggested by Boral et al. [2] in the Bubba project.

A database system must also provide an effective method of data access if it is to achieve a balanced workload and to be of practical use. This function is normally provided by the indexing system.

8.2   Indexing and Data Partitioning

The function of an indexing system is to record the location of a data tuple within a storage system, thus enabling the tuple to be retrieved and processed efficiently. In order to achieve this aim, an indexing system operating in a parallel database environment must also support the system's data partitioning strategy. As described by Scheuermann et al. [15], there are two principle data partitioning strategies in common use:

1. **Data Striping**, a technique that divides a file or table into a number of stripes. Each stripe consists of a number of data blocks. This technique is commonly found in RAID systems [14] and it was also used in the FIVE file system developed for the COMFORT Project [16].

2. **Declustering**, a technique that partitions data based on the value of one or more attributes. Declustering schemes can be found in a number of research (Bubba, Gamma, and Grace) and commercial systems (Terradata DBC/1012).

For the remainder of this chapter we will restrict our discussion to index systems which offer support for partitioning schemes based on data declustering.

8.2.1   Standard Systems

There are three types of data partitioning techniques in common use: Range, Round-Robin, and Hash partitioning. A summary of these techniques is presented here, a full discussion may be found in DeWitt and Gray [7].

Range Partitioning. This technique allocates to each processor in the system a range of primary attribute values. Data tuples are then distributed across processors based on the tuple's primary attribute value.

Round-Robin Partitioning. As its name implies, this partitioning technique allocates data tuples to processors by mapping the xth tuple to the $x \bmod n$ where 'n' is the number of processing units in the system.

Hash Partitioning. This technique distributes data tuples to processors based on the application of a hashing algorithm to the tuple's primary attribute.

8.2.2 Grid Files

There are two principal problems with the three partitioning approaches discussed above [8]. The first is that the approaches decluster tuples based on the value of a single attribute (the partitioning attribute) and as such are not capable of supporting multiattribute declustering without resorting to a secondary indexing structure. The second problem is that they offer no effective method of load balancing to account for insertions and deletions that occur within relations over time.

As a solution to these shortcomings, the Grid File Declustering (GFD) technique was devised by Hau and Lee [8]. The technique is based on a grid file structure described by Nievergelt, Hinterberger, and Seveik in [12]. The grid file consists of a number of linear scales that are used to specify key ranges on a multidimensional partitioning directory. Each cell in the directory contains the number of tuples assigned to the cell and the disk identification on which the tuples are stored.

The initial data declustering algorithm used by the GFD technique first constructs a partitioning directory or grid, with an axis for each key attribute. This is done by first determining the minimum and maximum attributes for each axis. Each axis is then partitioned into a linear scale, the number of intervals on each axis equalling the number of processing nodes on the system. The data is then allocated to cells that are sorted into descending order based on the number of tuples in each cell. Cell allocation is then carried out by allocating the cell with the most tuples to the processing node with the least total number of tuples. The GDF load balancing strategy seeks to distribute data tuples evenly across all processors in the system.

In normal database operations where tuples are inserted into and deleted from relations, data skew can become a problem. GFD corrects for any data skew by using three data reorganization algorithms. The first, a data rebalancing algorithm, seeks to re-establish a balanced system by redistributing cells among processor nodes. The remaining two algorithms are what Hau and Lee refer to as "Environment Adaptation Algorithms." These two algorithms allow large cells to be split in two and small cells to be merged with their neighbors.

GFD has two principle features.

1. It provides a declustering technique that allows multiattribute indexing.

2. It contains a strategy to balance processor load by minimizing data skew.

Grid file decluster is used in the MEDUSA system to provide a multiattribute indexing system which is amenable to a "heat"-based load method.

8.3 Dynamic Load Balancing

Earlier, it was pointed out that if parallel database machines are to reach their full potential they must exhibit a level of operational autonomy. This means the database machine must be capable of carrying out day-to-day management and performance-tuning functions with minimum intervention by human "experts." Critical to the attainment of this goal is the identification and automation of tuning parameters used by human "experts." A review of the literature has identified three parameters that would appear to be critical in the attainment of optimal query performance from a parallel database machine: Data Access Frequency, Data Distribution, and Query Partitioning.

8.3.1 Data Access Frequency

In von Neumann type architectures, database administrators have long realized the importance of balancing the I/O activity across all the I/O channels on a database system. Normally this involves an examination of the database logs to determine the relative file access frequencies. Information derived from this process is then used to move files to achieve a more balanced I/O load across the available I/O channels [5]. A method of load balancing in parallel database machines was suggested by Copeland et al. in [10] that uses data access frequency. Copeland et al. introduced the terms "Heat" and "Temperature," "Heat" being the number of times a relation is accessed and "Temperature" being defined as a relation's "Heat" divided by its size in bytes. While Copeland has shown the importance of "Heat" as a load balancing and hence performance parameter, he concluded that there was a need for better predictors of work. Copeland felt that the measurement of data access rates did not accurately reflect any single component of system load.

Weikum, Zabback, and Scheuermann in [17] describe the use of "heat" and "temperature" in the data placement algorithms developed for the FIVE file system, under the COMFORT project. They used "temperature" in a manner similar to Copeland et al. to balance the load across disk units, by allocating new files to the coolest disks. Weikum, Zabback, and Scheuermann extended the work of Copeland et al. by not assuming that all files are created at the same time and allowing for file creation and expansion. They use a combination of the "heat" of a disk unit and the amount and condition of its free space to select target disks for file expansion and creation. Weikum, Zabback, and Scheuermann were able to show that despite Copeland's initial reservations, "heat" and "temperature" are useful load balancing parameters providing good indicators of a processing node's I/O workload. Moenkeberg et al. in [11] were able to further demonstrate the use of "heat" as a load balancing metric using the FIVE file system simulator. This work was confirmed by results published in [15].

8.3.2 Data Distribution

Data distribution is seen by a number of authors [8, 1] as providing a good method of load balancing. However, it would appear that a lack of any correlation between a balanced data distribution and a balanced processor workload, except in a few unique cases, renders it unreliable as a load balancing method. In [6], DeWitt et al. noted: "In retrospect, we made a serious mistake in choosing to decluster all relations across all nodes with disks. A much better approach, as proposed in [10], is to use the "heat" of a relation to determine the degree to which the relation is declustered."

8.3.3 Query Partitioning

Query partitioning refers to the system's ability to exploit any inherent parallelism within a query. Query partitioning involves either the decomposition of a query into a number of concurrently executable subqueries, or the replication of the original query across a number of processor nodes [7].

8.4 The MEDUSA Project

The MEDUSA project is an attempt by the authors to construct a low-cost, practical, shared nothing data server which may be used as the basis for a parallel database machine.

8.4.1 The MEDUSA Architecture

The current MEDUSA prototype, as shown in Figure 8.1, implements a shared nothing architecture based on the INMOS Transputer. The Client Interface Processor (CIP) provides an interface to the host PC system which in turn can be used to connect MEDUSA to a wider network. The CIP provides basic I/O functions for the system as well as monitoring basic system parameters such as the transaction rate. Upon receipt of a query the CIP directs the transaction to the Transaction Processing Controller (TPC). The TPC then broadcasts the transaction to each processing node. The respective processing nodes then reply with their capability to service the transaction. At this stage the TPC constructs a table of all nodes which are actively processing the transaction. The TPC then monitors each of these active processors collecting the results of the transaction and passes it back to the CIP together with some relevant statistics such as the number of tuples recovered and the total time for the transaction. The CIP can then use these statistics to activate a load balancing cycle if required. At this stage there are three user-selected factors which may be used to activate a load balancing cycle. They are the number of tuples processed, the time since the last load balancing cycle was completed, or the current transaction data transfer rate. Once the criteria for a load balancing cycle have been met, the CIP sends a signal to the Load Balancing Processor (LBP). The LBP then recovers transaction data from each transaction processor node and formulates a load balancing strategy which it then executes. Each of the three transaction processing nodes used in the prototype consists of a T805 transputer with a T222 SCSI-1 interface to a Maxtor 180-Mbyte disk unit.

8.4.2 Software

The design of MEDUSA called for a data management system with the following characteristics:

1. modular and easily scalable within transputer network;

2. provide support for three basic data structures: sequential, indexed, and long;

3. be capable of supporting statistical data collection to facilitate load balancing; and

4. be designed to support data movement between processors in order to support load balancing.

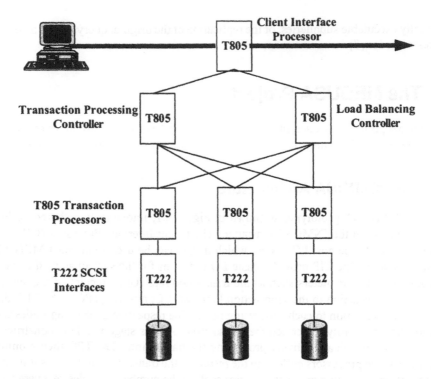

Figure 8.1: Schematic diagram of a MEDUSA cell. A cell consists of up to three nodes.

The MEDUSA Data Management System (MDMS)

The design of the MDMS is based on a model developed at the University of Wisconsin called WiSS (Wisconsin Storage System) [4]. WiSS formed the basis of the data management system used in the GAMMA database machine [6]. The declustering strategy used by MDMS is based on the grid file techniques described by Hua and Lee in [8].

Disk Space Allocation

The MDMS uses two data structures for the management of disk access and extent buffering: the *Volume Header* and the *Buffer Transaction Table*. MDMS divides a disk unit up into a number of extents. Each extent corresponds to a track on the disk unit, extents are in turn divided into sectors. On the prototype each sector contains 512 bytes and an extent is comprised of 36 sectors or 18,432 bytes. The first two extents on each volume are allocated to the Volume Header.

Volume Header.   The Volume Header has the following three main tables:

Volume Data, this table contains physical details pertaining to the volume: Volume Identification; Volume Name; size of each extent in sectors; maximum number of extents on the volume; number of free extents on the volume; maximum number of files on the volume; number of files on the volume; bitmap of free/used extents.

File Allocation, this table contains details of files on the volume: File Identification Number; a pointer to the first extent allocated to the file; the file storage type: sequential, index, or long;

Extent Allocation, this table contains details of the allocation of each extent: the address of the first sector in the extent; File Identification Number to which the extent is allocated; a pointer to the next extent allocated to the File Identification Number; the number of disk accesses made on the extent.

Like WiSS, MDMS uses a layered processing architecture consisting of three layers (Figure 8.2) with each layer being responsible for a single aspect of data management. The top level, level 3, is responsible for implementation of the three data structures supported by MEDUSA. Level 2 supports the collection of statistical information for load balancing and the provision of I/O buffering for higher levels. The lowest level, level 1, supports the physical I/O.

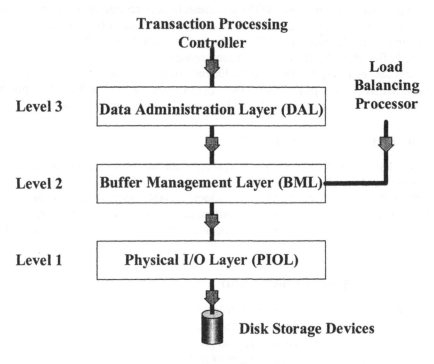

Figure 8.2: Architecture of MDMS.

Buffer Transaction Table. The Buffer Transaction Table records the following information: the identification number of the disk containing the buffered extent; the sector address of the buffered extent; the identification number of the process or processes currently holding locks over the content of the buffer; details of the type of lock held.

Data Administration Layer (DAL)

The Data Administration Layer (DAL) is responsible for the implementation of the three basic data structures supported by the MDMS: Sequential, Index, and Binary Large Objects (BLOb's). The Sequential data structure, as the name implies, stores data sequentially with no indexing. The Index data structure is based on a grid index, currently supporting two key attributes. The BLOb structure is designed to support objects such as images. The DAL supports basic read and write operations on these data structures. The format of these operators is dependent on the data structure being accessed.

Buffer Management Layer (BML)

The Buffer Management Layer has three functions: management of the Extent Buffer, recording the "heat" of each extent, and locking extents. When a transaction request is received from the DAL, the BML checks to see if the required extent is available in the Extent Buffer. If the required extent is in the Extent Buffer, then the BML checks the lock status of the extent and compares it with the transaction lock requested. If the lock requests are compatible, the BML passes the memory address of the extent back to the DAL; if the locks are incompatible, then the BML returns an error message. If the required extent is not in the buffer, then the BML passes a read request to the Physical I/O Layer (PIOL) and updates the "heat" on that extent in the Extent Allocation Table of the Volume Header. Currently, MEDUSA has provision for locking at the extent level only, with support for three types of locking transactions: *shared lock*, *exclusive lock*, and *release lock*.

Physical Input Output Layer (PIOL)

PIOL provides the interface between data management applications running on the transputer network and the SCSI TRAM's firmware. It provides functions such as the initialization of the SCSI interface, reading the *extent* allocation table, processing I/O requests, reading disk extents, writing disk *extent*, and writing the *extent* allocation table. A schematic diagram of the PIOL's control flow is shown in Figure 8.3, PIOL functional control diagram.

8.4.3   Grid File Implementation

The indexing method uses a hierarchical structure as shown in Figure 8.4. Each disk contains an index for the fragment of the data structure allocated to it. At the top of the hierarchy is the *Extent Index*. This is a logical grid file [8] used to partition data within data extents. Extent addresses stored in the *Extent Index* are absolute sector addresses for the disk. The *Extent Index* is stored in the first extent allocated to the indexed data structure on the disk. At the second level in the hierarchy is the *Sector Index*. This index partitions the data extent into sectors. Sector addresses stored in the Sector Index are offset from the first extent in the sector. *The advantage of this form of indexing is that all data extents are self-contained data modules and may be relocated within the system without the need for reindexing, thus aiding 'access load' balancing.*

The current indexing implementation on MEDUSA restricts the number of key attributes to two integers. The current data tuple size is restricted to 512 bytes.

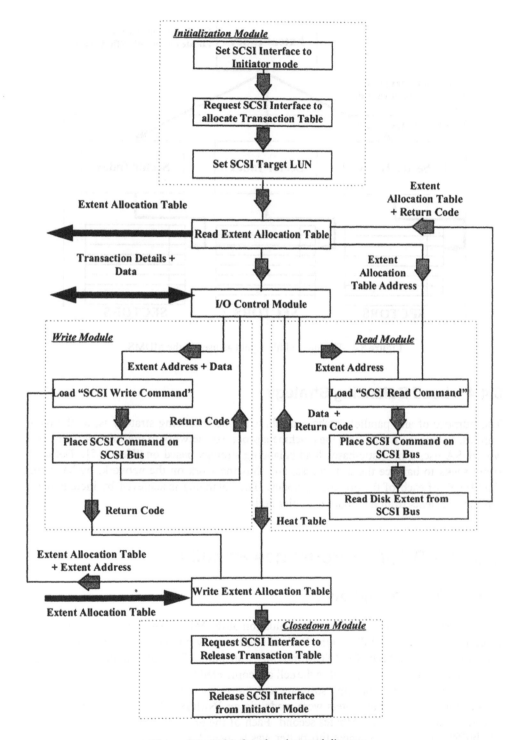

Figure 8.3: PIOL functional control diagram.

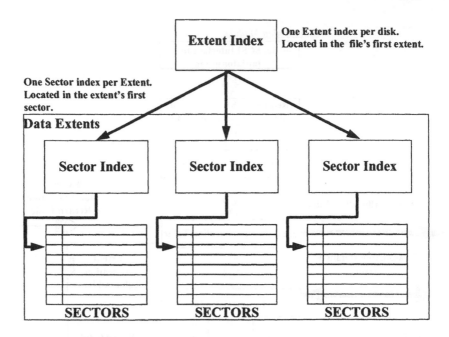

Figure 8.4: The indexed file layout as used in the MDMS.

8.4.4   Load Balancing Strategy

The purpose of any parallel database machine's load balancing strategy is, as the name implies, to balance load within the machine's processor network to optimize performance. MEDUSA uses a heuristic-based load balancing strategy based on "Heat" [5]. The algorithm seeks to balance the disk access, and thus the work on the network, by balancing the "Heat" of each of the processing nodes. The balancing is achieved by incrementally removing extents from hot nodes to cooler nodes.

8.5   MEDUSA Performance Results

8.5.1   Test Configuration

The hardware used in the performance evaluation of the MEDUSA data server consisted of three 150-Mbyte SCSI-1 disk units. Each of these units was interfaced to an INMOS T805 transputer via an INMOS T222 SCSI interface transputer. This configuration constitutes a cell. Each of the three nodes within the cell are connected to two INMOS T805 transputers, one running the load balancing software and the other interfacing to the client PC. All connections between transputers were made via an INMOS C004 link switch, giving an effective bandwidth of 1.9 Mbytes/second. Each of the processing nodes has a 180-Kbyte I/O buffer. In the results where this buffer was activated, it was "warmed-up" by cycling the file being processed once through the buffer.

8.5.2   Transaction Throughput

Sequential Structures

Figure 8.5 and Figure 8.6 show MEDUSA's read and write performance for a series of sequential files ranging in size from 368 Kbytes to 13,824 Kbytes. Sequential file operations involve significant amounts of communications traffic between the client PC and the data server as each extent must be sequentially requested by the client. As a consequence of these requests, these operations tend to be dominated by the system's bus transfer rate and disk I/O rate. The effect of buffering on the read performance for smaller files can be seen in Figure 8.6. The figure shows the increased throughput when small files can be completely held in the buffer. As would be expected, buffering has little effect on write transaction performance.

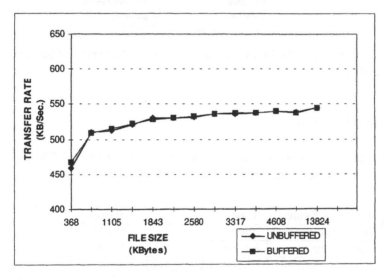

Figure 8.5: Performance results for a sequential write operation using one cell (three nodes) of the MEDUSA system.

Binary Large Objects

Figure 8.7 and Figure 8.8 show MEDUSA's read and write performance for a series of Binary Large Objects ranging in size from 368 Kbytes to 13,824 Kbytes. As these operations on Binary Large Objects involve the bulk transfer of data from the processing nodes to the PC, the performance tends to be dominated by disk I/O rates. This fact is highlighted by the effect of buffering on the read performance for smaller files (Figure 8.8) which can be totally buffered by the system. As with sequential operations, buffering has little effect on write transactions.

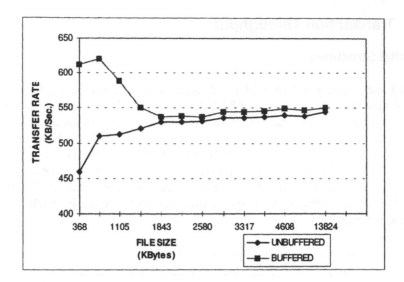

Figure 8.6: Performance results for a sequential read operation using one cell (three nodes) of the MEDUSA system.

Indexed Data Structures

MEDUSA's query processing performance was evaluated against a 1,000 tuple relation (Table 8.1) using a series of queries described in Table 8.2.

Attribute Name	Type	Range
Pri_Attribute	Integer	0-1000
Sec_Attribute	Integer	0-100
Non_Key_Attribute	Character String [12]	1% : GWFMoore1 10% GWFMoore10 89% GWFMoore89
Data	Character String [236]	

Table 8.1: Attribute specification for query processing evaluation.

The performance achieved is shown in Table 8.2. This table shows the query processing timings for a 1,000 tuple attribute table. The response time column gives the time taken to access the disk, select the tuples predicated by the selection criteria, and display the results on the PC. Due to the nature of the Grid File technique, the processing time for queries 1 to 5 (in Table 8.2) is dominated by the index search time. The consequences of queries such as 6 and 7 (in Table 8.2), which are dominated by disk access time and bus transfer rate, can be seen in the table. These queries (6 and 7) require the transfer of larger quantities of data before the completion of the query.

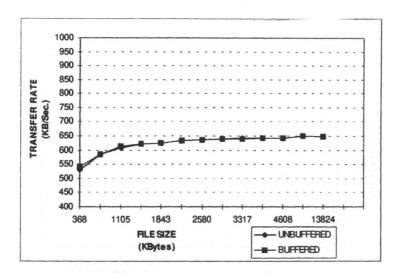

Figure 8.7: Performance results for a Binary Large Object write operation using one cell (three nodes) of the MEDUSA system.

Query Number	Description	Response Time (Sec.)
1	Single tuple selection via a unique index	0.2191
2	1% Selection via a unique index	0.6749
3	10% Selection via a unique index	5.4594
4	1% Selection via a nonunique index	2.0198
5	10% Selection via a nonunique index	6.8461
6	1% Selection via a nonindexed attribute	2.6471
7	10% Selection via a nonindexed attribute	7.3715

Table 8.2: Selection criteria and results for a 1,000 tuple attribute table using a three node system.

8.5.3 Speedup

Speedup is widely accepted as a key metric in evaluating the performance of a parallel database system [7]. Speedup is an indication of whether adding additional processors to the system will result in a corresponding decrease in the response time of a query. Figures 8.9, 8.10, and 8.11 show MEDUSA's speedup performance under the same test conditions described in the Transaction Throughput section above.

In Figures 8.9 and 8.10 MEDUSA has demonstrated near linear speedup. As discussed in the Transaction Throughput section, the performance and subsequent speedup gains of sequential file operations are limited by bus bandwidth and disk I/O transfer rate, whereas the performance of Binary Large Object operations tend to be limited mainly by disk I/O transfer rates.

Figure 8.11 shows the speedup gains obtained in index file operations; these tend to be not as marked as those shown in the previous Figures 8.9 and 8.10, reflecting the complex nature of indexed file operations, involving multiple index lookups and table searches.

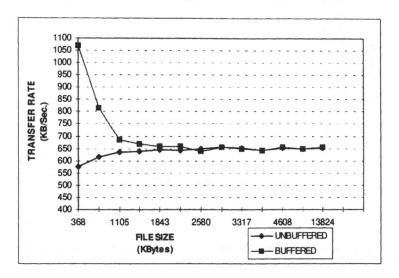

Figure 8.8: Performance results for a Binary Large Object read operation using one cell (three nodes) of the MEDUSA system.

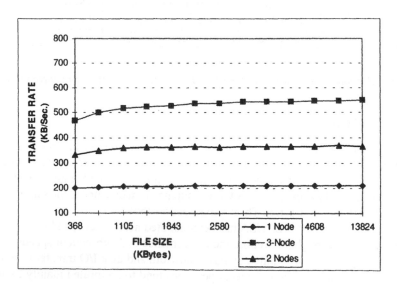

Figure 8.9: A diagram showing speedup from one node (bottom curve) to three nodes (top curve) for a sequential read operation.

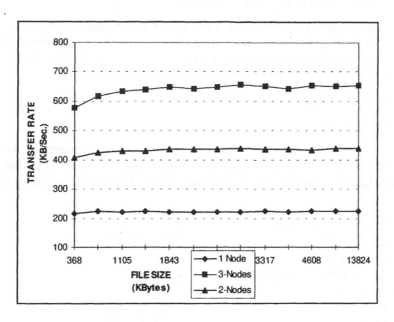

Figure 8.10: A diagram showing speedup from one node (bottom curve) to three nodes (top curve) for a Binary Large Object read operation.

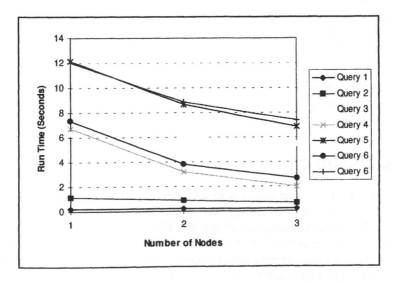

Figure 8.11: A diagram showing speedup for the series of indexed file queries described in Table 8.2.

8.5.4   Load Balancing Test Results

Using the load balancing algorithm developed by the authors, the following results were obtained. The details of the testing procedure can be found in Moore and Bryan [3].

The following values were allocated to the parameters used by the Heat Balancing Algorithm:

- the desired error limit ε, was set to 10;

- M was set to zero.

Setting the desired error limit to 10 means that a difference between the hottest and coldest disks must be at least 10 before load balancing will take place. M was set to zero to eliminate Qave from the first round of testing. The results of these tests are as follows:

Test A

Number of Disks Accessed	:	3
Initial Load Profile	:	50%, 30%, 20%
Number of Transactions	:	200
Number of Load Balancing Cycles	:	2
Initial Run Time	:	9 Seconds
Final Run Time	:	6 Seconds
Transfer Rate	:	614 Kbytes/Sec.

Test B

Number of Disks Accessed	:	3
Initial Load Profile	:	70%, 10%, 20%
Number of Transactions	:	200
Number of Load Balancing Cycles	:	5
Initial Run Time	:	9 Seconds
Final Run Time	:	5 Seconds
Transfer Rate	:	737 Kbytes/Sec.

The outcome of these tests would appear to confirm that the Heat Balancing Algorithm is capable of improving system performance. This is shown by the improvement in the transfer rate in Test A and Test B.

8.6   Conclusions

This chapter has presented an overview of the authors' work in developing the MEDUSA parallel data server. The data management system that has been developed is modular and robust. Performance testing has shown that the system can be easily used as either a research prototype or as a practical backend server to presently available conventional processors. The data management system supports three useful data structures that allow great flexibility in its application base.

The authors' aim in implementing an economic data server was achieved by the use of "off the shelf" INMOS Transputer components. The use of such modular components makes the system easily physically scalable.

The performance figures show the MEDUSA system behaves as a classic parallel shared nothing architecture exhibiting near linear speedup and scaleup.

Bibliography

[1] C. Ballinger, "Evolving Teradata Decision Support for Massively Parallel Processing with UNIX," *Proc. ACM SIGMOD Conf.*, Minneapolis, MN, May 24–27, 1994, p. 490.

[2] H. Boral et al., "Prototyping Bubba: A Highly Parallel Database System," *IEEE Trans. on Knowledge and Database Eng.*, Vol. 2, No. 1, 1990.

[3] G.M. Bryan and W.E. Moore, "Autonomous Data Management, a Future Direction in High Performance Multi-processor Database Systems," *Int'l Symp. on Next Generation Database Systems and Their Applications*, Fukuoka, Japan, Sep. 28–30, 1993, pp. 62–68.

[4] H-T. Chou et al., "Design and Implementation of the Wisconsin Storage System," *Software-Practice and Experience*, Vol. 5, No. 10, Oct. 1985, pp. 943–962.

[5] G. Copeland et al., "Data Placement in Bubba," *Proc. ACM-SIGMOD Int'l Conf. on Data Management*, Chicago, May 1988, pp. 99–108.

[6] D.J. DeWitt et al., "The Gamma Database Machine Project," *IEEE Trans. on Knowledge and Data Eng.*, Vol. 2, No. 1, Mar. 1990.

[7] D.J. DeWitt and J. Gray, "Parallel Database Systems: The Future of High Performance Database Systems," *Comm. of ACM*, Vol. 35, No. 6, June 1992, pp. 85–98.

[8] K.A. Hua and C. Lee, "An Adaptive Data Placement Scheme for Parallel Database Computer Systems," *Proc. 16th. VLDB Conf.*, Brisbane, Australia, 1990.

[9] M. Kitsuregawa, T. Hidehiko, and T. Moto-oka, "Architecture and Performance of Relational Algebra Machine GRACE," *Proc. Int'l Conf. on Parallel Processing*, IEEE, 1984, pp. 241–250.

[10] M. Livny, S. Khoshafian, and H. Boral, "Multi-Disk Management Algorithms," *ACM SIGMETRICS Conf.*, 1987.

[11] A. Moenkeberg et al., "The COMFORT Prototype: A Step Towards Automated Database Performance Tuning," *Proc. ACM SIGMOD Conf.*, Washington, DC, May 26–28, 1993, pp. 542–543.

[12] J. Nievergelt, H. Hinterberger, and K.C. Seveik, "The Grid File: An Adaptable Symmetric Multikey File Structure," *ACM Trans. on Database*, Vol. 9, No. 1, 1984.

[13] Y. Noguchi et al., "A Parallel Database Machine Using Transputers," *Proc. Int'l Conf. on Applications of Transputers*, Glasgow, UK, Aug. 28–30, 1991, pp. 674–679.

[14] D.A. Patterson, G. Gibson, and R.H. Katz, "A Case for Redundant Arrays of Inexpensive Disks (RAID)," *Proc. ACM SIGMOD*, June 1988, pp. 106–116.

[15] P. Scheuermann, G. Weikum, and P. Zabback, "'Disk Cooling' in Parallel Disk Systems," *IEEE Bulletin of the Technical Committee on Data Eng.*, Vol. 17, No. 3, Sep. 1994, pp. 29–40.

[16] G. Weikum et al., *The COMFORT Project: A Comfortable Way to Better Performance*, Technical Report, ETH, Zurich, Switzerland, 1990.

[17] G. Weikum, P. Zabback, and P. Scheuermann, "Dynamic File Allocation in Disk Arrays," *Proc. ACM SIGMOD Conf.* Denver, CO, May 29–31, 1991, pp. 406–415.

Part III

Partitioned Data Store

Chapter 9

System Software of the Super Database Computer SDC-II

Takayuki Tamura and Masaru Kitsuregawa

Abstract. *This chapter presents the design and implementation of the system software of the SDC-II, the Super Database Computer II. The SDC-II is a highly parallel relational database server aiming to provide high processing power for large scale and complex queries. In data analytical applications such as decision support systems, database management systems have to handle very large databases and process ad hoc queries which include heavy relational operators such as join, sort, and aggregate. The SDC-II employs an efficient data passing mechanism in the system software as well as architectural and algorithmic support for high performance database processing. The mechanism enables query executors to process data without the overhead of extra data copies and context switches per I/O operation. It can also efficiently support complex queries which involve pipelined joins. The evaluation results based on the TPC-D benchmark show that the SDC-II works quite efficiently.*

9.1 Introduction

The widespread adoption of relational database systems has led to the existence of very large databases. Users now use the databases to analyze the behavior of their customers and to provide new business plans. Queries issued to the systems in such analyses are ad hoc and intensively use heavy relational operators such as join, sort, and aggregate. Thus, very high performance relational database systems which can efficiently scan a large amount of data and have sophisticated processing algorithms for heavy operators are needed to build decision support systems of practical use.

Considerable research on parallel database processing has been done in the last decade, and the effectiveness of parallelization in improving performance has been proved through research [3, 5, 7, 2, 15, 4, 16]. Based on research results, several vendors are now shipping commercial parallel DBMS products running on commercial parallel platforms [1]. While research interests and efforts have concentrated on the parallelism exhibited in speedup and

scaleup characteristics, the efficiency of fundamental I/O operations has tended to be ignored. Few papers present analyses on I/O performance including disk transfer and network
communication on real parallel machines. Most of such machines have serious bottlenecks
in disk drives, busses, or interconnection networks, resulting in ill-balanced configurations
for large database applications. In addition, dynamic behavior of the internal states of the
systems, such as buffer consumption, processor workloads, and network traffic based on
runtime trace information, has also been disregarded.

This chapter presents the design and organization of the system software of the SDC-
II, the Super Database Computer II. The first prototype of the SDC (SDC-I) was finished
in 1991 [9, 6]. It consists of two data processing modules interconnected by a network,
where each module contains five MC68020 microprocessors and two SCSI 8-inch disk
drives. Although the SDC-I showed much higher performance than other parallel database
machines in those days, we could not prove the scalability of the system due to its limited
number of modules. As a solution to the problem, we developed the SDC-II [13]. The SDC-
II consists of eight data processing modules, where each module employs seven MC68040s
and four SCSI 3.5-inch disk drives with dedicated I/O processors for the disks and the
networks.

One of the key features of the SDC is its use of the Bucket Spreading parallel hash join
algorithm, which is robust in the presence of data skew [11]. This algorithm enables the
system to achieve a high degree of scalability under various data distributions. Furthermore,
we introduced additional hardware into the interconnection network to assist the algorithm.
It enables the network to automatically distribute the data load equally among the modules,
forming a flat bucket distribution. At the same time, the network is able to reduce the conflict rate to almost zero without introducing topological redundancy. In addition to these
algorithmic and architectural supports for parallel relational database processing, we have
directed our efforts to performance improvement of disk accesses and network communication. As a result, we designed a special I/O handling mechanism in the system software
of the SDC-II to enable efficient data transfer, eliminating various overheads found in conventional operating systems.

In Section 9.2, we describe the hardware implementation of the SDC-II. Section 9.3
presents the design and organization of the SDC-II system software, and describes how
it works during operations. The performance evaluation based on the standard TPC-D
benchmark is given in Section 9.4 and Section 9.5 concludes this chapter.

9.2   Architectural Overview of the SDC-II

Instead of employing a cluster of commercial workstations, we designed and built the SDC-
II hardware from scratch in order to obtain higher performance. As shown in Figure 9.1, the
SDC-II globally employs a distributed memory architecture where eight processing nodes
are connected through two kinds of interconnection networks: the data network (DNet) and
the control network (CNet). The data network offers high-speed channels for data transfers,
while the control network handles control information and supports communication with
the front-end machine. Two data networks are provided to divide the load of each network,
especially in the multijoin operations. The data network also provides the bucket flattening
support for the Bucket Spreading hash join algorithm.

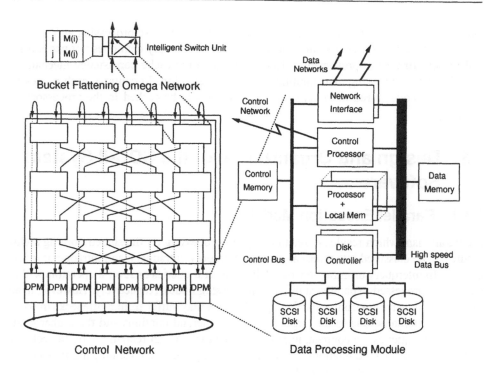

Figure 9.1: Architecture of the SDC-II.

Each processing node is called a data processing module (DPM), which has a shared memory multiprocessor architecture. It contains up to six MC68040 microprocessors operating at 25 MHz as data processors (DP), and one MC68040 as a control processor (CP). The CP manages all the activities of the DPM, such as initialization and synchronization of all DPs. It also contains the interface for the 10 Mbps Ethernet employed as the control network. Dedicated I/O processors are also provided for each of two disk controllers (DC), MC68340 microcontroller at 16 MHz, and two data network interfaces (NI), MC68020 microprocessor at 25 MHz. Each disk controller controls two Fujitsu M2624S 3.5-inch disk drives connected to individual SCSI busses. The I/O processors are responsible only for DMA channel setup. Data transfer itself is done by the DMA hardware using the FIFO buffer on each board.

The processors are connected through two common busses, one for high-speed data transfer (HBus, 100 MBytes/sec) and the other for handling interprocessor communication and mutual exclusion (CBus). The HBus is used solely for bulk data transfer. The local address space of each processor is mapped to a certain area of the global address space and is accessible from the other processors through the CBus. In addition, the location monitor is mapped into this area, which enables the other processors to send a signal to the processor by raising an interrupt. Shared memory is also composed of two portions: 32 MBytes of data memory (DM) for the raw tuple data and 2 MBytes of control memory (CM) for storing the control data structures such as page headers, hash table entries, and memory consumption statistics for each staging buffer. Since the database processing applications show poor temporal access locality, caching the shared memory data does not necessarily lead to performance improvements. Thus we omitted the cache consistency mechanism from the busses, resulting in a simplified bus implementation. In contrast, each processor executes the code stored in its local memory, which can be cached in the processor's I-cache.

9.3 Design and Organization of the SDC-II System Software

9.3.1 Parallel Execution Model

The parallelism which resides in relational query processing on the shared nothing architecture can be classified into three categories: interquery, intraquery, and intraoperator parallelism. In interquery or intraquery parallelism, several queries or several operators within a query are processed in parallel at different processing nodes, respectively. However, in ad hoc query-intensive environments, these parallelisms may suffer from bottlenecks in some queries or operators, due to the larger size of the operand relations and the higher complexity of the queries. In contrast, intraoperator parallelism can relax these bottlenecks by declustering the operand relations among all processing nodes and running multiple copies of the operator at all processing nodes.

The SDC-II system software is designed to fully exploit intraoperator parallelism in two levels according to the hardware architecture: inter-DPM level and intra-DPM level. Since we are interested in cases where no index is available for query executions, all queries are assumed to be broadcasted to all DPMs. If a query contains several pipelined operators, such as scan and hash table probe, all the operators are running at all DPMs. Note that each "pipe" which feeds the outputs of one operator to another is not a local (intra-DPM) entity but represents full connections among all the DPMs. Figure 9.2 depicts how pipelined operators are mapped to the entire SDC-II system.

One of the difficulties with exploiting intraoperator parallelism at inter-DPM level is to distribute the intermediate data (such as buckets in hash-based algorithms) equally among the DPMs. Although most hash-based algorithms work well when the bucket sizes are uniformly distributed, the distribution cannot always be guaranteed to be uniform for real queries. Once the distribution fluctuates, then bucket loading times, hash table creation times, and hash table probing times will vary among the DPMs. Moreover, certain buckets may not fit in main memory, incurring significant performance deterioration since the overflowed buckets require recursive hash partitioning. In such cases, the total execution time is limited by the slowest DPM. The SDC-II employs the Bucket Spreading hash join algorithm to avoid redistribution (bucket size) skew in the parallel hash join operations. Its essential idea is to defer assignment of buckets to DPMs until all the buckets are generated to utilize the statistics of bucket sizes at runtime. As for the join product skew problem, some different approach, such as dynamic workload migration, should be carried out, and is under development.

Similar to the DPMs, all the processors within a DPM execute the same set of operators. In contrast to inter-DPM level, workload balancing is easily accomplished at intra-DPM

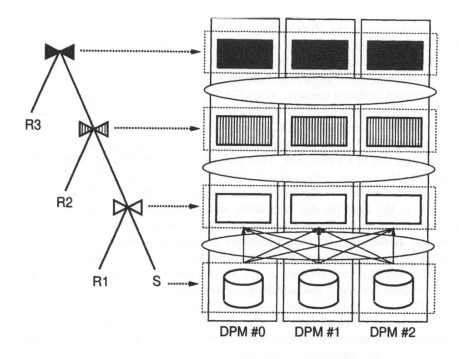

Figure 9.2: Parallel execution model for pipelined operators.

level by maintaining a centralized heap of data in shared memory, and assigning a chunk of the data to a processor on a request basis. Since shared memory in the DPM is used solely for data, each processor is running its own independent kernel code stored in its local memory (currently, the VxWorks 5.1 [8] real time kernel is used). The kernel provides various services including local process scheduling, interrupt handling, and debugging. Before a query execution starts, the program code for the query operators is loaded into each processor's local memory and the processes executing it are created and scheduled individually by the kernel on each processor. The role of the SDC-II system software is to provide the processes access to the global data and mechanisms to communicate with each other.

9.3.2 I/O Model and Buffer Management Strategy for Bulk Data Transfer

Because of the ad hoc nature of the queries issued to the SDC-II, the table scan method is assumed to be sequential access over the full contents of the file. In such circumstances, the efficiency of each I/O operation is critical for the total performance. In the SDC-II, sequential access to the disk file contents is performed through an FIFO, which is written by multiple disk controllers at one end and read by multiple processors at the other end. This enables the processors to bypass the overhead of the buffer cache mechanism which is intended to improve the random access performance.

In order to support the FIFO abstraction of the files, the disk controllers have to be intelligent enough to act as writer processes. When a sequential read operation of a file is initiated, a single command packet is sent to each disk controller. The command contains all of the block numbers to be read from the disk device and the address of the FIFO structure created in shared memory. In the SDC-II, the disk blocks for a file are allocated on an extent basis, and usually the permanent files consist of single extents. Thus each disk controller can issue a single SCSI command directing the disk device to read the entire contents of the file, instead of repeatedly issuing read commands with the block size at each completion of a block read. Then the disk controller splits the data stream from the disk into blocks, on-the-fly, and puts them into the FIFO. In addition, the sequential read operation must be interruptible since the free memory may be exhausted during the operation. In this case, the disk controllers send abort messages to the disk devices to discard the rest of the blocks, and save the positions where successive read should start on resumption. In this way, the reader processors do not have to issue the disk I/O requests except for the very first time, and the system can perform disk prefetching quite efficiently.

Another benefit of the FIFO abstraction is that workload balancing among the processors can be done implicitly. Because the processors take any data at the head of the FIFO in an FCFS manner, lightly loaded processors are more likely to receive the next inputs. Thus the processor workloads will be balanced at last. If the assignment of portions of data to the processors is determined beforehand, the workloads may vary among the processors, since the imbalance cannot be corrected at runtime.

Actually, the disk blocks are stored in the DM portion of shared memory by the DMA hardware. The DM is partitioned into fixed size pages, and every page has its header in CM. When the system boots, all the page headers are linked together in a linked list, called the free page list. Before starting DMA transfer, each disk controller CPU allocates a new page from the free page list and directs disk data to that page. On completion of the transfer, the disk controller links the page header at the tail of the FIFO which is located in CM. At the head of the FIFO, each processor extracts a page header, performs some operation on the page, and frees it by chaining the page header to the free page list.

As for the disk write operation, the behavior of the system is very different. Here, we ignore the update operations of existing file blocks, and focus on the files newly created for temporary files such as buckets or final results. For these files, the written pages are simply buffered as long as there are enough free pages. This corresponds to the dynamic destaging mechanism [10], where the bucket destaging is deferred as long as the aggregate buckets fit within main memory. At this stage, no pages are related to the physical blocks on the disk devices. Once the amount of free pages reaches a low water mark, the system starts to destage the buffered pages. First, the amounts of write pages per file are examined and sorted in descending order. Then, the largest file is picked up and the pages of that file are destaged to the disk devices after allocating a single extent of blocks on each device. The pages used to buffer the write data are freed and made available for other purposes. The destaging operation is repeated until there are enough free pages (greater than or equal to a high water mark).

In addition to the disk devices, the processors operate with the network devices. The network devices are FIFO in themselves, they are so implemented. However, in order to achieve higher throughput, the network packets are sent/received in clusters to/from the network interfaces. That is, several packets are put in a page, and the page is passed between the processors and the network interfaces. Here, again, a linked list of page headers is used to implement the FIFO.

Figure 9.3 depicts an abstract view of the I/O model of the SDC-II, where the hatched circles represent pages filled with tuples and white circles represent free (empty) pages.

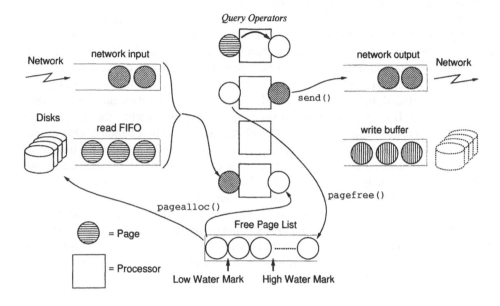

Figure 9.3: I/O model of the SDC-II.

9.3.3 Process Model and Efficient Flow Control Mechanism

When pipelined operations, as found in the probe phases of the right-deep multijoins [12], are executed on each processor, the most natural way of execution is to employ an individual process or thread for each operator. Usually, such threads take one input source and generate zero or more outputs. Except for the operator at the first stage of the pipeline, the input is the network stream. In this model, flow control and scheduling of these threads are done by suspending/resuming the threads on I/O operations. The threads are suspended on input operations when the input stream is empty or on output operations when the output stream is full, and they are resumed when the I/O streams become ready. Although this is simple and flexible, it may suffer from overheads of raising interrupts between the processors (when the wakeup operation is performed on the processor other than the sleeping processor) and context switches on suspend/resume.

To avoid such overhead, the SDC-II utilizes an event dispatcher method to schedule the execution of each operator. Each operator is realized as a callback routine attached to its input, and when the data is ready on the input, the dispatcher executes the routine with the data. Since there is only one process running, the dispatcher process can perform busy-wait on the input, thus eliminating overheads of interrupts and context switches.

In this model, multiple operators can be scheduled appropriately by prioritizing input streams to reflect the structure of the query execution tree. The priority of each input gets higher from the leaf (primary input) to the root (final result) of the tree resulting in avoidance of congestion at the middle of the tree. When several inputs are active, the callback of the input with the highest priority is executed first.

Although this model can handle input blocking of operators, it cannot handle output blocking properly. If an operator is blocked and the dispatcher process is suspended, then all other operators will be blocked. On the other hand, if the output blocking is ignored, the flow control mechanism does not work at all, resulting in explosion of the data contained in some I/O stream, and moreover, free page exhaustion not recoverable by destaging write buffers. In the SDC-II, this problem is solved by treating the limit set on each output stream as a "soft" limit. If the number of pages residing in the stream reaches the soft limit, the caller returns without being blocked after invoking some exception handler. One of such exception handlers is a routine to inactivate the input stream which generates the output. This is done by marking the stream not to call the callback routine. Though the outputs to the output stream may not stop immediately, they are likely to stop soon because the pages from the corresponding input stream are no longer consumed. When the suspended output stream reaches almost empty, another handler is called to undo the effects of the exception handler. If the input stream corresponding to the output stream is inactivated, the mark on the stream is removed to resume the execution of the operator which consumes the input. In this way, scheduling and flow control of multiple operators are realized without the overhead of interrupts and context switches.

9.3.4   Structure of the System Software Components

Figure 9.4 depicts the structure of the components of the SDC-II system software. Queries issued from the user applications are compiled and optimized at the front-end machine to produce executable object files. We did not take the interpreter mode for the query execution mode because of its overhead and inflexibility. The produced object file contains codes specific to the corresponding query, such as initialization and finalization code according to the query execution plans, and evaluation code for predicates. Commonly used code such as hash table manipulation routines and various utility routines are implemented as dynamic link libraries, and are not linked to each object file.

When the scheduler process directs the executor process to start execution of a query, the latter broadcasts the object file to each DPMC, DPM control process, running on the master CPU (CP) of each DPM. Each DPMC creates a new process for executing the query, and monitors exceptional events from that process or the executor. The exceptional conditions from the query processes are reported to the executor and cause other running processes to abort. Each of the newly created processes then sets up the I/O streams and the shared memory regions according to the contents of the object file, and performs parallel fork operation to start the copies of the process at slave CPUs (DPs). Slave processes on DPs inherit all I/O streams and shared memory regions set up by the master process, and then attach operators to each of the input streams as callback functions. On each DP, the dispatcher process called "pageiod" is running. This process keeps polling all the registered input streams and evaluates callback functions with delivered data. Thus, most of the processing is done within the context of the dispatcher process, and the forked process

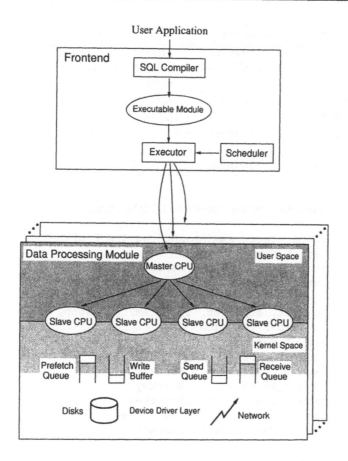

Figure 9.4: Structure of the SDC-II system software.

suspends until EOF conditions are met.

Once execution starts, the processors perform their operations without any centralized control. Barrier synchronizations are encapsulated within open and close operations of network connections to simplify the code. On completion of the network open operation, all the DPMs are guaranteed to be ready for receiving data, and on completion of the network close operation, it is guaranteed that no more data will arrive.

9.4   Evaluation of the SDC-II System

9.4.1   Details of a Sample Query Processing

Now we present the performance evaluation of the SDC-II system using queries of the TPC Benchmark^{TM} D [14]. Table 9.1 shows the test relations used in the benchmark. These relations are generated by a program provided with the benchmark. The total database with scale factor SF will occupy approximately SF GBytes.

Relation	Tuple length	Number of tuples
SUPPLIER	160 Bytes	$10000 \times ScaleFactor$
PART	156 Bytes	$200000 \times ScaleFactor$
PARTSUPP	144 Bytes	$800000 \times ScaleFactor$
CUSTOMER	180 Bytes	$150000 \times ScaleFactor$
ORDER	104 Bytes	$1500000 \times ScaleFactor$
LINEITEM	112 Bytes	$\approx 6000000 \times ScaleFactor$
NATION	128 Bytes	25
REGION	124 Bytes	5

Table 9.1: Test relations of the TPC-D benchmark.

```
select Nation, Year, sum(Amount) as Sum_Profit
from (select N_Name as Nation,
        extract(year from O_Orderdate) as Year,
        L_Extendedprice * (1 - L_Discount)
            - PS_Supplycost * L_Quantity as Amount
        from part, supplier, lineitem, partsupp,
            "order", nation
        where  S_Suppkey  = L_Suppkey
          and PS_Suppkey = L_Suppkey
          and PS_Partkey = L_Partkey
          and P_Partkey  = L_Partkey
          and O_Orderkey = L_Orderkey
          and S_Nationkey = N_Nationkey
          and P_Name like '%green%')
group by Nation, Year
order by Nation, Year desc;
```

Figure 9.5: Formal description of TPC-D query 9.

First, we examine a sample query to explain how the SDC-II processes the queries. Figure 9.5 shows a formal description of the TPC-D query 9 and Figure 9.6 depicts its execution tree in a right-deep way. The execution starts with building five hash tables from five relations on the left-hand side of the tree one by one, and ends with probing the hash tables with the tuples of relation LINEITEM. In the probe phase, five probe operations run simultaneously, and the inputs of a probe operation are fed from all DPMs through the network. Accordingly, I/O streams in shared memory are configured as shown in Figure 9.7 during the probe phase. The name of each stream corresponds to each of the parenthesized names on the right links of the execution tree. Note that between the buffer dr and the buffer $no0$ is a process which performs hashing on the join attribute of the input tuples (that is, LINEITEM.L_PARTKEY) and sends the tuples to the destination DPM according to their hash value.

Figure 9.8 shows the transition of memory consumption and the effective disk transfer rate during execution of the query 9 with scale 0.4 database. Table 9.2 shows the configura-

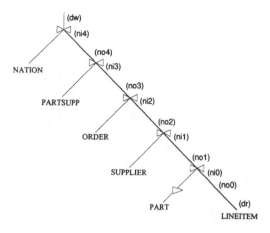

Figure 9.6: TPC-D query 9 execution tree.

tion of the SDC-II system used for the tests. The relations are declustered among the DPMs randomly and have no indexes. Since the total execution time is short, we can observe some startup delays and synchronization overheads at each transition between the build phases. In addition, the disk read transfer rate shows slightly lower values than the maximal rate of 1,100 pages/sec during the build phases. This is because the disk controllers autonomously limit the data transfer rate, detecting that the data processors cannot consume the inputs at the maximal rate. In the build phase of PART, the tuples are selected by performing a string matching operation. This is more expensive than a simple integer comparison, thus the processor becomes the bottleneck. The build phase of SUPPLIER is too short to measure the correct transfer rate. In the other phases, the tuples are short and the selectivity is 100 percent. While the I/O load is determined by the number of bytes transferred, the processor load is affected by the number of tuples processed. The processor load is relatively high due to the large number of tuples in these phases. In contrast, the disk transfer rate shows an almost maximal value in the probe phase. Thus, the SDC-II software model works efficiently even in the complicated right-deep operations.

Number of DPMs	4
Data Processors / DPM	4
Disk Drives / DPM	4
Memory Size / DPM	32 MBytes
Page Size	8 KBytes
Disk Transfer Rate	2.4 MBytes/sec
Network transfer rate	25 MBytes/sec at each port

Table 9.2: Configuration of the SDC-II system under test.

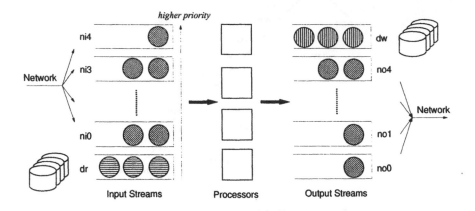

Figure 9.7: I/O streams configuration in the probe phase of query 9.

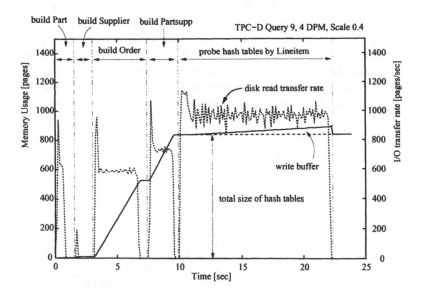

Figure 9.8: Memory usage trace of the query 9.

9.4.2 Comparison with Commercial Systems

Here, we make an informal comparison between the SDC-II and other commercial parallel database servers using the TPC-D benchmark queries. Since the benchmark is quite heavy, almost all of the reported systems employ parallel architecture. Here, we choose the systems with the top processing power record (NCR WorldMark 5100M running Teradata V2R2.0) and the top price/performance record (DEC AlphaServer 8400 5/440 running Oracle7) for comparison. Table 9.3 shows the configuration of the tested systems.

System Configuration	SDC-II	NCR WorldMark 5100M + Teradata V2R2.0 (1996/6/14)	DEC AlphaServer 8400 5/440 + Oracle7 (1996/11/22)
Architecture	SE + SN	SE + SN	SE
CPU	MC68040 25 MHz 21 SPECint92	Pentium 133 MHz 191 SPECint92	DECchip 21164 437MHz $\approx$ 500 SPECint92
# of CPUs	16 (4 × 4)	160 (8 × 20)	12
Memory Size	32MB × 4	1GB × 20	2GB × 12
Disk Capacity	4GB × 16	2GB × 400	4.3GB × 84
DB Size	1GB/10GB	100GB	100GB

Table 9.3: TPC-D benchmark test environment.

Although both NCR and DEC used a 100-GB database, 1-GB and 10-GB databases are used in the SDC-II because of the limited total disk capacity. All the relations except for NATION and REGION are horizontally partitioned among the four DPMs. The relations NATION and REGION are stored at a specific DPM (DPM 0) because they are tiny. We employ range partitioning instead of the hash partitioning for the partitioning method to avoid intentionally advantaging our hash join algorithms. In addition, we do not make use of indexes to force the full scanning over the input relations.

Because the test database sizes are different, we cannot directly compare the benchmark results of the SDC-II with those of the commercial systems. So, we use normalized results for comparison though they may be inaccurate. First, Figure 9.9 shows the execution times of TPC-D queries normalized with database size. We can observe that the SDC-II is about eight times slower than NCR's machine. This is caused by the limited hardware resources and the avoidance of data placement optimization (horizontal partitioning and indexing). To take account of the available resources, Figure 9.10 shows the execution times normalized with database size and total CPU power. Now the SDC-II shows much better performance than the commercial systems. Moreover, normalized results based on memory size (Figure 9.11) and number of disks (Figure 9.12) show that the SDC-II performs much better than the other two systems. We can conclude that the SDC-II works quite efficiently with fewer resources, though actual measurement with a scaled up system is still necessary.

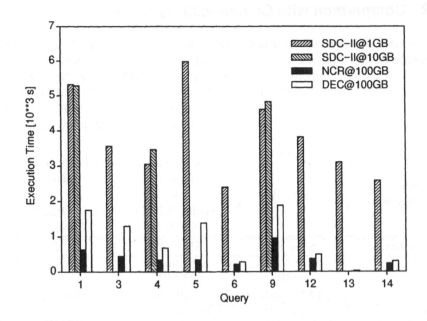

Figure 9.9: Execution times of selected TPC-D queries normalized by database size.

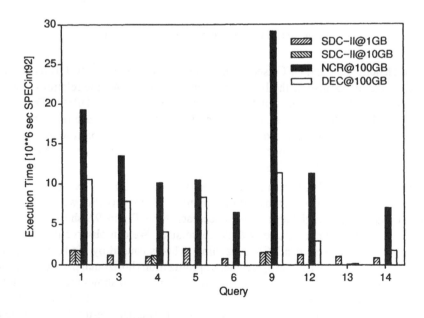

Figure 9.10: Execution times of selected TPC-D queries normalized by database size and total CPU power.

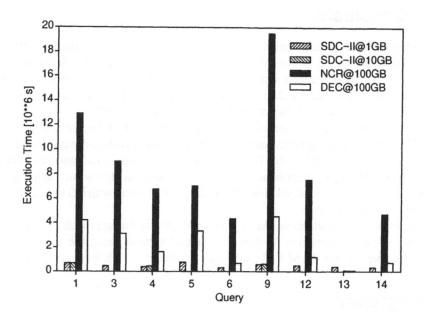

Figure 9.11: Execution times of selected TPC-D queries normalized by database size and memory size.

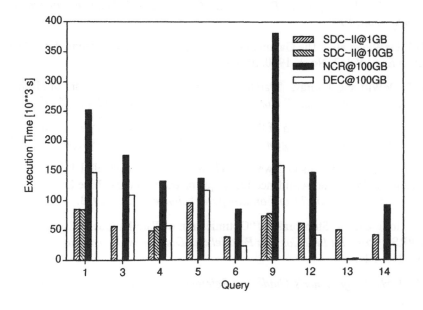

Figure 9.12: Execution times of selected TPC-D queries normalized by database size and number of disks.

9.5 Conclusion

We presented the design and implementation of the system software of the SDC-II parallel relational database server, and examined its performance on pipelined hash join operations based on the standard decision support benchmark queries. Synergy of a sophisticated parallel join algorithm, dedicated parallel hardware, and specially tailored system software enables the SDC-II to attain high performance over complex queries.

The data-driven process model of the SDC-II system software handles the flow of data with little overhead and efficiently multiplexes many operators running simultaneously during pipelined hash join processing. The disk controller can take full advantage of prefetching and write buffering by determining when to start reading or start writing autonomously. In I/O bound application, computation time overlaps completely with I/O time, resulting in an almost ideal performance.

The performance evaluation results convinced us that our approach is effective and promising. The comparison with other commercial systems using the standard TPC-D benchmark revealed that the SDC-II worked quite efficiently with fewer resources.

Bibliography

[1] C. Baru et al., "An Overview of DB2 Parallel Edition," *Proc. Int'l Conf. on Management of Data*, ACM SIGMOD, 1995, pp. 460–462.

[2] B. Bergsten, M. Couprie, and P. Valduriez, "Prototyping DBS3, A Shared-Memory Parallel Database System," *Proc. 1st Int'l Conf. on Parallel and Distributed Information Systems*, 1991.

[3] D.J. DeWitt et al., "The Gamma Database Machine Project," *Trans. Knowledge and Data Eng.*, Vol. 2, No. 1, 1990, pp. 44–62.

[4] D.J. DeWitt and J. Gray, "Parallel Database Systems: The Future of High Performance Database Systems," *Comm. ACM*, Vol. 35, No. 6, 1992, pp. 85–98.

[5] G. Graefe, "Encapsulation of Parallelism in the Volcano Query Processing System," *Proc. Int'l Conf. on Management of Data*, ACM SIGMOD, 1990, pp. 102–111.

[6] S. Hirano and M. Kitsuregawa, "A High Performance Parallel I/O Model and its Deadlock Prevention/Avoidance Technique on the Super Database Computer (SDC)," *Proc. 26th Hawaii Int'l Conf. on Computer Sciences*, IEEE, 1993.

[7] W. Hong and M. Stonebraker, "Optimization of Parallel Query Execution Plans in XPRS," *Proc. 1st Int'l Conf. on Parallel and Distributed Information Systems*, 1991, pp. 218–225.

[8] *VxWorks Programmer's Guide and Reference Manual*, Wind River Systems, Inc., 1993.

[9] M. Kitsuregawa et al., "The Super Database Computer (SDC): Architecture, Algorithm and Preliminary Evaluation," *Proc. 25th Hawaii Int'l Conf. on Computer Sciences*, IEEE, 1992, pp. 308–319.

[10] M. Kitsuregawa, M. Nakayama, and M. Takagi, "The Effect of Bucket Size Tuning in the Dynamic Hybrid GRACE Hash Join Method," *Proc. 15th Int'l Conf. on Very Large Data Bases*, 1989, pp. 257–266.

[11] M. Kitsuregawa and Y. Ogawa, "Bucket Spreading Parallel Hash:A New Parallel Hash Join Method with Robustness for Data Skew in Super Database Computer (SDC)," *Proc. 16th Int'l Conf. on Very Large Data Bases*, 1990, pp. 210–221.

[12] D.A. Schneider and D.J. DeWitt, "Tradeoffs in Processing Complex Join Queries via Hashing in Multiprocessor Database Machines," *Proc. 16th Int'l Conf. on Very Large Data Bases*, 1990, pp. 469–480.

[13] T. Tamura et al., "Implementation and Performance Evaluation of the Parallel Relational Database Server SDC-II," *Proc. 25th Int'l Conf. on Parallel Processing*, 1996, pp. I–212–I–221.

[14] *TPC Benchmark^{TM} D (Decision Support)*, Standard Specification Revision 1.1, Transaction Processing Performance Council, 1995.

[15] P. Watson and P. Townsend, "The EDS Parallel Relational Database System, Parallel Database Systems," *Proc. PRISMA Workshop*, 1991, pp. 149–166.

[16] A.N. Wilschut, J. Flokstra, and P.M.G. Apers, "Parallelism in a Main-Memory DBMS: The Performance of PRISMA/DB," *Proc. 18th Int'l Conf. on Very Large Data Bases*, 1992, pp. 521–532.

Chapter 10

Data Placement in Parallel Database Systems

M. Howard Williams and Shaoyu Zhou

Abstract. *The way in which data is distributed across the processing elements of a parallel shared nothing architecture can have a significant effect on the performance of a parallel DBMS. Data placement strategies provide a mechanical approach to determining a data distribution which will provide good performance. However, there is considerable variation in the results produced by different strategies and no simple way of determining which strategy will provide the best results for any particular database application. This chapter considers five different data placement strategies and illustrates some of the problems associated with the placement of data by studying the sensitivity of the results produced by these different strategies to the changes in a number of environmental factors, such as the number of processing elements participating in database activities and the size of database. The study was conducted by using an analytical performance estimator for parallel database systems, in the context of a shared nothing parallel database system using the transaction processing benchmark TPC-C. It provides some insight into the effect that different types of strategies can have on the overall performance of the system.*

10.1   Introduction

Data placement is an important issue in shared nothing parallel database systems. It is concerned with the way in which data is divided up and distributed between the different nodes in the system. In a relational database system this refers to the way in which individual relations are divided into subsets (fragments) and these fragments assigned to different processing elements (PEs). The way in which this process is carried out can significantly affect overall system performance. A poor data distribution can lead to higher loads and/or load imbalance and hence higher cost when processing transactions.

Various data placement strategies have been developed by researchers to provide a mechanical approach to the process which will produce data distributions capable of realizing much of the performance potential of shared nothing database systems. Since the complexity of the problem is NP complete [8], there is no guarantee that even a feasible solution, let alone an optimal one, can be found in a reasonable amount of time, without using heuristic procedures. For this reason researchers have been working on various heuristic methods to achieve the objectives of data placement.

Generally, a *static* data placement strategy can be divided into three phases. They are:

1. **Declustering** phase in which relations are partitioned into a number of fragments which will be allocated to the disks of a parallel machine in the placement phase;

2. **Placement** phase in which the fragments obtained from the declustering phase are allocated to the disks of a parallel machine;

3. **Redistribution** phase in which data is redistributed to restore good system performance after the load has become unbalanced and overall system performance degraded.

Dynamic data placement is concerned with dynamically reorganizing relations during execution in order to increase the degree of parallelism, reduce response time, and improve throughput. It usually takes the form of generating temporary relations (that is, intermediate relations). The placement of base relations resulting from the initial data placement scheme is not changed.

There is no simple way of determining which data placement strategy would provide the best results for any particular database. Currently, few comparative studies have been performed on these strategies to assess their relative suitability to different database architectures and different database applications. This chapter illustrates some of the problems associated with the placement of data by studying the performance of several types of data placement strategies and their sensitivity to changes. The study has been conducted in the context of a shared nothing parallel database system using the transaction processing benchmark TPC-C, and provides some insight into the effect which different strategies can have on the overall performance of the system. The study concentrates on the placement phase of *static* data placement strategies and used an analytical system throughput estimator, STEADY (System Throughput Estimator for Advanced Database sYstems) [14], which can estimate system throughput for a given benchmark or a given set of queries over a given database and a given data placement strategy.

10.2   Overview of Data Placement Strategies

As stated in the previous section, a *static* data placement strategy can generally be divided into three phases—*Declustering*, *Placement*, and *Redistribution*. These three phases are not completely independent as the approach chosen for placement sometimes limits the choice of the declustering and redistribution methods.

10.2.1   Declustering and Redistribution

The declustering phase of data placement is concerned with the problem of partitioning an entire data space into subspaces, which may be overlapping or nonoverlapping. In the case of relational databases, this partitioning can be either *horizontal* or *vertical*. A fragment in a horizontal partitioning consists of a subset of tuples from a relation, while a fragment in a vertical partitioning consists of a projection of a relation over a set of attributes. These two types of partitioning can also be combined, which results in a *mixed* approach. A discussion on the complexity of operations over a mixed-partitioned relation is given in [11].

For horizontal partitioning, which is the most widely used, there are three basic approaches: *range, hash,* and *round-robin*. The range declustering method partitions a relation into fragments by dividing the domains of some attributes into sections. The hash declustering method partitions a relation into fragments according to the hash value obtained by applying a hash function to the chosen attributes. These can be performed on both single or multiple attributes. Other partitioning methods include using bit-wise operators [7] and space filling curves [3]. However, since hash join algorithms have been widely adopted in parallel database systems, the *hash* method is the most popular as it fits nicely with the requirements of a hash join algorithm.

As insertions and deletions are performed on the local data associated with each PE, the size of the local partition of data may change so that gradually a nonuniform distribution of data will appear. This causes an unbalanced load on PEs which in turn degrades overall system performance. In this situation, a redistribution of data is necessary to resume good system performance. Although the redistribution of data can always be performed with the original declustering and placement strategies, it may require the movement of large amounts of data in complex ways resulting in a cost that is even higher than that of processing data under the skewed circumstances. While this data movement could be done in the background, throughput would be severely degraded in a heavily loaded system. In such cases redistribution should be infrequent and should involve as little data movement as possible.

In the study described in this chapter, the performance of the placement phase of a number of *static* data placement strategies has been assessed. For simplicity, a hash-based declustering method was used for all the data placement strategies under study.

10.2.2 Placement

Various placement strategies have been developed for parallel database systems. These can be classified into three categories according to the criteria used in reducing costs incurred on resources such as network bandwidth, CPUs, and disks, namely: network traffic based [1], size based [4, 5], and access frequency based (although some methods can be considered as combined strategies [2]). The main idea behind these approaches is to achieve the minimal load (for example, network traffic) or a balance of load (for example, size, I/O access) across the system using a greedy algorithm.

Size-Based Strategies

Size-based strategies were developed for systems utilizing intraoperator parallelism, where the CPU load of each PE depends on the amount of data being processed. Since the declustering methods are built around the ideas of hashing and sorting of relations, relation operations applied to the partitioning attribute can be performed very efficiently. However, queries that involve nonpartitioning attributes are naturally inefficient.

Hua et al. [4] proposed a size-based data placement scheme which balances the loads of nodes during query processing. Each relation is partitioned into a large number of cells using grid file structure. These cells are then assigned to the PEs using a greedy algorithm so as to balance the data load for each element. This algorithm is executed by putting all cells into a list and then allocating the first cell in the list to the PE which currently has the largest disk space available. The cell is then removed from the list. This process is repeated until the cell list becomes empty. This initial placement scheme was also used in [5], where the concept of a cell was generalized to any logical unit of data partitioning and movement, that is, all records belonging to the same cell are stored on the same PE.

For the study of data placement strategies described in this chapter, a size-based strategy called *size* has been derived from the Hua strategy by retaining the basic principles while enhancing it particularly for the parallel DBMS architecture used in this study. A notable difference between the *hua* strategy and this size-based strategy is that the hua strategy puts fragments of all relations into the cell list and applies the greedy algorithm only once, while the derived strategy applies the algorithm for each relation in turn (starting from the largest to the smallest), with the list of fragments of the current relation as the cell list.

Access-Frequency-Based Strategies

Access-frequency-based strategies aim to balance the load of disks across PEs since disks are most likely to be the bottlenecks or hotspots of the system. Sometimes, the relation access frequency is taken into account together with the relation size due to the fact that some parts of the relations may be RAM resident and do not require disk access. This has resulted in some size- and access-frequency-based strategies.

The *bubba* [2] method defines frequency of access to a relation as the *heat* of the relation and the quotient of a relation's heat divided by its size as the *temperature* of the relation. Heat is used in determining the number of nodes across which to spread the relations. Temperature is used in determining whether a relation should be RAM resident. The strategy then assigns fragments of relations to nodes, taking account of each node's temperature and heat. It puts relations in a list ordered by their temperatures and assigns the fragments of the relations in the list to PEs using a greedy algorithm to ensure that the heat of each PE is roughly equivalent to the others. The heat of each relation can be estimated for initial placement and tracked for redistribution.

There are several disk allocation algorithms developed for multidisk systems [10], which can be classified as access frequency based. The *disk cooling* method [10] uses a greedy procedure which involves both placement and redistribution phases. It tries to achieve an I/O load balance while minimizing the amount of data that is moved across disks. As the disk cooling procedure is implemented as a background demon which is invoked at fixed intervals in time to restore the balance of I/O load across different disks, the heat of each data block can be tracked dynamically based on a moving average of the inter-arrival time of requests to the same block. Alternatively, it can also be tracked by keeping a count of the number of requests to a block within a fixed timeframe. The problem with these heat tracking methods is that for application sizing, it would be very difficult to track block heat dynamically for initial data placement, as there is no ready system running for the tracking exercise.

Following a similar approach to that for the size-based strategies, an access-frequency-based strategy called *heat* and a size- and access-frequency-based strategy called *size-and-heat* have been developed by retaining the basic principles while enhancing the strategy for the particular DBMS architecture used in the study. The heat of each relation is estimated by analyzing the effects of all the queries on the relation. In the *heat* strategy, only the balance of the *heat* (access frequency) of each relation is considered, while in the *size-and-heat* strategy, both the size and the access frequency are considered. This strategy attempts to balance the product of normalized values of a relation's heat and size for each relation. It tries to strike a balance of consideration between the disk loads and CPU loads.

Network-Traffic-Based Strategies

Network-traffic-based strategies aim to minimize the delay incurred by network communication for transferring data between two nodes. They were originally developed in a distributed database environment where the PEs are remote from each other and running independently but connected together by a network.

Apers [1] presented an algorithm based on a heuristic approach coupled with a greedy algorithm. In this algorithm, a network is constructed with the fragments of a relation as its nodes. Each edge represents the cost of data transmission between two nodes. Each pair of nodes is then evaluated on the basis of the transmission cost of the allocation. The pair of nodes with the highest cost is selected and united. This process is repeated until the network is unified with the actual network of machines. This algorithm was later extended by Sacca and Wiederhold [9] for shared nothing parallel database systems, in which a first-fit bin-packing approach was used to allocate selected fragments.

Ibiza-Espiga and Williams [6] developed a variant of Apers' placement method. It pre-assigns the clusters of relations (each cluster contains relations which need to be colocated due to hash join operations) to groups of PEs, taking into account the available space of the PEs, so that each cluster is mapped to a set of PEs. The idea is to find an appropriate balance among the work load of the PEs and an equitable distribution of the space. Then the units within each cluster are assigned to the set of PEs associated with the cluster using Apers' method.

Following the same approach as for size- and access-frequency-based strategies, a network-traffic-based strategy called *network* has been developed based on the Apers method for the performance comparison described in the next section. Apart from this, another network-traffic-based strategy called *distributed-database* has also been developed particularly for the parallel DBMS used in the study. It classifies relations into a number of clusters on the basis of the frequencies with which they are joined in the database queries. The fragments of the relations in the same cluster are grouped into a number of units. The fragments with the same hash value on the declustering attribute are placed on the same PE. This strategy enables exploitation of local access phenomena, in which the number of local accesses is far greater than the number of remote accesses. For example, in the transaction processing benchmark TPC-B [12] which describes a bank application, there is an assumption that only 15 percent of the transaction requests received by a bank branch are for other branches (that is, the accounts concerned in the transactions are held in other branches). Exploitation of this local access phenomenon reduces the amount of data transmission through the network required in processing transactions.

10.3   Effects of Data Placement

In order to illustrate some of the effects of data placement, some results will be presented for different types of data placement strategies for the transaction processing benchmark TPC-C running on a shared nothing DBMS platform. In particular, their sensitivity to changes in several environmental factors such as the number of PEs participating in database activities and the size of database are considered. The study has been performed on an analytical throughput estimator for parallel database systems, which was configured to model the target shared nothing DBMS. The *size* (typical of size-based strategies), *heat* (typical of access-frequency-based strategies), *size-and-heat* (typical of combined strategies), *network* (typical of network-traffic-based strategies), and *distributed-database* strategies are compared in this study. The inclusion of the *distributed-database* strategy is due to the fact that it is quite different from the traditional network-traffic-based strategies.

10.3.1   STEADY and TPC-C

STEADY (System Throughput Estimator for Advanced Database sYstems) [14] is an analytical tool for performance estimation of shared nothing parallel database systems. Apart from a graphical user interface, it consists of four major modules: **DPtool** is used to generate various data placement schemes for a parallel database using different strategies; the **Profiler** is a statistical tool primarily responsible for generating base relation profiles and estimating the number of tuples resulting from data operations; the **Modeller** is responsible for producing the benchmark workload profile for a particular benchmark or application with assistance from the Profiler; the **Evaluator** takes in workload profiles and predicts the utilization of each resource and from it the system throughput values and bottlenecks.

For this study, STEADY has been configured to model a shared nothing parallel DBMS which consists of a number of PEs and a Delta network. Each PE has a processing unit, a communication control unit, and a number of disks. The parallel DBMS utilizes inter-transaction parallelism. The transaction log comprises a log file on each PE. Disk access is through a distributed file system. Locking is coordinated across all the PEs by a distributed lock manager.

TPC-C [13] is a transaction processing benchmark which exercises the database components necessary to perform tasks associated with transaction processing environments emphasizing update-intensive database services. It is a mixture of read-only and update-intensive transactions that simulate the activities found in complex OLTP application environments. TPC-C comprises a set of basic operations designed to exercise system functionalities of OLTP applications in a lifelike context. The workload is centered around the activity of a wholesale supplier, and includes operations such as verifying and updating customer credit, receiving customer payments, entering and delivering orders, checking on order status, and controlling the inventory of multiple warehouses [13]. In this study, the mixed workload consists of a large amount of order entries and receipts of customer payment, and a relatively small amount of delivery and order status checks.

10.3.2 Dependence on Number of Processing Elements

In this scalability study, the number of processing elements participating in database activities varied from one to 60, while the number of disks attached to each PE remained fixed at four. The size of each relation of the TPC-C database used in this study is given in Table 10.1.

Relation name	Number of Attributes	Tuple size (bytes)	Tuple number	Total size (bytes)
Warehouse	5	100	70	7K
District	7	100	700	70K
Stock	3	20	70K	1400K
Item	7	100	5K	500K
Parts	3	50	11K	550K
Customer	18	400	700K	280000K
Order	7	50	700K	35000K
New_order	4	20	7K	140K
Order_line	10	50	7000K	350000K
History	6	50	6300K	315000K

Table 10.1: TPC-C relations.

Figure 10.1 illustrates the overall performance measured in terms of throughput obtained from the data distributions generated by each of the strategies for TPC-C as the number of PEs varies from one to 60. The system throughput value varies from about 0.000361 tps to 0.019565 tps. In each case the bottlenecks predicted by STEADY are disks attached to particular PEs.

When the number of PEs is less than 35, all five strategies (that is, *network*, *distributed-database*, *heat*, *size*, *size-and-heat*) produce similar performance behavior, with the *heat* strategy producing the worst performance in almost all cases. For numbers of PEs above 35, there is significant variation (maximum variation is 36.6 percent) between the performance figures obtained for these five approaches. The *distributed-database* approach produces best performance for almost all cases in the range of PEs studied.

For the *size* strategy, the performance does not improve linearly with increasing numbers of processing elements but is characterized by a step function. There are two main reasons for this. First, there are several large relations in the TPC-C database, that is, *Order_line*, *History*, and *Customer*, the sizes of which are similar. Of these three relations, *Customer* and *Order_line* are accessed more frequently in the mixed workload of TPC-C than other TPC-C relations. Second, the numbers of disk read/write operations required for small relations, such as *Warehouse* and *District*, are relatively small in the mixed workload of TPC-C. As a result, the placement of the two large relations, *Customer* and *Order_line*, has the largest effect on performance. Due to the similarity in size of the fragments of the three large relations, the large relations can be distributed fairly evenly across the PEs, with minor variations in performance depending on the fit between the number of fragments and the number of PEs. This results in a relatively steady performance improvement as the number of PEs increases.

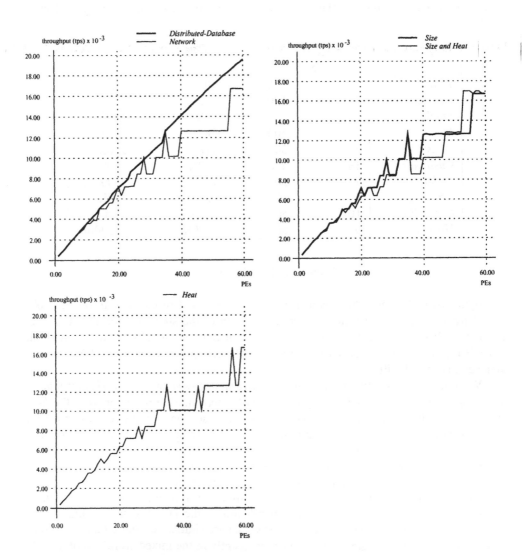

Figure 10.1: Variation of performance obtained using different types of data placement strategies with varying numbers of processing elements.

Due to the high access frequency of the *Order_line* and *Customer* relations, the PE with the maximum number of the *Order_line* and *Customer* fragments assigned to it becomes the bottleneck in the system, and thus determines the overall throughput value. When the number of PEs is small, the increase in the number of PEs has a noticeable impact on the performance, as it significantly reduces the maximum number of the *Order_line* and *Customer* fragments assigned to a PE and hence reduces the disk accesses on the bottleneck PE. However, as the number of PEs increases, a small increase in the number of PEs does not necessarily change the maximum number of *Order_line* and *Customer* fragments on a PE but may simply reduce the number of bottleneck PEs (that is, the PEs which have the maximum number of *Order_line* and *Customer* fragments). This causes the steps in the performance curve of the *size* strategy observed in Figure 10.1. The larger the number of PEs, the longer the steps.

In addition to the steplike behavior, the performance curve for the *size* strategy also has a number of performance peaks. The reason for this is that the *size* strategy applies the greedy algorithm to each relation in turn, starting from the largest to the smallest. As a result, the two largest relations, *Order_line* and *History*, are usually distributed fairly evenly. However, the *Customer* relation can be distributed evenly for certain numbers of PEs, but less evenly for others. As an example, in Figure 10.1, at 35 PEs, a balance has been achieved and the maximum number of *Order_line* and *Customer* fragments on a PE is four. However, when the number of PEs increases to 36, this balance is disturbed, resulting in some PEs having five *Order_line* and *Customer* fragments in total. This results in a drop in performance.

The *heat* and *size-and-heat* strategies produce similar behavior patterns, each with a few performance drops as the number of PEs increases. There are several levels of performance, due to the different maximum numbers of *Order_line* and *Customer* fragments assigned to a PE which determine the performance. For each of the two strategies, the performance reaches a peak at 35 PEs, when two fragments of each relation are assigned to each PE to achieve a balance of the respective weights. However, when the number of PEs increases beyond 35, this balance is disturbed and the difference between the numbers of *Order_line* and *Customer* fragments assigned to different PEs could be relatively large. This results in relatively large differences among the numbers of disk I/O operations required for different PEs and causes a subset of the PEs to become bottlenecks. This is evidenced by the drops immediately following the peaks at 35 PEs for both strategies.

The *size-and-heat* strategy demonstrates a combination of the performance characteristics of both the *size* and the *heat* strategies. The performance achieved using this strategy for TPC-C gives a pattern of steps, as the size factor has been considered when distributing data. Moreover, the balance of combination of heat and size (the products of proportioned values of relation heat and size) also displays some characteristics of the *heat* strategy.

The performance obtained using the *heat* strategy for TPC-C has a behavior pattern consisting of steps with some peaks (such as when the number of PEs is 35 or 45) and drops (such as when the number of PEs is 15 or 46), similar to that obtained by using the *size* strategy. The reason for these steps, peaks, and drops is similar to that given for the *size* strategy, except that heat is used instead of size. However, the *heat* strategy provides generally worse performance in the range of numbers of PEs studied.

The reason for the relatively bad performance of the *heat* strategy lies in the method adopted in the *heat* strategy to estimate the heat of a relation, in which the queries are analyzed to give the number of accesses to a particular relation. The storage structures and access methods of relations are not taken into account. Whereas the *heat* strategy does attribute a relatively high heat to the *Order_line* and *Customer* relations, the proportion of the heat does not reflect the extremely high frequency of access to these two relations which is caused by their storage structures and access methods. In some cases (such as when the number of PEs is 27 and 46), compared with other PEs, one PE is assigned relatively more fragments of these two relations although its estimated heat is at the same level as those of other PEs. Hence this PE requires a much larger number of disk I/O operations and becomes the system bottleneck. This in turn may result in a relatively bad performance.

Of the two network-traffic-based strategies, the *network* strategy uses *size* as a measure for network traffic. Its performance is similar to that produced by the *size* strategy. Although the *network* strategy focuses on network traffic and uses a different algorithm, the performance curves of *network* and *size* are almost identical. The best performance is produced by the *distributed-database* strategy, which shows a near-linear increase in the performance curve with increasing number of PEs for TPC-C. This is due to the utilization of local access phenomena, in which the number of local accesses is far greater than the number of remote accesses. This not only reduces network traffic, but also sometimes reduces the possibility of forming bottlenecks due to heavy load on a particular disk, as this strategy tries to localize the access to disks. However, the degree of scalability of the *distributed-database* strategy is sensitive to the number of units generated in the major relation clusters, relative to the number of processing elements. A detailed study of this sensitivity is presented in the next subsection.

10.3.3 Dependence on Database Size

To investigate the sensitivity of data placement strategies to changes in database size, the number of warehouses in the TPC-C database was varied from 20 to 100. Suppose the number of warehouses is n. Table 10.2 shows the relative size of each TPC-C relation used in our study. The tuple size and number of attributes of each relation remain unchanged.

Relation name	Relative Number of Tuples	Relative Size (bytes)
Warehouse	n	$100n$
District	$10n$	$1000n$
Stock	$1000n$	$20000n$
Item	$71.43n$	$7143n$
Parts	$157.14n$	$7857n$
Customer	$10000n$	$4000000n$
Order	$10000n$	$500000n$
New_order	$100n$	$2000n$
Order_line	$100000n$	$5000000n$
History	$90000n$	$4500000n$

Table 10.2: The relative sizes of TPC-C relations (n = number of warehouses).

The number of processing elements participating in database activities is taken to be 14 and the number of disks attached to each PE is four. This corresponds to a 16-node parallel processing system with two nodes dedicated to nondatabase activities.

Figure 10.2 illustrates the performance measured in terms of throughput obtained from the data distributions generated by each of the strategies for TPC-C as the database size changes (the number of warehouses varies from 20 to 100). The system throughput value varies from about 0.016692 to 0.003159 and the bottlenecks are disks attached to particular PEs in each case.

The performance curve for the *size* strategy shows a pattern in which there are peaks at regular points in an otherwise steplike curve. There are peaks when the number of warehouses, n, is 21, 28, 35, 42, 49, 56, 63, 70, 77, 84, 91, and 98. The drops in performance which form downward steps occur when the number of warehouses, n, is 25, 32, 39, 46, 53, 60, 67, 74, 81, 88, and 95.

As noted before, the performance of the TPC-C mixed workload is determined to a large extent by the PE with the largest number of fragments of the *Order_line* and *Customer* relations. Thus this peculiar performance behavior of the *size* strategy can be explained as follows.

The *size* strategy starts by distributing fragments of the biggest relation, *Order_line*, among the 14 PEs. If the number of warehouses, n, is a multiple of 14 this will result in an equal number of fragments on all PEs. Next, the fragments of the second largest relation, *History*, are distributed among the PEs. If n is a multiple of 14, the two relations will have an equal number of fragments on each PE; if n is a multiple of 7, the total number of fragments on each PE will be the same and will be odd (seven PEs will contain one extra fragment of *Order_line*, the other seven an extra fragment of *History*). In the next step fragments of the relation *Customer* will be distributed among the 14 PEs.

After distributing the fragments of *Customer*, three cases arise:

1. n is divisible by 14. In this case there will be an equal number of fragments of each of the three relations on each PE and performance will be a maximum.

2. n is divisible by 7, but not by 14. In this case, since the sizes of *History* fragments are slightly smaller than those of *Order_line*, one will end up with each PE having the same total number of fragments of the two relations, *Order_line* and *Customer* (although seven PEs will have an extra fragment of *Order_line*, while the other seven have an additional fragment of *Customer*). Once again performance will be a maximum.

3. n is not divisible by 7. In this case the total number of fragments of the two relations, *Order_line* and *Customer*, varies across PEs, some having one or two more fragments than others. Those PEs with the extra fragments become bottlenecks and performance is no longer optimal. Once again, steplike behavior would be expected and the detailed pattern observed can be explained by a full mathematical analysis.

The performance obtained using the *heat* strategy behaves in a similar manner. Once again, there are peaks when the number of warehouses is a multiple of 14, that is, 28, 42, 56, 70, 84, or 98. Between the peaks, there are two-level steps with drops in performance at 22, 29, 36, 43, 50, 57, 64, 71, 78, 85, 92, and 99. This is caused by the change in bottleneck immediately after a multiple of 7.

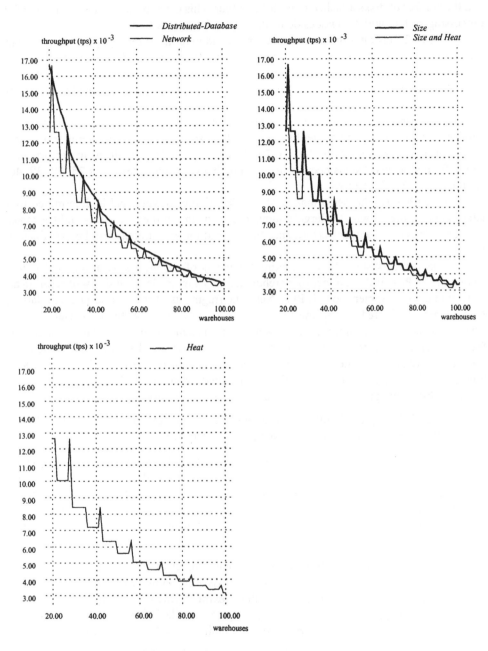

Figure 10.2: Variation of performance obtained using different types of data placement strategies with varying database size.

Unlike the *size* strategy, in this explanation, the weight of a relation fragment is estimated from the access frequency to this fragment (that is, estimated heat), rather than its size. The weight of a PE is the accumulated heat of all fragments assigned to the PE. As stated in the previous subsection, the accuracy of heat estimation directly affects the performance of the strategy. If one already has measurements of the heat of fragments, these can be used to obtain accurate predictions from the *heat* strategy. However, if one does not have such measurements, it can be very difficult to obtain an accurate estimate of the heat by simply analyzing the relation storage structures and application queries. This has caused the performance achieved by using the *heat* strategy to be not as good as expected. In the case of TPC-C, the *heat* strategy used in this chapter put the *Customer* relation, together with the *Order* relation, as the fourth most frequently accessed relation (its heat is 7.1 percent), while *Stock* (36.7 percent), *Order_line* (20.0 percent), and *Item* (18.4 percent) are the top three most frequently accessed relations. However, in reality, due to the data storage structures used in our study, the *Customer* and *Order_line* relations have much higher access frequencies than other relations. Consequently, the performance obtained by using the *heat* strategy is generally worse than that obtained by using the *size* strategy.

The results obtained using the *size-and-heat* strategy once again contain a combination of features from the results obtained using the *size* and the *heat* strategies. The general pattern is that it reaches peaks at the same points as the *heat* strategy. The overall performance is worse than that obtained by the *size* strategy in almost all cases. Suppose the number of warehouses, n, is $14p + q$. When q is 0, 1, 2, 3, 8, 9, or 10, the performance obtained by using the *size-and-heat* strategy is generally close to or better than that obtained by using the *heat* strategy. When q is 4, 5, 6, 11, 12, or 13, the performance obtained by using the *size-and-heat* strategy is close to or worse than that obtained by using the *heat* strategy. The peaks and drops can be explained using a similar approach to that for the *size* strategy, except that the combined factor of both size and heat should be used as the weight of a relation fragment.

Of the two *network-traffic-based* strategies, the *network* strategy provides a performance curve almost identical to that of the *size* strategy. This is due to the fact that the *network* strategy uses the data size as a measure for the amount of traffic incurred on the network, while the *size* strategy tries to balance the data size across the PEs. In the case of 14 PEs, the results produced by the two strategies are very similar. The *distributed-database* strategy takes advantage of local access phenomena, in which the number of local accesses is far greater than the number of remote accesses. It provides the best performance at most points, except at some peaks of the *size* strategy such as when the number of warehouses is 21, 35, 49, 63, 77, and 91 (that is, multiple of 7 but not 14).

However, the degree of scalability of the *distributed-database* strategy depends on the comparison between the fragmentation degree of relations and the number of processing elements. This is evidenced in Figure 10.3. In this figure, part (a) illustrates the variation in throughput obtained from data distributions generated using the *distributed-database* strategy as the number of PEs increases for the case where all relations are partitioned into 14 fragments. The performance of the *distributed-database* strategy scales up well until the number of PEs reaches 14, after which there is very little improvement in performance. Part (b) of Figure 10.3 illustrates the variation of performance obtained from data distributions generated using the *distributed-database* strategy as the database size decreases. Once again the number of PEs used is 14, but the number of warehouses ranges between 5 and

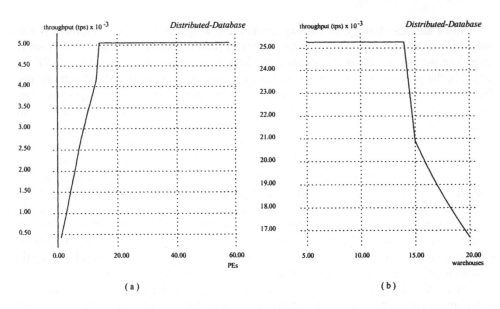

Figure 10.3: Restrictions of the *distributed-database* strategy.

20. The performance achieved by the *distributed-database* strategy scales up well until the number of warehouses decreases to 14, below which there is little change in performance.

This variation in performance depends on the number of units in the relation clusters, which in turn depends on the number of fragments in the relations resulting from the declustering process. In TPC-C there is a major cluster generated which is much larger in size than any of the other clusters. The number of units in this cluster largely depends on the number of warehouses, which is used as the partitioning attribute for all relations in the cluster. When the number of PEs approaches the number of units in the major clusters or the number of units in the major clusters decreases but is still above the number of PEs involved, the performance of this strategy improves steadily as more PEs are used for placing the units of the major clusters. Once the number of PEs exceeds the number of units or the number of units decreases below the number of PEs involved, only a subset of PEs is required to place the units of the major clusters, while the other PEs share little disk I/O load. Hence the performance improvement is limited by the disk load on the subset of PEs selected for placing the major relation cluster. Thus the scalability of the *distributed-database* strategy relies heavily on the number of fragments in the relations resulting from the declustering process. The good scalability observed in Figures 10.1 and 10.2 is due to the fact that the number of PEs used in the study never exceeds the fragmentation degree.

10.4 Conclusions

The way in which data is distributed across the PEs of a parallel shared nothing architecture can have a significant effect on the performance of a parallel DBMS. Data placement strategies provide a mechanical approach to distributing data among the PEs although there is considerable variation in the results produced by different strategies.

Five data placement strategies have been considered in detail, representing three general categories, namely, size based, access frequency based and network traffic based. These five different strategies have been applied to the transaction processing benchmark TPC-C in situations in which the number of processing elements has varied, and the database size has varied.

Some conclusions from this study might include the following:

- The access-frequency-based and size-based strategies provide comparable performance for TPC-C. However, for complicated applications such as TPC-C, the performance obtained using the access-frequency-based strategies largely depends on the accuracy of the estimation of heat. While it is difficult to estimate heat of relation fragments accurately for an initial placement, dynamic heat tracking in established systems may provide more accurate heat information for relation fragments in subsequent placement procedures.

- The traditional network-traffic-based strategy provides almost identical performance to that of the size-based strategies, as it utilizes size as a measure for network traffic. In middle-to-heavyweight read-write-oriented applications, the disks generally become the system bottlenecks. Although there is a cost difference between a remote disk access and a local disk access, the difference is mainly related to network communication and has little impact on disk access cost. Hence improvements made to other factors such as reduction of network traffic and CPU cost will not enhance the performance significantly.

- Another network-traffic-based strategy, the *distributed-database* strategy, scales up well when the number of units in relation clusters is larger than the number of processing elements participating in database activities. The main reason for this lies in its utilization of local access phenomena. However, the degree of the scalability of this strategy is sensitive to the comparison between the fragmentation degree of relations and the number of processing elements. If the fragmentation degree of relations results in a number of units in relation clusters which is smaller than the number of PEs, there is little improvement in performance as the number of PEs increases or the database size decreases.

- As the number of PEs increases or the database size decreases, the performance obtained from data distributions generated using the size-based and access-frequency-based strategies generally scales up. However, there are peaks and drops at particular numbers of PEs, depending on the maximum number of most heavyweight fragments assigned to a PE. To obtain the best performance using a placement strategy mechanically, database administrators may have to choose a good configuration providing peak performance. Alternatively, the initial data layout generated by a data placement strategy may need to be fine tuned manually to produce the final layout.

To avoid complexity, this study of data placement strategies has focused only on the PE level. The distribution of relation fragments among multiple disks attached to each PE is assumed to be round-robin. However, data placement at this level is also important to system performance, as an individual disk on a disk string attached to a PE could become a bottleneck due to poor placement of data at this level. The design of multidisk structures provides room for parallel I/O accesses. This complicates still further the process of determining the best data distribution for a particular database application, and reinforces the need for tools to experiment with data placement strategies.

Acknowledgments

The authors acknowledge the support received from the European Union under the Esprit III programme for this work which was done under the Pythagoras project. Particular thanks are due to Mr. P. Broughton and Mr. A. Fitzjohn of ICL, Dr. H. Taylor and Mr. N. Tomov of Heriot-Watt University, and Professor M. Kersten of CWI for their support and assistance with the work.

Bibliography

[1] P. Apers, "Data Allocation in Distributed Database Systems," *ACM Trans. Database Systems*, Vol. 13, No. 3, Sep. 1988, pp. 263–304.

[2] G. Copeland et al., "Data Placement in Bubba," *Proc. ACM SIGMOD Conf.*, 1988.

[3] C. Faloutsos and P. Bhagwat, "Declustering Using Fractals," *Parallel and Distributed Information Systems*, Jan. 1993, pp. 18–25.

[4] K. Hua and C. Lee, "An Adaptive Data Placement Scheme for Parallel Database Computer Systems," *Proc. 16th VLDB Conf.*, Brisbane, Australia, 1990, pp. 493–506.

[5] K. Hua, C. Lee, and H. Young, "An Efficient Load Balancing Strategy for Shared-Nothing Database Systems," *Proc. DEXA'92 Conf.*, Valencia, Spain, Sep. 1992, pp. 469–474.

[6] M.B. Ibiza-Espiga and M.H. Williams, "Data Placement Strategy for a Parallel Database System," A.M. Tjoa and I. Ramos, eds., *Proc. Database and Expert Systems Applications 92*, Springer-Verlag, Spain, 1992, pp. 48–54.

[7] M.H. Kim and S. Pramanik, "Optimal File Distribution for Partial Match Queries," *Proc. ACM SIGMOD*, June 1988, pp. 173–182.

[8] D. Sacca and G. Wiederhold, *Database Partitioning in a Cluster of Processors*, KBMS Project, Stanford Univ., Computer Science Dept., Mar. 1983.

[9] D. Sacca and G. Wiederhold, "Database Partitioning in a Cluster of Processors," *Proc. 9th VLDB Conf.*, Florence, Italy, Oct. 31–Nov. 2, 1983, pp. 242–247.

[10] P. Scheuermann, G. Weikum, and P. Zabback, "'Disk Cooling' in Parallel Disk Systems," *IEEE Data Engineering*, Vol. 17, No. 3, Sep. 1994, pp. 14–28.

[11] C. Thanos and C. Meghini, "The Complexity of Operations on a Fragmented Relation," *ACM Trans. Database Systems*, Vol. 16, No. 1, Mar. 1991, pp. 56–87.

[12] Transaction Processing Performance Council (TPC), "TPC Benchmark B," *The Benchmark Handbook for Database and Transaction Processing Systems (2e)*, J. Gray, ed., Morgan Kaufmann, San Mateo, CA, 1993.

[13] Transaction Processing Performance Council (TPC), "TPC Benchmark C," *The Benchmark Handbook for Database and Transaction Processing Systems (2e)*, J. Gray, ed., Morgan Kaufmann, San Mateo, CA, 1993.

[14] S. Zhou, M. H. Williams, and H. Taylor, "Practical Throughput Estimation for Parallel Databases," *Software Engineering Journal*, July 1996, pp. 255–263.

Contributors

Mahdi Abdelguerfi Computer Science Department, University of New Orleans, New Orleans, LA, 70148, USA, email: mahdi@cs.uno.edu

Carel A. van den Berg Faculty of Logic and Computer Science, University of Amsterdam, Kruislaan 403, Amsterdam, The Netherlands, email: carel@wins.uva.nl

Eike Born Information Systems, Siemens-Nixdorf

Lothar Borrmann Corporate Research and Development, Siemens AG, Munich, Germany, email: lbo@shams.zfe.siemens.de

George M. Bryan Department of Computing, University of Western Sydney, Nepean, P.O. Box 10, Kingswood NSW 2474, Australia, email: gbryan@st.nepean.uws.edu.au

Felipe Cariño Jr. NCR Parallel Systems, 100 N. Sepulveda Blvd., El Segundo, CA 90245, USA, email: Felipe.Cariño@ElSegundoCA.ncr.com

M.L. Kersten Center for Mathematics and Computer Science, Kruislaan 413, Amsterdam, The Netherlands, email: mk@cwi.nl

Masaru Kitsuregawa Institute of Industrial Science, University of Takayuki Tokyo, 7-22-1 Roppongi, Minato-Ku, Tokyo, 106, Japan, email: kitsure@tkl.iis.u-tokyo.ac.jp

Fred Kwakkel Data Distilleries, Kruislaan 419, Amsterdam, The Netherlands, email: fred@ddi.nl

Chiang Lee Institute of Information Engineering, National Cheng Kung University, Tainan, Taiwan (R.O.C.), email: leec@dblab.iie.ncku.edu.tw

Lory D. Molesky Oracle Corporation, One Oracle Drive, Nashua, NH 03062, USA, email: lory@us.oracle.com

Wayne E. Moore School of Information Technology, Charles Sturt University, Mitchell, Bathurst, NSW 2795, Australia, wmail: wmoore@scu.edu.au

Krithi Ramamritham Department of Computer Science, University of Massachusetts, Amherst, MA 01003-4610, USA, email: krithi@cs.umass.edu

Björn Schiemann Corporate Research and Development, Siemens AG, Munich, Germany, email: Bjoern.Schiemann@mchp.siemens.de

Warren Sterling NCR Parallel Systems, 100 N. Sepulveda Blvd., El Segundo, CA 90245, USA, email: Warren.Sterling@ElSegundoCA.ncr.com

Takayuki Tamura Institute of Industrial Science, University of Takayuki Tokyo, 7-22-1 Roppongi, Minato-Ku, Tokyo, 106, Japan, email: tamura@tkl.iis.u-tokyo.ac.jp

Patrick Valduriez INRIA, Domaine de Voluceau, Rocquencourt, B.P. 105, 78153 Le Chesnay Cedex, France, email: patrick@rita.inria.fr

M. Howard Williams Heriot-Watt University, Department of Computing and Electrical Engineering, Edinburgh, Scotland, email: howard@cee.hw.ac.uk

Kam-Fai Wong Department of Systems Engineering and Engineering Management, The Chinese University of Hong Kong, Shatin, N.T. Hong Kong, email: KFWong@se.cuhk.edu.hk

Mohamed Zaït Oracle Corporation, Redwood Shores, CA, USA, email: mzait@us.oracle.com

Shayou Zhou email: shayou@informix.com

Mikal Ziane Université René Descartes, Paris, France

IEEE
COMPUTER
SOCIETY

Press Activities Board

IEEE Computer Society Publications

The world-renowned Computer Society publishes, promotes, and distributes a wide variety of authoritative computer science and engineering texts. These books are available in two formats: 100 percent original material by authors preeminent in their field who focus on relevant topics and cutting-edge research, and reprint collections consisting of carefully selected groups of previously published papers with accompanying original introductory and explanatory text.

Submission of proposals: For guidelines and information on Computer Society books, send e-mail to cs.books@computer.org or write to the Project Editor, IEEE Computer Society, P.O. Box 3014, 10662 Los Vaqueros Circle, Los Alamitos, CA 90720-1314. Telephone +1 714-821-8380. FAX +1 714-761-1784.

IEEE Computer Society Proceedings

The Computer Society also produces and actively promotes the proceedings of more than 130 acclaimed international conferences each year in multimedia formats that include hard and softcover books, CD-ROMs, videos, and on-line publications.

For information on Computer Society proceedings, send e-mail to cs.books@computer.org or write to Proceedings, IEEE Computer Society, P.O. Box 3014, 10662 Los Vaqueros Circle, Los Alamitos, CA 90720-1314. Telephone +1 714-821-8380. FAX +1 714-761-1784.

Additional information regarding the Computer Society, conferences and proceedings, CD-ROMs, videos, and books can also be accessed from our web site at http://computer.org/cspress

Printed and bound by CPI Group (UK) Ltd, Croydon, CR0 4YY

27/10/2024

14580344-0003